TOM'S WAR

TOM'S WAR

Flying with the U.S. Eighth Army Air Force in Europe, 1944

James T. Hammond
Journalist, Historian

Cynthia,
I hope you
remember Tom.

James T. Hammond

iUniverse, Inc.
New York Lincoln Shanghai

TOM'S WAR

Flying with the U.S. Eighth Army Air Force in Europe, 1944

iUniverse books may be ordered through booksellers or by contacting:

iUniverse
2021 Pine Lake Road, Suite 100
Lincoln, NE 68512
www.iuniverse.com
1-800-Authors (1-800-288-4677)

The views expressed in this work are solely those of the author and do not necessarily reflect the views of the publisher, and the publisher hereby disclaims any responsibility for them.

ISBN-13: 978-0-595-41539-7 (pbk)
ISBN-13: 978-0-595-67916-4 (cloth)
ISBN-13: 978-0-595-85886-6 (ebk)
ISBN-10: 0-595-41539-3 (pbk)
ISBN-10: 0-595-67916-1 (cloth)
ISBN-10: 0-595-85886-4 (ebk)

Printed in the United States of America

To my father, Thomas Donald Hammond, who died sixty years after he fought for America in World War II. In my earliest years, I knew he had done something brave and survived great peril. And to his eight crewmates—Victor Radke, Scott Alexander, Charles Delcroix, Sam Clay, Joe Hagerty, Frank Nutt, Edward Smith, and William Galvin. Together with my father, these men flew into the hell of German flak and fighter planes thirty-five times and came home alive. They were physically unhurt. But my father and many others were emotionally wounded by the threats to their own well-being and by the injuries and deaths of others they saw around them. Sam Clay said Tom had a steely calm as he helped Vic fly a B-17 Flying Fortress bomber. Tom's pain from the terror in the skies over Germany would come later—in sleepless, traumatized nights after he returned home. For these men, I leave this record to ensure that future generations will know what they sacrificed to preserve our way of life.

Contents

▼

Illustrations

Acknowledgments

My wife, Elizabeth, made possible the time I needed to finish this project. She and Walter Edgar provided the encouragement I needed to write this book. My mother, Callie, gave me the precious content: her thoughts and those of my father, written in letters to each other during World War II. My father's comrades, Scott Alexander and Sam Clay, gave me details about their service with Tom. Dudley and Glenn Nutt, Susan Radke, Sarah Nachin, Karen Sayko, and Lyle Graesser provided valuable information about their fathers. Janice Lanou helped me find Scott Alexander. Jan Zdiarsky helped me understand the battle in which Earle Johnston died. Frances Goddard and Howard Johnston shared memories of their brother. Bob Mercer's sisters, Louise and Nolie, likewise recalled their brother for me. Jacques De Ceuninck showed me the place where Bob Mercer died. Chris Boughton helped me explore Horham, the Suffolk village where my father was stationed in England. Bill Bramlett, Fred Rector, Nestor Celleghin, David Taylor, and Hubert Fackrell told me about their combat experiences. Robert Huff also shared his combat experience, and his wife Helen's 1945 diary. Eugene Fletcher provided valuable guidance on operations of the Ninety-fifth Bomb Group. My wife, Elizabeth, along with Walter Edgar, Lyn Riddle, Patricia George, Jeff Burke, and Polly Worthy (Tom's sister) read the manuscript and suggested changes.

Introduction

I began thinking about this book in 2004, during the final six months of my father's life. I was working on a United States Senate campaign and spending time whenever possible at my parents' home in Greenville County, South Carolina. Along with my brother Mike and my sister Susan, I helped my mother, Callie, care for my father, Tom, as his emphysema grew steadily worse. It was increasingly apparent that Tom was nearing the end of his life. I had been working for several years on adding detail to the list of my father's World War II combat missions as co-pilot of a B-17 bomber crew. Eventually, as my father's memory began to fail, and I accumulated more and more detail from his records and other people, I realized that, in a very real sense, I had become his memory. If his experience was to be shared with his descendants, preserving it would be up to me.

After Tom died on September 21, 2004, Callie gave me about 150 letters she and Tom exchanged during 1944 and 1945. His pilot's logbook surfaced, as well as other records I had never seen. I now had a detailed picture of his airman training, his combat tour, and the months that followed his return to the United States, complete with his courtship of my mother, which was detailed in letters that they'd written almost daily. My father had always spoken with great excitement about flying. He loved it and was proud of his accomplishments in the United States Army Air Forces. He spoke often about the other eight men on his crew, for whom he felt great affection, even if he did not have much contact with them in the half-century following the war. Navigator Scott Alexander and gunner Bill Galvin completely disappeared from his world. But he talked about them as if their shared experience in England were only yesterday. His letters to my mother opened many doors and created many questions, some of which I would ultimately answer, and others that I may never be able to resolve. I'd have liked a chance to ask him about them while his memory was clear. But the clock could not be turned back, and I would have to paint the rest of this picture without him.

In his letters, Tom wrote about friends who died, and I have tried to recreate profiles of those brave men. I do not want those who died too young, such as Earle Johnston and Bob Mercer, to be forgotten. They will live as long as someone speaks their names.

I have built the story around my father's training, combat, and post-combat experience. I have also tried to leave a record of the men with whom he served. And I have tried to show, in a small way, how the United States Army Air Forces not only came to be regarded as the most glamorous service of World War II, but also as the most life threatening. The air campaign in Europe created an odd sort of war in which young men enjoyed London's social life one day and fought for their lives over Germany the next. These airmen came home after completing a certain number of combat missions. But heavy bomber groups based in England had one of the highest casualty rates of the war. The odds against completing the magical number of twenty-five, then thirty-five, missions were staggering. Tom preserved the orders that sent him overseas, and those twenty pages name 730 airmen. At least one-quarter of those men became prisoners of war or were killed in action—a horrific toll. Early in the war, bomber crews were sent home after twenty-five missions. As the war progressed, and the pressure to defeat Germany increased, airmen were required to fly more missions. Missions over the original benchmark of twenty-five were called Doolittle's missions, after Eighth Air Force Commanding Officer General Jimmy Doolittle.[1] The high command never actually set a cap on the number of missions, but as the war raged on, group and squadron commanders, and medical officers unofficially settled upon a limit of thirty-five combat missions for bomber crews. In the winter of 1944, some crews, including Tom's, began to grumble about the increase in required missions that took effect about the time they arrived in England. They and other crews took to writing on their after-mission interrogation reports, "30 missions and DFC (Distinguished Flying Cross)." Tom and his crew completed the requisite thirty-five missions. Others did not come home alive.

Chapter 1

▼

A Hankering to Fly

Tom Hammond was born December 3, 1922. That year, James Joyce published his epic novel *Ulysses* in Paris. The Lincoln Memorial was dedicated in Washington, D.C. Actress Judy Garland was born. The German currency began to collapse in value because of heavy World War I reparation demands by France and other nations. That set the stage for hyperinflation and the rise of Adolf Hitler's Nazi Party. Warren Harding was the first U. S. president to broadcast by radio, and in Britain, the British Broadcasting Company was founded, ushering in the era of mass communications. And on December 30, Lenin proclaimed the formation of Communist Soviet Union.

But Tom grew up in an insular, Southern world, deeply colored by his family's Christian faith, generations of military service, and loyalty to family.

Tom's father, Thomas Alexander Hammond, carried the name of their ancestor Alexander Peden, who arrived in America as a teenager from Ireland on the eve of the 1776 Revolution and fought against Britain. Thomas Alexander Hammond's grandmother was Nancy Caroline Peden, granddaughter of Alexander Peden. Defending the American nation was bred into young Tom Hammond. His father had been a naval gunner on the USS *Delaware* during the Great War and saw action in the North Sea and the Atlantic. His uncle, John Hammond, was a Navy seaman on the USS *Antigone*, and another uncle, Francis Marion Hammond, was an infantryman with General John "Black Jack" Pershing's army in France. His father's cousin Samuel Raymond Hammond, a mechanical engineer and graduate of Georgia Tech, became an officer in Pershing's army.

Tom was born in his grandfather's house on Suber Road in the Pleasant Grove community of Greer, in the upcountry of South Carolina.

On Christmas night 1921, almost a year before Tom was born, the Hammond home burned to the ground. The family escaped the blaze, after making a heroic effort to get Grandmother Ella's piano out the front door. It was saved, but scorched by the fire. Neighbors held a house-raising to build a replacement home, the one in which Tom was born.

His grandfather, Thomas Herbert Hammond, known simply as Herbert, was a young boy during the Civil War and had seen his father, John Sidney Hammond, go off to serve in Wade Hampton's Legion in Virginia. After the war, Herbert attended school at Reidville Academy in Spartanburg County, South Carolina. He became an engineer for the Richmond & Danville Railroad and moved his family to Atlanta for several years before resettling in Greenville, South Carolina, to work for Southern Railway. By the time young Tom was born, Herbert had retired to the farm on Suber Road. But Herbert still loved the railroad. He knew the schedules of all the trains that passed through Greer, and he knew all of the conductors and engineers. He would schedule trips to Greenville with his grandson, Tom, to coincide with the passing trains. Herbert would set the little boy on his lap, between his chest and the steering wheel of his Ford A-Model car. They would arrive at a stretch of road parallel with the railroad track at just the right time. Herbert would allow the boy to steer the car as they raced alongside the steam locomotive barreling down the tracks. As long as he could still drive, the old man never tired of greeting his old railroad buddies in this way.

Tom's father moved with his wife, Pauline, and their son to Oakfield, New York, where brother Francis Marion Hammond had married Eva, a local girl, and settled down to the life of a gypsum miner. Tom's father worked in the mines for a couple of years, and another child, Helen, was born in 1925, while the family lived in upstate New York. But Grandfather Herbert and Grandmother Ella were aging, the farm was not doing well, and Tom's father sent money home to help keep the tax collector at bay. Finally, Tom's father gave up the lucrative mining job and returned home to South Carolina to help with the family farm. While they were in New York, Tom's father bought a new Ford T-Model truck, which the family drove until it fell apart decades later. They bought a violin for Tom's father. And they made many photographs of little Tom. They enjoyed their income. The family would never again in Tom's father's lifetime have as much disposable income. He built a small house on the

Suber Road farm to give his growing family a place of their own. Another child, Nancy, was born in 1927.

Tom's life revolved around family. He had little social life outside that circle, and starting school was a difficult transition. Always painfully shy, he fought going to school. A family photograph of the little boy shows him standing in the middle of the road in front of his grandfather's home, his book satchel hanging from his shoulder, jaw clinched in defiance, and clearly unhappy. He recalled, in later life, fights with older boys who saw his vulnerability. Fistfights became common events on Tom's walks home from school. He began then to develop a combative personality that marked him for life.

In 1931, Grandmother Ella died on the first birthday of Martha, the Hammonds' fourth child. Ella, who had lived through the Civil War as a young child, was seventy-four when she died. Tom's father had moved the family to Abbeville County, to a farm about sixty miles south of Greer. Tom, just nine years old, was given the task of driving a team of horses pulling a wagon with the family's possessions, alone, on the trek to their new home. It was a harbinger of the responsibilities and burdens the child would face in the next decade, as the Great Depression loomed over his family and the country.

By now, Tom was the oldest of four. His father arranged to buy the Abbeville farm, but a bank failure interrupted the transaction, and he never won the title to the land. They stayed only a little more than one growing season, and then moved back to Greenville County to be near and often to live with relatives in Greer and nearby Taylors. At times they would rent drafty, old tenant houses near Pauline's relatives on Hudson Road. Not until 1939, when Tom's father purchased a farm on Groce Meadow Road, in northern Greenville County, did they own their home.

Meanwhile, Tom milked cows, tended crops, and drove a school bus to help out his growing family. In 1933, Tom's brother James Herbert joined the family, and finally, in 1937, sister Linda Pauline (Polly) arrived to fill out the family of six Hammond children. Tom had to grow up fast to help raise his siblings and handle a man's chores on his father's farm.

Tom had been taught early by his railroad engineer grandfather to love technology and speed. The death of Tom's beloved grandfather in 1933 did not dampen his growing enthusiasm for new things. Tom bought a battery-operated, shortwave radio from the Sears Roebuck catalog, and his inquisitive sisters and brother knew not to mess with Tom's prized possession. And he grew more and more fascinated with the barnstorming airmen who would occasionally land their World War I-era biplanes in the community and take people for rides. Tom even accompanied his father when they hired out themselves and their team of horses and wagon to work on the airport runway that was being built just outside Greenville. The horse-and-buggy economy was making a quantum leap to the jet age, as draft animals prepared the path for airplanes. The wagon was stripped of its usual cargo box, and loose planks were spread over the frame. Soil would be shoveled onto the bed of planks by a host of laborers and the wagon pulled by the horses to the deposit site for the dirt. Then Tom's father would simply loosen the planks from under the soil, and the soil would spill through to the ground.

Tom was almost finished with high school, in the eleventh grade in those days, when his family moved to the farm on Groce Meadow Road. The 175-acre tract was sandwiched between the road and the South Tyger River. It was a combination of cleared farm fields and forest. Tom's father obtained the property through a Depression-era program that encouraged the purchase of family farms. For a $7,500 mortgage ($103,827 in 2006 dollars, adjusted for inflation), they got the land, a new home, a barn, a chicken house, an outhouse, a well with a well house, and a smokehouse. Tom's father was forty-three years old, and having his own place was the realization of a long-held dream.

The two Toms were cut from the same cloth. They loved mechanical things and challenges. They were good at making something new out of something old. When they tired of digging post holes by hand, they built a post-hole auger that operated from the back of the tractor using discarded iron bedrails and an old automobile gear box. They also converted an old mule-drawn drag pan to work behind the tractor. They rebuilt an A-Model Ford car into a truck to use on the farm. They used an acetylene torch to cut the body off the car, just behind the front seats. Then they built a wooden frame, turning it into a truck. The car had headlights that were attached to the front fenders, sitting quite high. Polly and Herb would straddle the lights and ride down the rough, washed-out trails to the back fields on the farm. And they attached an engine recycled from another vehicle to the handle of the water pump. They did not have running water piped into the house, but that old engine raised water from the well, saving a lot of time, especially when drawing water for the animals or washing clothes. The farmhouse had no indoor plumbing, so they built a wooden tower about ten feet tall, put a fifty-five-gallon drum on top with a hose running from the bottom of the barrel to a shower head. The creation made a very effective outdoor shower for bathing.

Tom graduated from high school at Mountain View in the spring of 1941 and went to work at Southern Bleachery, a nearby textile plant that employed hundreds of people from the surrounding farming communities. He was paid $11 ($152) a week for forty hours of work. He bought a 1933 Ford for $150 ($2,077) and carried two or three riders to the bleachery for a few extra dollars. And he continued to work on the farm with his father.

Four days after Tom's eighteenth birthday, Japanese warplanes attacked Pearl Harbor, and Tom was among the first to answer the call to arms. Just five weeks later, on January 13, 1942, Tom entered Army basic training at Fort Jackson, near Columbia, South Carolina.

A half-century later, Tom told his grandson, Thomas Hart Hammond, about his early obsession with flight: "I wasn't resigned to being a mechanic. I had a fair amount of that on the farm growing up. I went to gunnery school to become an aircraft gunner. Those two things went together. In combat, many aircrew members had to be qualified in several different specialties, such as how to keep an engine running, how to operate a radio, or how to be a navigator. But all along, I had it in the back of my head that I wanted to be a pilot. That goes back to a time in my life in the '30s when I heard a noise overhead. I looked up, and there went a biplane. That was when Lindbergh was very famous.

"Seeing airplanes was unusual in those days. Dad took me to the downtown Greenville airport sometime during that period. That planted the seed that made me end up where I did. I eventually got into the pilot training program, and the first step was academics. They taught us about the principles of flight, the things we had to know. The basic aircraft, the first plane I had occasion to ride in was a PT-17, a twin-wing airplane with a big, 600 HP engine on it. It wouldn't go very fast, but it sure would do a lot of maneuvers. That was the fun part of it," Tom told his grandson.

Figure 1: Airman Cadet Tom Hammond prepares for a solo flight in a PT-17 trainer aircraft at Hawthorne Field in Orangeburg, South Carolina.
(Photo from Tom Hammond's collection.)

Chapter 2

▼

First Steps to Becoming a Pilot

More than two years of training at bases around the southeastern United States lay ahead of Tom to earn his lieutenant's bars and pilot's wings. He was just one of thousands of young men who learned to fly airplanes they would never have had the opportunity to pilot, but for America's entry into World War II. Suddenly, America had to train and equip legions of airmen. And South Carolina would play a critical role to supply the men and the training bases. Tom learned to fly at bases in Columbia, Orangeburg, and Sumter, South Carolina. Most did not exist before World War II and were hastily built to meet the war's staggering needs.

Tom was among a steady stream of young men from his region and state who answered the Army's call for volunteers. In his photo collection is a snapshot of five young privates in crisp, new uniforms. On the back of the photo, which included him, Tom wrote: "Greenville boys. Jack Durham, Bill Iseman, Charles Vaughn, D. A. Scarborough." The Upstate supplied the lion's share of soldiers, airmen, and Marines who served in the military services from South Carolina. That fact is reflected in the War Department's casualty list at the end of the war; 24 percent of South Carolina's war dead came from three counties—Anderson, Greenville, and Spartanburg.

Nationwide, South Carolina's contribution was not out of line with its share of the population. South Carolina contained 1.41 percent of the U. S. population in 1940; the state contributed 1.2 percent of those who entered the Army. Of the men and women of South Carolina who went to war, 2.85 percent, or 3,423 service members, did not return. South Carolinians comprised 1.11 percent of the Army's total dead and missing.[2]

To defeat Germany and Japan, America was mobilizing on a scale never before undertaken. In 1940, the American military stood at just 700,000 men. Four years later, on January 1, 1945, Director of War Mobilization Jimmy Byrnes reported to Congress that America's armed forces had grown to 11.9 million. The total comprised 8.1 million in the Army; the remainder in the Navy, Marines, and Coast Guard.[3]

Tom began his climb to the cockpit in the enlisted ranks, and in school, he began training to repair airplanes. He arrived at Keesler Field, Biloxi, Mississippi, on January 18, 1942, for Air Corps Technical School. Six months later, on June 23, Tom graduated with a certificate as an airplane mechanic.

Tom also began to explore the world. He and his buddies decided one weekend to hitchhike to New Orleans. The only problem was that gasoline, tires, and other necessities for cars were rationed. Traffic was extremely light. After a long wait, an elaborate limousine approached, with a large, well-dressed white woman in the back seat and a uniformed black chauffeur at the steering wheel. The car stopped in front of the three soldiers, and the well-to-do woman offered them a ride all the way to New Orleans. It was a fitting introduction for the country boys to the opulence of the Big Easy.

On August 11, 1942, Private Hammond graduated from Aerial Gunners (Flexible) training in the Army Air Forces Gunnery School, at Tyndall Field, Panama City, Florida. He also earned a promotion to staff sergeant. Flight engineers had to be prepared to share the gunnery duties when the bombers came under attack from enemy fighter planes.

Tom was transferred to Turner Field, near Albany, Georgia. Built in 1942 as a training center, Turner Field began as a school for navigators and later also offered basic and advanced twin-engine pilot training. Tom's records covering this period are thin on detail, but he took navigation training there.

Upon finishing navigator training, he was transferred to Columbia Army Air Base, South Carolina, to continue his training as a bombardier—a new specialty, as bombers grew in size and complexity. At any stage of his training, he could have received orders to join a combat crew, in which case he never would have made it to pilot training. Sam Clay, for example, received orders for pilot training in 1945, after he completed his 1944 combat tour on Tom's crew. But because the end of the war was in sight, the orders were canceled, and Clay never received pilot training. Tom wrote in a letter from Miami, following his combat tour, that the crew's bombardier, Lt. Chuck Delcroix, had visited him on his way to pilot training.

Now and then Tom was reminded of the grim reality of flight operations. One day while Tom was on watch at Columbia, a rookie pilot approached the airfield, slowed too much, and lost the lift under his wings. The B-25 two-engine bomber plunged to the earth at the end of the runway. When Tom arrived at the wreckage, he found the pilot dead, impaled through the chest by the yoke of the plane's flight controls.

As a student bombardier, Tom practiced targeting bombs on the islands in Lake Murray, the giant new lake built on the Saluda River northwest of Columbia. And he continued to hope for acceptance into pilot training.

On April 19, 1943, Tom was in an Army classification center in Nashville where the Army tested young men and decided what specialty to which they would be assigned. Tom learned that his grandmother Martha Duncan had died. He had spent many happy hours in her home east of Greenville, and he wanted to be with his family. But he was denied permission to attend her funeral, and that incident remained a source of resentment toward bureaucratic inflexibility all his life.

Eventually, he received the orders that fulfilled his wildest dreams; he would be taught to fly. "I knew what I wanted to do when I went in, but I didn't know if I could get there," Tom said years later.

Basic training started in South Carolina, at a hastily constructed airstrip beside the railroad tracks running south from Orangeburg. During World War II, an already famous aviator, Bevo Howard, began training pilots for the Army Air Corps from Hawthorne Field at Orangeburg.[4] In 1941, Howard had received a contract to operate a primary flying school. In Army jargon, the base was known as the 2162nd AAFBU (Army Air Force Base Unit). Across the nation, in Tennessee, Ohio, Texas, and many other states, civilian flying schools trained pilots for the Army Air Forces. In South Carolina, there were also civilian schools at Camden and Walterboro.

Tom entered Hawthorne School of Aeronautics in class 44-B, meaning he would graduate in February 1944. The basic training aircraft was the Boeing PT-17, an open cockpit biplane known as the Kaydet. Hawthorne Field was home to one hundred Stearman trainers, painted bright blue with yellow wings. Each cadet spent two months in training, six days a week. One hundred lower classmen would take basic flying and academic lessons for four weeks. They were required to fly solo within twelve hours, or be washed out of the program. If they passed reviews by civilian and military instructors, they advanced to four more weeks as upper classmen. Graduates logged sixty-five hours of flying time, including all aerobatic maneuvers, except an outside loop. The railroad track running beside the airfield was an important landmark for the beginner pilots, who had no radios in their open-cockpit airplanes. The newest pilots were restricted to the eastern side of the railroad track and used an auxiliary landing strip off Highway 178 called Hagood Field. The advanced cadets were restricted to the airspace west of the railroad track. Following their eight weeks in basic training, cadets moved on to eight weeks of primary training, then another eight weeks of advanced training.[5]

Bill Strohmeier, who taught at the school from its opening in 1941 to its closing in 1945, said the academic program comprised a "very stiff ground school." Students learned many survival lessons, including how to recognize friendly aircraft versus enemy planes. Hawthorne School of Aeronautics was so successful that of the fifty-eight civilian contract pilot training schools nationwide, it was the last one the Army Air Forces closed as the war ended. As a treat for the new pilots, Strohmeier said school owner Bevo Howard would put on an aerobatic show at each graduation ceremony.

Strohmeier said Hawthorne Field was "all scraped out of a cotton field," with barracks, classrooms, and other buildings arranged in an oval, and a parade ground in the middle. There were no paved runways, just dirt strips, ironically better suited for the PT-17, which was prone to ground loop (an out-of-control spin) on hard-surface runways.

One memorable cadet Strohmeier recalls was Yves Negaret, a French trainee who was having a difficult time meeting the deadline to qualify in aerobatics. Strohmeier learned from talking to the young Frenchman that he and his family had fled to Paris ahead of the German Army. In the French capital, Negaret witnessed his wife shot dead in the street by Nazi soldiers, and his son spirited away to safety in a location unknown to him. Rather than wash him out of training, Strohmeier had the young pilot set back a class, and helped him through completion of his aerobatic maneuvers. Strohmeier said Negaret later wrote that he had found his son safe with the child's grandparents.[6]

A high point of a cadet's training was the day his instructor would remain on the ground and order him to take the ship aloft alone. Solo flight marked entry into an elite culture of the military. On August 14, 1943, at 8:18 in the morning, twenty-year-old Tom piloted Stearman trainer number forty-seven into the sky above Orangeburg alone. He was not the only cadet to pass that threshold. Six other cadets, including L. A. Szmagaj, R. D. Hammond, Andy Griparis, and Charles S. Coe also passed the critical test. Afterward, they all signed their names on a one-dollar bill along with the details to record the flight.

Tom's next step was in the larger single-engine trainers, the BT-13 Vultee "Valiant," and the AT-6. The Vultee aircraft was called the Vibrator by the young pilots, because it shook so much when the engine was running.

Once while flying a cross-country training mission, a line of threatening thunderclouds moved in between Tom and his base. He flew this way and that, watching his compass, and trying to get around the storm front. His gasoline gauge began to show a dangerously low level of fuel. He kept in touch with his base by radio and received directions from the control tower. Just as he was beginning to look for an open field or a long, straight road to put the trainer plane down, he found a break in the clouds. When he taxied to the hangar as the sun set on a tense day of training, he knew his fuel tank had hardly more than fumes left in it.

Hazards and mishaps were common with dozens of student pilots flying above Orangeburg. In January 1943, one Airman Cadet Upshaw, described as "one of Hawthorne's most promising students," descended through a cloud cover and landed, only to discover he had mistakenly put down at Hagood Field, an auxiliary field.[7]

Local residents became accustomed to objects falling from the skies. In June, Airman Cadet J. Welch was reported by *Prop Wash*, the Hawthorne Field newspaper, to be "practicing the fine art of bombardiering as well." The cadet surprised a grazing cow when the starter crank fell off his plane and landed in a pasture.[8]

In September, farmer C. J. Stroman reported a PT-17 crank handle landed just a few feet away as he plowed in his field. Stroman was becoming accustomed to objects dropping from the sky. A few weeks earlier, a cadet landed in his field after the hapless airman was thrown from his trainer plane during a spin because he forgot to fasten his seatbelt. Fortunately, the airman cadet opened his parachute, and was unhurt by the surprise descent. Two instructors from Hawthorne Field also had unexpectedly fallen from their planes when they accidentally unbuckled their seatbelts.[9]

In 1942, Harold Libby Foster, a pilot-instructor and squadron commander at Hawthorne Field, parachuted safely to the ground after his safety belt unexpectedly released when a student pilot put the open cockpit Stearman into an outside spin. Foster was thrown clear of the aircraft and opened his parachute. Foster formed a local chapter of the Caterpillar Club, an informal grouping of people who have used parachutes to save their lives.[10] (World War II parachutes were made of silk, which was made by caterpillar worms.)

Hawthorne also helped integrate women pilots into the nation's defense. They included Caroline Etheredge of Saluda, South Carolina, who became an instructor pilot at Orangeburg after graduating from the University of South Carolina's flying course in 1940, the first woman in the South to finish commercial pilot training.[11]

In January 1945, Betty Morton, a Columbia, South Carolina, native, rejoined Hawthorne School of Aeronautics after serving a tour of duty as a Women's Auxiliary Service pilot in the Army. Morton, "rated by veteran pilots as not only one of the cutest, but one of the best women pilots," learned to fly at Hawthorne Field. She returned there as an instructor pilot after the WASPs were deactivated on December 23, 1944. At twenty-two, Betty Morton was about the same age as Tom Hammond and had accumulated 900 hours of flying time. As a WASP, she was a test pilot for the Vultee BT-13 aircraft, and the 650 HP AT-6 trainers.[12]

As he progressed into more complex training, Tom moved to Shaw Field, near Sumter, South Carolina. He flew Beech AT-10 twin-engine trainer airplanes. One day, Tom had to fly a long practice mission cross-country. No one noticed the ordinary road map tucked into his flight suit. He followed the roads and railroad tracks until his twin-engine trainer arrived over the Hammond farm. He buzzed the house, and then proceeded to the nearby Mountain View School, which he also buzzed. His brother Herb and sister Polly both vividly recall the episode. Polly, then in first grade, said it made her proud to know it was her big brother flying overhead. He rocked his wingtips back and forth, and then set his course to return to Shaw Field, about 150 miles away, east of Columbia.

Showboating by young and inexperienced aviators was officially frowned upon by the Army Air Forces. Such an incident was reported in the *Greenville News*: "Col. Oliver H. Stout, commanding officer of Greenville Air Base, requested anyone having definite information as to the identity of the pilot of a plane which 'buzzed' Greenville during the morning to notify him at the base so disciplinary action may be taken."[13]

Greenville residents apparently were equally unamused: "Col. Stout reported that the plane that buzzed Greenville had been identified as a Marine plane from the base at Congaree, and that details had been forwarded to the base commander for whatever disciplinary action the latter may deem advisable."[14]

During his training at Shaw Field, Tom was landing a twin-engine AT-10 trainer with an instructor pilot when the landing gear suddenly collapsed, and the plane made a noisy and scary belly landing. Tom said the presence of the instructor pilot to verify that the mishap was caused by a mechanical failure kept him from being washed out of pilot training. It was a night landing. "Everything was going fine until the propellers started eating concrete. The landing gear folded up under the aircraft. You had red lights to indicate retracted gear, and green lights to indicate locked gear. It was green, but it wasn't locked. It was a fiery ride," Tom told his grandson many years later.

Tom was in and out of Turner Field at Albany, Georgia, for several months at the end of his primary training to become a pilot. On December 7, 1943, S. Sgt. Tom Hammond had "qualified for flying" Class One pilot, written into his records at Turner Field.

Overseas, American airmen were fighting and dying to stop the Nazi advance. The Army Air Forces had waged war against Germany alone for more than a year. Thousands of airmen had been killed or captured before the first squad of American infantrymen crossed the English Channel. But the tide was turning. The bombers, which had fought their way to targets deep in Germany and back home again without fighter support, now had company. The Associated Press reported on January 11 that a new fighter aircraft was escorting the waves of bombers, possibly all the way to their targets. The P-51 Mustang, now the longest-range single-engine plane in the world, could accompany the bombers into the deepest parts of Germany, engage enemy fighters, and return to friendly bases.[15] On January 16, the Associated Press reported that Gen. Dwight D. Eisenhower had arrived in London to assume command of the planning for the Allied invasion of Europe. "On his journey from the Mediterranean to the United Kingdom he had conferences with the President and the prime minister," the AP reported. The former commander of Allied forces in North Africa had spent "a few days" in Washington where he conferred with President Roosevelt and Gen. George C. Marshall, chief of staff, the AP reported.[16]

The American airmen in training clearly were impatient for action. At Shaw Field, a poll taken in January among officers and enlisted men indicated they expected Eisenhower to act quickly. The consensus of the poll was that the Allied invasion of France would take place by March 15. One-quarter of those polled thought the attack would take place as early as February.[17]

On February 7, 1944, S. Sgt. Tom Hammond received a discharge from enlisted service to accept a commission as second lieutenant. On February 8, 1944, 2nd Lt. Tom Hammond passed his instrument flight test at Turner Field.

As Tom was finishing up his pilot training, the tempo of American industry was changing, and the momentum against the Nazis and Japanese was accelerating. On February 28, the Army announced contracts with three companies for the construction of training airplanes were being ended to convert production to combat aircraft. When the war started, and America faced a dire shortage of trained airmen, about 60 percent of aircraft production had been of training airplanes. Two years later, thousands of airmen were in the pipeline, and plenty of training airplanes dotted North American airfields.[18]

On March 6, 1944, Lieutenant Hammond had his pilot physical record, with his immunization record, stamped at Turner Field, Sixteenth ATU, Flight Three.

Tom was transferred to Tampa, Florida, to a replacement depot at Plant Park, a tent city thrown up on a college football field. He had little to do but report for muster, and spent his time looking for a friend from home, Vance Clayton, on a nearby base. Tom visited St. Petersburg, and its Gulf shore beaches. He even made a weekend trip to Silver Springs at Ocala, where he went swimming. "That's about the nicest town I've seen in the whole state of Florida," he wrote in his first letter to Callie Barnette, a neighbor and former classmate at Mountain View High School.

Every flyer wanted to be a fighter pilot, but not all could be. On March 15, 1944, Tom wrote to Callie about his disappointment at being assigned to a bomber command:

"From here I guess I will go to Avon Park, Fla., which is about eighty miles south of here. I'll be flying B-17s or Flying Fortresses as they are called. I don't like the idea much but there isn't a lot I can do about it."

When Tom reported to Avon Park, to meet his new crew and begin training, he already had 207 hours of flying time. Tom's crew, under chief pilot Victor Radke, assembled at Avon Park in April 1944. By the time he wrote again a month later, Tom was busy learning to fly the big four-engine bombers.

"I don't know why I'm trying to write letters tonight. I've been flying all afternoon and I'm so tired I can hardly see straight, but I thought I had better thank you for the Easter card that you sent. Thanks a lot. It was real nice. I hope you had a nice Easter Sunday. You can imagine what I was doing, well, I was flying and didn't even get to go to church," Tom wrote to Callie on April 18.

Tom had driven his 1933 Ford to Florida before his crew shipped out. He had a flat tire, and could not buy a new one because of the rationing. He had no choice but to sign over the title to a local mechanic and abandon the car. Tom owned many cars during his life, but he talked about that 1933 Ford all of his life as if he had been forced to give up a Cadillac or a Lincoln.

Figure 2: Callie Barnette began a correspondence by mail with Tom Hammond while he was training to fly the B-17 in Florida. (Photo from Callie Barnette's collection.)

Chapter 3

▼

Showing Off and
Shipping Out

The twenty-one-year-old pilot eased back on the throttles of the big, four-engine bomber, let it settle well below the minimum altitude permitted for practicing military aircraft, and set its line of flight along Groce Meadow Road. As the B-17 Flying Fortress descended below 2,000 feet, he spotted the small, white farmhouse with red shutters where high school classmate Callie Barnette lived. The road running along the crest of the ridge was about 1,000 feet above sea level, and he was now fighting ground turbulence, screaming along only a few hundred feet above the treetops.

"I couldn't wait any longer than now to write and tell you that I saw you fly over this afternoon. When I saw the plane flying so low and what kind it was I knew then it must be you. Was you at the controls? Boy, it sure was a pretty thing, I'll bet it really flies good. How much longer do you have before you go over? Or maybe I shouldn't be asking. But the last time I saw your folks they said you only had a short time then, was what made me ask," Callie wrote in a letter to the young pilot later that day.

It was June 6, 1944, and Lt. Tom Hammond was on his way home to South Carolina to see his family. The Hammonds lived on a hilltop west of the South Tyger River, on a northern Greenville County farm.

Many of his neighbors in the Mountain View community already were engaged in battle. On that very day, American troops were landing on the beaches of Normandy. Bill Sammons was piloting a Higgins boat in the English Channel to land Army troops on Omaha Beach. He said in a 1994 interview that the experience was like his own personal vision of hell, with boats blown apart around him and blood and body parts raining down on him and his boat. Bill's brother, Sgt. Frank Sammons, was in the Army, and he would lose his life on December 7, 1944, in the European war. Rudolph Lynn had fought the Germans across North Africa, Sicily, and Italy. Tom Hammond still had his combat experience ahead of him. But this day, he was showing off his success in the United States Army Air Forces.

As he roared over Callie's house, he could see his own farmhouse a half-mile ahead. Within seconds, the bomber swept over the top of his parents' home. He had not expected that this unauthorized flight would give him such a thrill. Less than three years earlier, he had been milking cows and plowing corn and cotton on the hillsides now passing under his wings.

The first pass over the Hammonds' new house on the hill brought his brother Herb and sister Polly, and his parents, Tom and Pauline, hurrying out the front door. It took only seconds for ten-year-old Herb to realize that his brother Tom had just buzzed the farm. By the time the bomber roared a few hundred feet overhead the second time, Herb was in the front yard, shielding his eyes from the summer sun and peering up to see details of Tom's plane. Herb remembered Tom's fly-over of the previous year when Tom had buzzed both the farm and nearby Mountain View School in the much smaller AT-10 twin-engine trainer.

The crew eased the bomber back up to authorized altitude and set a course for Greenville Army Air Base,[19] a training center for B-24 and B-25 air combat bomber crews. They landed and lounged around the base until Tom's family, alerted by his fly-over, could drive across the county to see Tom.

Afterward, Tom's crew flew the B-17 bomber back into the summer sky on their return flight to Avon Park, six hundred miles away in central Florida. S. Sgt. Joe Hagerty invited his fellow airmen to his radio room to hear the broadcast news of the D-Day invasion of Normandy. "The martial music calmed the fear and renewed the resolve to go out and get the dirty 'Hun,' to do or die," wrote Sgt. Ed Smith, the assistant radioman and aerial gunner, years later.[20]

Like all airmen leaving America for combat, Tom set his personal affairs in order in case he became a casualty of the European war. On Wednesday, June 7, 1944, the day after he buzzed the farm, Tom signed his "Last Will and Testament," making his parents, Pauline Duncan Hammond and Thomas Alexander

Hammond, his beneficiaries should he be killed. He also signed a power of attorney, making his father his legal representative.

Five days later, the crew had orders to leave Avon Park. They were among seventy-three crews sent to Hunter Field, Savannah, Georgia, where the Eighth Air Force was mobilizing an air armada to send to the farmlands east of London. Ed Smith wrote that fifty of the crews would be traveling by ship to England, the "lucky" ones, in his opinion, while the rest would be flying new B-17 bombers across the Atlantic. That just meant those flying across would enter battle a month sooner, Smitty thought.

As they trained for battle in Europe, Tom's and Vic's crew logged more than one hundred hours of flying time over the swamps of South Florida, the Gulf of Mexico, and the red hills of South Georgia. During June alone, they flew fifty-one hours in just nine training flights. They spent ten hours flying at night. S. Sgt. Sam Clay, the flight engineer, began to see the complementing temperaments between Tom, the barely five foot six co-pilot, and Vic, the six foot four chief pilot. Vic was six years older and fifty pounds heavier than Tom. The enlisted crewmen called them Mutt and Jeff respectively behind their backs, after the newspaper cartoon characters. Sam sat between the pilots. On his left was Vic, who liked the thrill of dashing the four-engine bomber in and out of towering cloud formations. Vic was more at home in the big airplane because he had served as a four-engine flight instructor before being assigned his own crew. Tom, on the other hand, had only been flying the B-17 for a few weeks. He was steady and conservative. Scott Alexander, the navigator, said Vic and Tom made a good team. "Vic was a hard-headed SOB, but we'd fly anywhere in the world with him," Scotty said. But in tight formation, Scott said Tom had the steadiest hand on the wheel when dozens of B-17s were lined up, their wingtips sometimes only a dozen feet apart. "It always seemed smoother when Tom was flying the plane," Scott said.

While much time was devoted to building competence and cohesion as a crew, mischief was always just around the corner. Scott recalls buzzing the apartment building where Vic's wife Erna lived with some other military wives.

Erna and Vic had been together during most of the war. Vic was born June 23, 1916, the son of a Montello, Wisconsin, miner. His mother cleaned houses for better-off folks to help her family put food on the table. Vic grew up Lutheran and attended the Lutheran school across the street from his home for ten years. For many young men from small-town America, the military offered a way out of poverty and out of rural settings that offered little opportunity. Vic was assigned to Sheppard Field in Wichita Falls, Texas. One day in 1942, he was walking down the street in the small Texas town with a buddy when two attractive, young women pulled up alongside them in a beige 1928 Studebaker. Erna Renard was behind the steering wheel, and she invited them to get into the car. Erna's father, Frank Renard, was a college music professor in Dallas and had come to Wichita Falls that day to give piano lessons to a woman and her daughter. The daughter did not want to hang around the older folks when her lesson was finished, so she suggested to Erna that they go for a ride in town. The two lonesome-looking airmen offered a diversion from the slow pace of small-town life.

It was not long before Vic was traveling to Dallas regularly on weekends. Mrs. Hines, the Renards' next-door neighbor, had a spare room with an outside entrance and offered it to Vic and his friends when they were in town to visit Erna's home on St. John's Street. Vic and Erna became a regular item, attending dances at the Continental in Dallas.

Vic had volunteered for service in the Army and, like Tom, enlisted as a private, with a promise of an opportunity to serve in the Army Air Forces. He became an airman cadet, wearing the prized winged propeller symbol on the collar of his uniforms. He received his first pilot's training at the Air Corps Basic Flying School in Greenville, Mississippi, in Class 43-J, which meant he was scheduled to graduate in October 1943.

It took Vic a year to work up the nerve to ask Frank Renard for permission to marry his daughter Erna. Renard had emigrated from Europe, and such formalities were important to him. Erna traveled to Lafayette, Ohio, to pin Vic's wings on his uniform when he graduated from advanced flight training. They were married in Dallas on December 8, 1943.

Vic had been admitted to fighter pilot school, but after a while, Air Force officials told the tall, muscular pilot that his size made it awkward for him to fly the small fighter planes. He'd be better off behind the wheel of a heavy bomber, they said. So Vic was transferred to bomber training. He went to Boca Raton, Florida, where he trained other bomber crews. By the time Vic was assigned his own combat crew, he was a highly skilled pilot, more so than most of the chief pilots leading crews into battle in Europe.

At Hunter Field, their assembly base near Savannah, Georgia, the crew's mischief was not confined to practice flights. Two nights before they shipped out for Europe, Scotty Alexander met Gloria, from Oak Park, Georgia, at a local soda shop. They enjoyed each other's company. Liquor and the wartime contempt for consequences led to a twenty-four-hour courtship and marriage. Georgia law prohibited such quick unions, so Scotty and Gloria drove to South Carolina to get married. They did so with relative ease because South Carolina was just across the

Savannah River. The day after they were married, Scotty and the crew departed for New York. "I didn't know what she looked like for about two months. I had to write and ask her for a picture so I'd know what she looked like," Scotty said.

Twenty-three-year-old Scott Eugene Alexander was from Orange, Massachusetts. Born on July 21, 1921, and the son of the town doctor, Kirke Locke Alexander, and his wife Florence, Scotty had attended Dartmouth College for one year. His ancestors had been in Massachusetts since the mid-seventeenth century. His father wanted him to be a doctor, but medicine didn't appeal to Scotty. He was a restless young man, unsure of what he wanted to do. When the war came, he was single and without a clear plan for his life. Military service offered a chance to put career decisions on hold. On October 1, 1942, Scotty joined the Army at Springfield, Massachusetts, as a reserve officer. He was sent to navigator training school in Monroe, Louisiana.

Vic's crew included nine young men, including Lt. Charles M. Delcroix, the bombardier, age twenty and single. Chuck had signed up for service September 2, 1942, in his hometown of Pittsburgh. Chuck was a high school graduate who had enlisted to become an Army reserve officer.

Sam Clay, the flight engineer, was born in 1920 in Texas. When he enlisted June 15, 1942, at Camp Shelby, Mississippi, he was married to Martha and living in Forrest, Mississippi. He had attended college for one year. Before being assigned to a combat crew in Florida, Sam had trained in Tucson, Arizona; El Paso, Texas; and Pueblo, Colorado.

Joseph A. Hagerty III, the twenty-three-year-old radio operator, was the only member of the crew who had graduated from college when they went into combat. He was one of four children born in Germantown, Pennsylvania, to Joseph A. Hagerty Jr., a Philadelphia city treasurer and a founder of the Provident Building and Loan Association. Joseph III graduated from Germantown High School in 1939 and worked two jobs to pay his tuition while attending Villanova University. He was the only non-scholarship player on the college baseball team. He graduated from Villanova in 1943, and immediately entered the Army Air Forces as a radio operator and gunner. He was single when he enlisted at Philadelphia on April 14, 1943.[21]

S. Sgt. Frank Nutt, the twenty-three-year-old ball turret gunner, was a brave man, already recognized as such by his country, which issued a commendation for bravery under fire at Wheeler Field, Honolulu, on December 7, 1941, as he fought back when Japanese warplanes attacked the American air bases in the Hawaiian Islands.

But Frank's bravery did not end with the defense of Wheeler Field. For six months in 1944, he was the ball turret gunner on Vic's crew. He joked a lot about crawling into the tiny space of the ball turret to protect the bomber from attacking German fighter planes. But everyone knew it took a special kind of man to get into the ball turret, a position that left the airman feeling as if he were suspended in space. Born on August 23, 1921, a New York state native and unmarried when he enlisted in the U. S. Army Air Forces in July 1940, Nutt had served in the Forty-sixth Pursuit Squadron of the Eighty-first Fighter Group in Hawaii.

Thirty-one-year-old S. Sgt. William C. Galvin, the tail gunner, was born October 17, 1913, and was the oldest member of the crew. He was from Elwood City, just outside Pittsburgh. He was not married when he enlisted April 10, 1942, at Pittsburgh. His formal education had ended in grammar school.

Edward Smith, the waist gunner and assistant radio operator, was born January 13, 1915, in Tuscola, Illinois, the oldest of five boys. He spent his youth in St. Charles, Missouri, where his father was a painter. After graduating from high school, Ed worked in the Civilian Conservation Corps and as a bookkeeper before entering the U. S. Army Air Forces.

It turned out that Vic's crew was one of the lucky ones, according to Ed Smith, that got to travel to England by ship. In late June 1944, the crew traveled by train from the combat crew center at Hunter Field to Camp Kilmer, New Jersey, thirty miles south of New York City. Camp Kilmer was built in 1942, the first base designed solely to embark troops. It was the largest staging area in the United States and handled more than two-and-a-half million troops during the war. With a few days before departure, Ed Smith and his fellow airmen spent a night in New York City, made calls home from the Telephone Center, visited Jack Dempsey's Bar, and saw other sites in the Big Apple. On June 30, 1944, the crew rode the train to New York City, and then took a ferry to Brooklyn. A band met them at the pier, as well as Red Cross workers with coffee and doughnuts. They boarded the *Monticello*, formerly the Italian ocean liner *Conte Grande*. At 5:00 AM, July 1, the ship, confiscated from the fascist Italian government, hit the seas.[22]

Crossing took about a week. The ship had 7,500 troops aboard, the weather was rough, and the inner compartments of the ship stank from the vomit of hundreds of sick airmen. Tom and other officers, assigned to the upper decks, escaped the worst of the stench. Vic, Tom, Scotty, and Chuck went below as often as possible and brought their enlisted crew members topside for some fresh air. They landed in Liverpool, England, and in a few days were at their base at Horham, Suffolk, east of London.

*Figure 3: Tom Hammond earned his pilot's wings and lieutenant's bars in 1944.
(Photo from Tom Hammond's collection.)*

Chapter 4

▼

Joining the Eighth Air Force

Eighth Air Force commanders included the famous aviator Jimmy Doolittle, who had led the first air raid on Tokyo in 1942, with land-based planes launched from the deck of the aircraft carrier USS Hornet. Brig. Gen. Ira C. Eaker took the Eighth Air Force headquarters to England on February 20, 1942, locating it at High Wycombe, thirty miles northwest of London. In April 1942, Maj. Gen. Carl Spaatz arrived in England, where he established Headquarters of the Eighth Air Force at Bushy Park, fifteen miles southwest of London.

In 1944, the Eighth Air Force comprised 200,000 men and women. In the course of World War II, more than 350,000 Americans served in the Eighth Air Force, which could send more than 2,000 four-engine bombers and more than 1,000 fighters on a single mission on its best days. But 28,000 men became prisoners of war. Half of the Army Air Forces' casualties in World War II were suffered by the Eighth Air Force; more than 47,000 casualties with more than 26,000 dead. For comparison, all of the Eighth Air Force suffered one killed in action out of every thirteen men who served. Meanwhile, the U. S. Navy, with 4.1 million serving and 37,000 killed, suffered a casualty rate of one killed in action out of every 110 who served.[23]

But the casualty rate among air crews was much higher than for the general population. The rate for the 730 men listed on Tom's 12 June 1944 orders to depart Avon Park, Florida, for example, was one out of eight killed in action. Another one out of eight became prisoners of war. One-quarter, or at least 196, of those 730 airmen became casualties.

Greenville, Tom's home county, suffered the highest number of deaths (324) in the Army and Air Forces among South Carolina's 46 counties.

There would be no let-up until Germany unconditionally surrendered. American industry expected to produce a hundred thousand airplanes in 1944. Fewer of them would be training planes, and more would be heavy bombers. And they would all need crews, new young men quickly trained to fly the new weapons systems into battle.[24]

Most of the young airmen were fatalistic about the danger, steeling themselves to the likelihood they would not return from dangerous missions. In March 1944, Associated Press correspondent Mel Most was freed from imprisonment in Germany. Under the headline, "It's The Percentage, Airmen Say About Being Shot Down," he wrote an article quoting American airmen he had met and interviewed behind the barbed wire of a German POW camp. "If you go out often enough, you expect to get it sooner or later," he quoted one American veteran of twenty raids.[25]

Chapter 5

▼

Flying the Four-Engine Fighter

Tom had been assigned to fly the most famous bomber of World War II, the B-17 Flying Fortress. It was neither the largest, fastest, nor most numerous aircraft in the Allied inventory. But it came to symbolize the American assault on the Axis like no other airplane.

It was first flown as a prototype in 1935. The first B-17s were flown into combat by British Royal Air Force airmen in 1941 for high-altitude missions. The B-17E, the first modification to be built in large quantities, featured nine .30-caliber machine guns and could transport 4,000 pounds of bombs. Later models had increased armaments of eleven .50-caliber guns and could carry 6,000 pounds of bombs. Perhaps its most distinguishing feature was its enormous vertical tail, enlarged from the prototype to ensure control and stability on high-altitude missions. Flying Fortresses assigned to the Pacific were nicknamed "four-engine fighters" by Japanese pilots who feared their formidable guns. They were tough airplanes, able to absorb massive battle damage and still bring their crews back to friendly bases. Stories were legendary of whole sections shot away from planes that landed at bases back in Britain, hundreds of miles from where they were attacked.[26]

There were 12,726 of the B-17 heavy bombers built during World War II. Boeing, the company that designed the plane, built 6,981 of the bombers, while aircraft builders Douglas and Lockheed-Vega built an additional 5,745.[27]

The B-17G had a range of about 3,400 miles in ferry configuration, but was limited to about 2,000 miles when loaded for combat. It could carry 3,630 gallons of high-octane gasoline.

The planes were built in plants from the Midwest to the West Coast. The bombers were moved to Europe over a system of ferrying routes that carried them to the eastern-most Canadian provinces to Greenland or Iceland, Ireland, and finally to their bases in England. The Army Air Forces used some combat crews who were on their way to join bomb groups in East Anglia to transport some of the planes. They also used ferry pilots of the Air Transport Command. One such pilot was Tom's French-American cousin, Raoul Jacques Hammond, born in Paris in 1920 to a former American Army officer, Samuel Raymond Hammond of Spartanburg County, South Carolina, and Raymonde LaMotte, a French woman whom the officer met while serving in France during World War I. When World War II began in 1939, Raoul joined the American Volunteer Ambulance Corps and served on the front lines as an ambulance driver. He was captured by the German army at Saarbrucken and later released because the United States was not yet engaged in the war against Germany. Raoul was awarded the French Croix De Guerre medal. He left France and traveled to North America, where he stayed with his Grandmother Hammond in Spartanburg, South Carolina. In 1942, he joined the Canadian Air Force, which taught him to fly. In 1944, he transferred to the United States Army Air Forces, and was assigned to the Air Transport Command in Long Beach, California. He flew most types of multi-engine aircraft to the jumping-off base at Gander, Newfoundland, including B-17 Flying Fortresses. There, the aircraft were picked up by combat crews to finish the journey to England.

The B-17s were supplied in the largest numbers to the Eighth Air Force in England and were G models, identifiable for the distinctive chin turret featuring two machine guns. The G model, late in the war, was manned by a crew of nine: two pilots, a bombardier, a navigator, a flight engineer, radio operator, waist gunner, ball turret gunner, and tail gunner. In the last stages of the war, when the bombers flew in formations of dozens or hundreds of planes, a lead bombardier would sight the target, and other planes would release bombs simultaneously. Some crews at that stage of the war simply had a crew member designated as a toggler, eliminating the need for a trained bombardier.

Some of the fliers escaped death under almost miraculous circumstances. On March 29, newspapers carried a story, cleansed of identifying detail by the censors that said "7 U. S. Fliers Bail Out Fortress That Is All But Shot in Half." German gunners had hit the Flying Fortress over Reims, France. The direct hit on the plane nicknamed *Who Dat* blew off thirty feet of the fuselage behind the radio room. According to the report, just four slender, metal frame pieces and the thirty-inch-wide catwalk continued to attach the tail to the front of the airplane. Lt. Daniel C. Henry of St. Albans, New York, the pilot of the plane, pulled the stricken aircraft out of a 5,000-foot dive after it was hit, despite the elevator and rudder control cables being shot away. "Maybe the Lord was back there steering it," Daniels was quoted as saying. The correspondent described the airplane as it appeared back over England as flying in two pieces. The plane was too damaged to attempt a landing. The seven surviving crew members bailed out and were saved by their parachutes, while the doomed plane crashed with the bodies of the two waist gunners killed by the German anti-aircraft fire.[28]

Chapter 6

▼

Greenville's Sacrifice

Already, Greenville families had learned that service in the Army Air Forces was taking a heavy toll on their young men. On February 23, 1944, the local paper noted that Lt. William A. League was killed in action in Europe on February 6. League was a graduate of Greenville High School and had attended Furman University.

On March 9, 1944, the *Greenville News* informed its readers that a local football legend, Lt. Lake Hugh Jameson of Easley, had been reported missing in action while flying a B-17 Fortress over Germany. Jameson was a Clemson College graduate and a member of the storied 1940 Cotton Bowl team. And on March 28, 1944, the *Greenville News* sports columnist Carter "Scoop" Latimer wrote in his column that Walter "Booty" Payne, a legendary tailback on the Greenville High and Clemson football teams, had been missing over Germany since March 9.[29] Scoop Latimer described sports fans as "shocked" by the news of Payne's disappearance while flying a B-17 bomber.

"For two whirlwind football seasons, the Clemson tailback from Greenville flashed across the consciousness of America as one of those stars whom sports alone can create. Missing and dead, or prisoner? Perhaps. But everyone fervently trusts that Booty Payne will be found safe and well with it. He was one of the greatest football punters of them all in his day at Greenville High School and Clemson, and his fame extended from Boston to New Orleans, where his marvelous kicking against Boston College, Tulane, and many other teams gained national recognition. He was also a brilliant broken field runner and a capable passer. His spectacular individual achievements helped fashion sensational victories in crucial games. He could have remained at Clemson a year longer, but patriotism dictated he volunteer immediately," Latimer wrote.

Booty Payne's family was about as committed to the war effort as possible; he had three brothers in the military. Latimer got the answer he wanted to his question: Booty Payne spent the rest of the war in prison at Stalag Luft One, Barth-Vogelsang, Prussia.[30]

Lake Hugh Jameson also survived when his Flying Fortress, nicknamed *Dixie Jane*, was shot down on February 8, 1944, near St. Pierremont, France following a raid on the Frankfurt rail yards. And he, too, ended up in Stalag Luft One for fifteen months, with so many other Allied bomber and fighter pilots.[31]

Lt. Fred J. Rector, a former postal worker from Greer, South Carolina, and a B-17 pilot in the 306th Bomb Group based at Thurleigh, Bedfordshire, became a prisoner of war on February 22, 1944.

It was mission number eleven for Fred. He wasn't even scheduled to fly on that Tuesday. He rose before dawn with the other crews.

Fred had become an orphan of sorts. Following a mission earlier in his tour, he had developed a bleeding nose, and his co-pilot urged him to see the flight surgeon. When he did, he was promptly grounded. On January 5, 1944, he lingered in his barracks as the 306th, and his crew led by a young captain piloting his thirty-fifth mission, revved up their engines for an attack that would not include Fred. Bomber after bomber thundered down the runway at Thurleigh. The pitch of their spinning propellers changed as the big Wright engines bit into the air to pull the gasoline-and-bomb-laden planes aloft.[32]

Suddenly, he heard the muffled *thu-rump* of an explosion that he instantly recognized. It was a B-17 exploding on takeoff. He raced outside to discover within minutes that his crew and the young captain on his last mission were dead, consumed in the maw of 3,000 gallons of burning, high-octane gasoline and exploding bombs.

Fred was a lead pilot, often tapped to take combat command of his squadron's component of the 306th Bomb Group as it merged into an even larger combat wing and division. Now he was a replacement pilot, without his own crew, but always available to lead a mission.

This morning, as he entered the briefing room, he scanned the mission board. OK, he thought, Uncle Fred's not up there. But the pilot listed to lead the 367th Squadron that day did not show up for the briefing. Eager to move the briefing along, the officer in charge looked about the room, spotted him, and said, "Rector, you take his place."

He donned his flying suit, the wool-lined jacket and pants with electrical wiring that connected to the airplane's electrical system and provided heat to ward off the deadly freezing temperatures five miles high in the European winter skies. The crew did the checklist to ensure that the bomber was working properly, and then they waited for the signal to take off. As Fred frequently did before a mission, he pulled out his small Bible and read from Psalms over the aircraft intercom. Their target was Bernburg, near Berlin, and no one objected to a little reassurance from the Old Testament, even his Jewish navigator, Herb Edelstein.

When the flare arched over the airfield from the control tower to begin the mission, Fred added power, eased onto the runway, and then firmed up his touch on the yoke and rudder pedals as the B-17 leapt to life and roared down the runway. He knew he must not hesitate, because at twelve- to fifteen-second intervals a dozen more of the big bombers would be following him.

The jet stream was particularly strong that day and pushed them through the air at dizzying ground speeds. They made it to the target, dropped their bombs and turned back toward England, and right into the teeth of the same strong winds. They were bucking a 140-knot headwind, which meant they might be going as little as thirty miles per hour over the ground. They were sitting ducks for German fighters unfettered by American escort fighters that were off chasing other bandits.

Fred began feeling pressure on his right rudder. He pressed harder and harder on the pedals to keep the airplane stable, until he had to ask co-pilot Pat Pierce to help. Suddenly, the lumbering, four-engine bomber snap-rolled, spinning on the axis of its fuselage, and yawing out of the formation. By the time Rector and Pierce got the plane under control again, they trailed their squadron by a good distance. Fred thought it a minor miracle they had spun out of the formation without hitting one of the five other planes that had been following him. Then the obviously broken airplane rolled again, and Fred knew he could not long control it and he would have to get his crew out.

Thinking and planning a way to abandon the plane was not easy. The flight engineer, Elmer Waibel, kept firing the top turret. Its twin .30-caliber guns, emitting a staccato *bam, bam, bam,* sounded like a big hammer banging on the metal fuselage. And now, Fred added to the noise the bell alerting all the crew members to get out of the plane as soon as possible. Fred stayed at the controls until he believed everyone else was out. Once he released the controls, if the auto pilot did not work, the plane could spin so violently that no one else would be able to escape. Every time he added power, the plane started bucking again.

When he finally left his position to try to save himself, Fred was subjected to the full violence of a giant bomber spinning out of control. Centrifugal force took over. He was slammed against the ceiling of the plane, against the floor, and the sides of the airplane. Everything he tried to do was countered by the out-of-control forces of gravity. His only hope of escape was through a hatch at the navigator's position. He had to climb through the spinning maze of the doomed airplane from the cockpit on top of the fuselage to the navigator/bombardier compartment in the bottom. It tested his physical strength and will to live to crawl the ten feet or so from his pilot's seat to the escape hatch, which was already thrown open by the crew members who left the plane ahead of him. After fighting his way to the hatch, and poised to push himself through it, he had to pause briefly until it appeared the position of the spinning plane would throw him away from, and not into, the flailing propellers. He did not know how long it would take his stricken plane to descend to the ground, but he believed he only had minutes to save his life. The bailout bell was still ringing in his ears, adding to his sense of urgency to avoid having the airplane be his coffin.

When he finally pushed himself out of the stricken bomber, he could see the terrible damage to the tail section that had cost him the flight controls.

It was Tuesday afternoon and the dead of winter. He stayed in free-fall as long as he felt he could safely do so, to make it more difficult for German troops to track his descent. He could see his airplane falling through the air, and then disintegrate as it struck the earth. He could see that the ground was covered with snow. And he felt very alone. Another airman had cautioned him that if he ever had to parachute into alien territory, he should cross his legs to minimize damage from a fence, vegetation or other obstacles.

He landed in the snow, his mind a blur as he calculated direction, cover, and threats that might come from a nearby town. This was a hilly region, similar to his home in the Piedmont of South Carolina. He was determined to try to go to the English Channel, perhaps to France, where a strong secret guerilla force was fighting the Germans and helping fugitive airmen. He was alone, but he had a high level of confidence that he could succeed. He walked a quarter-mile in the mountainous territory. The first night, he could hear trains as he walked west and south. He found a town with rail tracks and freight trains. He spent Wednesday on one of those little mountains, building himself a leafy arbor and hiding the rest of the day.

That night he found the trains in the town, and as they were shifting through the marshalling yard, he climbed aboard one going west. He came very close to being captured there. Some Germans saw him. They appeared about as scared as he was and ran off blowing their whistles. But when they came back looking for him, they did not find him. The freight wagons had little cabooses on individual cars and he found a cubbyhole on one end where he could hide. Blackened by soot and hungry, he rode that train for the rest of the week, until he was discovered and captured.

Fred was sent to the prison camp for Air Force officers at Barth. There he joined Booty Payne. Fred remembered listening to Friday night high school football games between Greenville High and Parker High, in which Payne's skill at kicking the ball usually gave Greenville High the edge. Now, in the prison camp, Fred played football in the yard with Payne and other captured airmen. Together they sat out the war in enforced idleness.

Chapter 7

▼

Tom Joins the Ninety-fifth Bomb Group

When Tom Hammond joined the Ninety-fifth Bomb Group, it already had been in the thick of battle from the earliest days of American bomber raids on Germany. Its planes with the letter B inside a square of black paint on the tail were the first American bombers over Berlin. Tom's crew arrived at the Ninety-fifth base at Horham, near the Channel coast. They lived in Nissen huts (named after British mining engineer Peter N. Nissen), sheet metal buildings that looked like a tomato juice can half-buried in the ground, equipped with primitive stoves to fight off the English chill.

The bucolic English county of Suffolk contained thirty-two airfields at the height of World War II. Neighboring Norfolk County contained an additional thirty-seven airfields. Every six to ten miles in every direction, Royal Air Force engineers selected the best high ground for runways, taxiways, aircraft hard-stands, ordnance bunkers, barracks, and administration buildings for the British and American fighter and bomber groups that were hastily assembled to assault the German military and industrial heartland. Most of the new bases were built to a standard design for bombers, with three intersecting runways. The main runway typically would be 2,000 yards long and fifty yards wide. The other two runways typically would be 1,400 yards long. Much of the fill material for the bases comprised rubble from bombed-out blocks of London, turning the German Luftwaffe's damage to the English capital into launching platforms for bombs bound for attacks on Hitler's war machine.[33]

The base at Horham, designated Station 119, stretched across windswept farmers' fields and engulfed the tiny villages of Horham and Denham. Begun in late 1941 and completed in September 1942, it briefly hosted other aviation units before the Ninety-fifth Bomb Group settled there in April 1943. Horham featured a centuries-old church built by the wealth of the wool trade, and featuring the oldest peal of eight set of bells in England. There was also a small pub called the Green Dragon. There were precious few local inhabitants and little entertainment for the more than three thousand young men stationed on the base. When granted much-sought-after recreational passes, the airmen would catch trains from nearby Diss, or Ipswich, to London.

Tom and his crewmates had left New York by ship on July 1, for an Atlantic crossing that usually took a week. The troop transport docked in Liverpool.

On July 18, Tom wrote to Callie from Horham that he was now with the Ninety-fifth Bomb Group.

"We have been moving around so much that I haven't had time to write to anyone," he said. He expressed some frustration with getting used to the local customs.

"It's pretty hard for us to write letters now that we are in a war zone because of the censorship. There's so much that you can't say and so little that you can say. It's pretty hard to get acquainted with the customs over here. It seems that almost everything is done backwards. I haven't been here long enough to find out much about the English but I have talked to a few of them and at first it's very hard to understand what they say. The worst part is getting used to the money. The first thing we had to do was get all of our money changed into English before we could buy a thing," he wrote.

(A second lieutenant, with no family to support, had a generous amount of money to spend. Base pay was $150 a month, and those flying in combat received an additional seventy-five dollars a month. The $225 monthly total was the equivalent of about $2,600 in 2006 purchasing power.)

"How's everything going back in the states? Sure would like to see some good old American ground. Do you know of any more of the boys who are over here now? Could be that I might be able to look them up sometime. This is sure beautiful country. Most of it is farming country and everything is green," he wrote.

On July 21, Tom continued his travelogue for Callie:

"I got my first mail today in over a month and it's the first word I've had that you had been hurt. I sincerely hope that you are better now. The last letter that Helen wrote me said that you were getting better now and I was kinda puzzled as to what had happened until I read another one telling me what had happened.

"It usually takes our mail a little better than two weeks to get over here but the V-mail gets here much faster. One from the folks came in exactly nine days. That's pretty good service, don't you think?

"You know I really think you would enjoy seeing this country. It's really beautiful. Of course it can't compare with what it was before the war as far as the towns and cities go, because everything has been turned into war production.

"In this part of the country though there are rolling hills very much like those around home only these aren't heavily wooded. Every available piece of ground is planted and made up of small farms which are kept in the best of condition. Everything is as green as it can be.

"The weather here is nice too, it's just about like the late fall at home when the nights get to be rather cool and the days are pleasant. Contrary to the fact that you hear that England is all fog and rain, it hasn't rained at all since we've been here and has been clear and pretty. I guess there are exceptions to it though and we will probably see plenty before we get away.

"During this time of the year the sun doesn't set until just about eleven o'clock and it's dark then about eleven thirty, and sunrise is around seven o'clock.

"There aren't many cars left in Britain now that are in use because there isn't much gasoline and too a car owner must pay such high taxes in order to drive his car. The car tax on an American car over here would be about five or six hundred dollars per year and due to this most of the people have parked the cars and started riding bicycles. You've never seen such a cycling bunch of people in your life."

On July 27, Callie wrote to Tom, explaining how she had been hurt in an accident:

"I received your nice letter and certainly was glad to hear from you again. I thought you must be taking a longer trip than usual. So glad that you made the trip over alright.

"The weather is terrible hot these days. About the first week in July we had some cool weather, but we haven't had any since.

"But for me I am standing it pretty good. I'm not working just now, so I can usually find kind of a cool place around here. The whole reason I'm not working is because I've had another little accident. Our Sunday School class had been over to Paris Mountain on a picnic, in a truck. I was sitting with my feet hanging out the back and fell out. I just had a few skinned places, but I had pretty bad bump on the back of my head. I stayed in the hospital two weeks. I have been home three weeks. I stay up all the time, but I'm still not so strong yet. But I'm going to be O.K., with no after effects. I went back to see my doctor yesterday and he advised me not to go back to work for a couple of months yet. I'm going to have an extended vacation. But it's sure lonesome around here. There's never anything doing. In a way I'll be glad to get to go back to work.

"I don't believe I know of any of the boys being over where you are just now. There are several I know in Italy, but I haven't heard of any I know being in England. One of my girl friends' husband was there but he is in France now. While he was there he visited in an English home and the lady of that home wrote his wife a very sweet letter. I read the letter and could tell by the way she wrote that they must speak quite different from us. I hope that you soon get used to the people and their ways. I am sure it will be much better when you have.

"Mother has been canning peaches today. They sure are good after doing without any for a couple of years. There ain't so awfully many, but more than the preceding years.

"Well I guess that is about all for now. So long and much luck. I'll close hoping to hear from you again soon."

Figure 4: Tom's crew at Hunter Field, Savannah, Georgia: (Front, left to right) Chuck Delcroix, Vic Radke, Scott Alexander, and Tom Hammond; (Rear, left to right) Frank Nutt, Joe Hagerty, Sam Clay, Ed Smith, Bill Galvin, and Ed Watress. (Watress was dropped from the crew before they flew their first combat mission.) (Photo from Tom Hammond's collection.)

Chapter 8

▼

Preparing for Battle

Tom's crew flew three practice missions before receiving their first combat orders. On August 9, they took part in a two-hour, fifteen-minute training flight with five other B-17s. On August 14, they were part of a five-hour, thirty-five-minute training mission that comprised thirty-six aircraft practicing formation flying. On August 17, they were part of an eighteen-ship training mission. It was all part of conditioning the new crews that had not yet been battle-tested. The formation flying they were being taught would give them maximum protection from their massed .50-caliber machine guns when German fighter aircraft attacked.

Calibrating the airplane's air speed indicator involved flying back and forth between two railroad tracks that were exactly a mile apart. Scotty remembered Vic having to climb sometimes to avoid hitting unexpected trains on the tracks. Once while flying low up the channel of an English canal, he recalls having to look up to see passengers on the deck of a canal boat.

On August 16, Vic recorded his first combat mission, an attack on Zietz, near Liepzig, Germany. Tom did not participate in that mission, and he would have to fly a make-up mission with another crew later in order to finish with his crew. His absence from the mission is unexplained in the Ninety-fifth Bomb Group's records.[34]

The young airmen spent their off-hours getting to know the East Anglia countryside. In an August 10 letter to Callie, Tom describes an excursion by bicycle.

"I've been out bike riding all afternoon, and as I'm not used to such, I'm just the least bit fatigued. Everybody and his brother over here has a bicycle, that is, all except me and I expect to acquire one soon. I guess it was silly to go riding all over the country on a bike, but I was curious as to what it looked like around here, so I borrowed a couple of bikes for my Bombardier (Lt. Chuck Delcroix) and myself and we took off. We had a rather nice ride though, and as I hadn't been off the base before, I enjoyed it lots."

Tom also praised the balmy weather they were enjoying in their early days in England.

"We've been having some very nice sunny days for the past two weeks. As a general rule it usually rains over here about every day but something must have happened for such a pleasant change as this."

He would soon change his tune, as rain and poor flying weather beset the region for most of the rest of his combat tour. Tom had the first encounter with old friends from back home, also serving in the Air Corps.

"I've met several fellows over here from Greenville. One of them joined the Army the same day that I did and went to Keesler Field with me but I hadn't seen him since I left there over two years ago. It's sure a small world and you meet people you know almost anywhere. I have two cousins over here that I think I'll look up when I get a pass. We can leave the post almost anytime we want to but can't go any great distance without a pass. I guess that's in case they want us for a raid," he wrote to Callie.

Tom's June 12 orders that started his crew's journey to Europe included detailed lists of seventy-three combat air crews. They were dispersed across eastern England as replacement crews to many different bomb groups. Cross-checking that list against the National Archives database of World War II casualties shows some on that June 12 list already had died in combat or been made prisoners of war by the time Tom went into combat himself. On August 9, Pilot Clayton Child became a prisoner of war and four members of his crew were killed in action when their B-17 from the 305th Bomb Group was hit over Karlsruhe. Pilot Harry F. Bowling, flying his first mission of the war with the 305th over Karlsruhe, also was shot down and captured with four other members of his crew that same day. Four members of Bowling's crew were killed.

On July 31, Callie wrote to Tom:

"I wasn't expecting to hear from you quite so soon, but I really was glad to. I'm sure glad to hear that you have gotten some mail. A month is a terrible long time to have to go without getting any. Now that it's caught up with you, maybe you will get it regularly. My letter from you today was only ten days getting here. It made the trip in almost the time the V-mail from your folks did.

"Boy, this sure has been a gray, gloomy day and rather chilly too. And it has only now begun to rain. We had a couple of showers yesterday though. We have been well supplied with rain this summer, not too much, but enough to keep the crops in good condition. They're looking swell in this section. In the farming sections over there do they grow chiefly food crops? And what type of soil is there?

"You bet I would enjoy seeing the country over there. I sure do enjoy travel and would have like to seen those countries before the war. I imagine it really gives one a thrill to see all those old places. And I imagine they are old and historical like, for after all it is a rather old country. Maybe I shouldn't ask so many questions, but you can answer them if you want to and if you don't it will be alright. What I would like to know, does the towns near you show much damage done by German bombs? And something else, are the towns very big, or about like ours?

"Gee, I can hardly blame those people for parking their cars. If tax was that high here we probably wouldn't see quite so many. And too, gas is so much more plentiful here. But I'll bet it does seem strange to not see any cars hardly. I've always heard that the English rode bicycles lots, and since the war I suppose they have gone all out for it. But after all riding bicycle isn't so bad. I rather enjoy it myself, when the weather isn't so hot.

"I don't believe I know any news this time. Since I've been staying home so much I don't hear of things happening. The boys you know from around here are so scattered I can't keep up with them. You know that James A. Neves had to go to the Army didn't you? He is in the infantry at Camp Blanding, Fla. He was home for a weekend not so long ago and he sure was brown and his lips were blistered and peeling off. I can't think of them if any of our class except you are across. I haven't heard it if they are.

"Well, I guess I had better sign off now. I almost forgot to tell you that I am feeling fine, but am still lazy as ever. I hope this finds you in tip top condition.

"So long and write every chance you can for I really enjoy your letters."

Chapter 9

▼

Mission One: Attacking the Gasoline Supply

Tom's first combat mission on Friday, August 18, lasted eight hours and forty minutes. It was the 196th mission for the Ninety-fifth Bomb Group. The B-17s attacked an oil storage depot at Pacy-Sur-Armacon, southeast of Paris, in German-occupied France. American ground troops had been in France for three months and were still fighting their way out of the beachhead region of Normandy. Hitting the oil depot would strangle German Army units' fuel lifelines.[35]

Tom read the takeoff check list for Vic, as he had done many times on practice missions, while Vic adjusted the throttles, checked the flaps and kept firm pressure on the brakes to line up ninth in order for takeoff. Ahead of them was R. G. Boudon, the lead pilot of the high squadron; behind them was Charles Wicker, who lived in the barracks with Vic and Tom. The lead aircraft would be pushed well down the main runway of the small airfield to allow the remaining dozen planes to line up for takeoff.[36]

The main runway was laid out across farmers' fields on the highest ground for miles around. The terrain fell away gradually as the runway ended. A mile or so in the distance stood a farmer's house with chimneys rising at both ends of the structure. More than once, lumbering fortresses, heavy with fuel and bombs, struggled to gain altitude, drifted towards the farmhouse, and clipped the chimneys off with their landing gear. Each time, the base commander sent workmen to rebuild the chimneys. The lead aircraft always had to struggle most to get airborne because it had less runway space to gain momentum before lifting off.[37]

Boudon, then Radke, then Wicker, lifted off, each a minute apart. The last plane lifted off at 10:27 AM. The high squadron spiraled skyward to assemble over the base at 8,000 feet. Assembly required flying a corkscrew pattern over the base, a pattern that could be dangerous with other bomber groups doing the same thing every five to ten miles away at other airfields in every direction. It was a good day for flying as English weather went: Stratocumulus columns filled about half the sky starting at 1,500 feet and rising in places to 5,000 feet. The crews could see easily for five to seven miles. At 8,000 feet, where they would meet in formation, the air was clear. At mission altitude of 10,000 to 12,000 feet, they would have clear visibility for twenty to thirty miles all the way to the target.[38]

The Ninety-fifth Bomb Group was the lead group of the Thirteenth Combat Wing that day. Thirteen aircraft took off between 10:15 AM and 10:27 AM and assembled over Horham. They arrived at the wing assembly point at Luton six minutes early and made a 360-degree (full-circle) turn to lose time before assembling with their sister One Hundredth and 390th Bomb Groups. On their left, they could see London hemming in the Thames River. They turned left, heading south toward Portsmouth. They crossed the English coast at Selsey Bill, east of Portsmouth, at 10,000 feet at 12:23 PM and forty minutes later, at 1:03 PM, they crossed the French beaches at Normandy. Ruined hulls of boats, tanks, artillery pieces, and individual soldiers' combat gear still littered the beaches, as well as the prefabricated docks that the Allies had built in England and towed across the channel to use as artificial harbors on the invasion beaches. They continued flying south over several low mountain ranges until 1:33 PM, when they turned due east toward their target.[39]

They reached their Initial Point, a set of map coordinates where they would begin their bomb run, at 2:22 PM. The lead bombardier could not see the target on the first two runs. They made a series of circles in formation, and on the third run at 3:20 PM they fixed on the target and dropped their bombs. Vic's crew flew in the high squadron, wing-tip to wing-tip with Charles Wicker. The lead squadron hit the oil storage tanks, while the high squadron let loose on dispersed railroad tank cars. In his after-mission report, navigator Robert Gammon said about half the group's bombs fell on the target, but "the target did not burn as if there was any gas there." Each of the thirteen planes delivered twenty bombs of 250 pounds each, making more than thirty-two tons of explosives dropped on the fuel depot.[40]

Scotty Alexander recorded that their bombs made a "direct hit" on the target. As they traversed the French countryside approaching their target, Scotty made notes about potential enemy troop or material movements. At 2:07 PM, over Pithiviers, south of Paris, he noted fifty to seventy-five freight cars. Eleven minutes later, over Soupers, he saw ten to twelve barges in a waterway beneath them, and at 2:32 PM, another thirty to forty freight cars. He also noted that the crew saw no enemy aircraft, but experienced medium anti-aircraft fire, or flak, that was "fairly accurate." The mission commander cut the corner off their inbound route as they flew back toward the English Channel to reduce flight time. But the route took them over a hotly contested battleground. Ground fire came from a pocket of German troops southwest of Falaise, where American and British troops were closing in on stalled German forces. Navigator Gammon complained in his after-mission report that "we would not have seen (the enemy guns) if we were on briefed course." At 5:27 PM, they crossed the French Normandy coast heading toward the Portsmouth coast. At 5:50 PM they turned east just north of London toward their base in the Suffolk farm country.[41]

At 6:27 PM, Vic set the plane down at Horham airfield, just seconds behind Wicker. All thirteen planes of the Ninety-fifth had made it to the target, and all thirteen returned safely to base with minimal damage from enemy fire. Vic's plane, number 42-31992, nicknamed *Mirandy*, had brought them home safely, but it was limping with just three engines. They had been forced to shut down the number two engine during the mission.[42]

Chapter 10

▼

Mission Two: The Gauntlet across Germany

Vic and Tom did not fly again for almost a week. But on Thursday, August 24, they pulled one of the longest and most dangerous missions in the Eighth Air Force playbook. The mission would require eight hours, thirty minutes to strike Ruhland, near the Polish border and sixty-five miles east of Leipzig.[43]

Vic and Tom were third in line to take off and were airborne at 8:02 AM, just behind Lt. John Hofsaes. It took about forty minutes for the group to climb to 6,000 feet and achieve formation. They flew toward the channel coast. At 9:30 AM an oil line in one of Hofsaes' engines broke, forcing him to turn back. Hofsaes was on Vic's wing-tip, directly behind lead pilot J.W. Streeton. Lt. John Wyatt, bringing up the rear of the Ninety-fifth A Group, moved his plane into position just off Vic's right wing-tip, close enough for Tom to look out his window and exchange hand signals with Wyatt. They turned north toward Great Yarmouth, and at 9:32 AM they departed the security of the English coast and began a long climb over the North Sea. On their right they could see the Dutch and then the German coast.

At 10:40 AM they began a forty-minute turn to the right that would bring them over the German mainland at 20,000 feet. Wyatt, who had pulled into

Hofsaes' position outside Tom's window in the lead squadron, could not keep up with the formation. As they started the climb from 20,000 to 25,000 feet over Germany, Wyatt's cranky B-17 began lagging. He could not maintain 150 miles per hour, and an engine began to overheat. Wyatt had flown number 1876 before, and he knew its peculiarities. He tried adjustments to the engines that had worked before, but at 22,000 feet, he was hopelessly behind and falling further away from the formation. Wyatt decided to turn back at 11:50 AM. He selected the runway at Norhulz as an alternate target for his ten 500-pound bombs, scoring hits on the enemy airfield. Seeking to further make some purpose of his aborted flight, Wyatt responded to an Air Sea Rescue to search for nine crew members who had bailed out. But after thirty minutes they found no one.[44]

Lt. Eugene Fletcher and many others in the formation saw Berlin for the first time, but from a safe distance. They were just outside range of the German capital's flak guns. Fletcher had no desire to see it any closer.[45]

Lt. P. A. Kroos left the trailing position in the lead squadron and filled the slot off Tom's wing for the final run to the target. One hour and thirty-two minutes after entering German air space, they unleashed their bombs from 25,100 feet on the synthetic oil plant at Ruhland. Flak bursts over the target were moderate, but inaccurate. The nine aircraft of the Ninety-fifth A Group that made it to the target dropped ninety 500-pound bombs on the oil plant. Targeting was difficult because of a deliberate smoke screen and smoke from previous bombing attacks. Lieutenant Lemmon, the lead navigator, could not observe the results of their attack. But strike photos showed part of the Ninety-fifth A Group's bombing pattern flew short of the intended target. The Ninety-fifth B Group's bombs fell in the smoke-obscured area, and damage could not be assessed.[46]

Tom said it was the "nastiest mission we had"—a lot of anti-aircraft fire, or flak. Fires of oil targets ablaze were visible at many places on the route home.

Lt. D. J. Schmidt, flying with the Ninety-fifth B Group, lost his number two engine over the target. He left the formation under control and joined another B-17 that had feathered an engine. At 1:50 PM Schmidt's plane was observed with the number four engine feathered, and losing altitude over the German town of Holzminden, southeast of Osnabruck. Their fellow airmen could not assess their fate, knowing only that no parachutes, smoke or fire were observed. But Schmidt and his crew spent the rest of the war as prisoners of the Germans.[47]

Eighth Air Force bomb groups sent 135 B-17s to strike oil and industrial targets. The Ninety-fifth Bomb Group lost one aircraft. It was the last mission of the Third Bomb Division B-24s. Vic reported light flak and no enemy fighter aircraft. His crew dropped ten 500-pound bombs.[48]

The after-mission evaluation by the Thirteenth Combat Wing was that the bombing had been poor to fair. The first group over the target missed it entirely. Smoke covered the plant when the second and third groups crossed the plant. Many bombs were dropped late or after the group had released their weapons. The analysts chastised group bombardiers to work on improving their bomb salvo techniques. They estimated the oil plant could be back to 50 percent production with only minor repairs.[49]

The strategy of "precision bombing" often proved a myth in the murky European weather and confusion created by the German flak guns. But for many of the bomber crews crossing Germany and trying to return safely to their English bases, it looked like a nation ablaze. Frank Dimit, Fletcher's bombardier, noted that most of the oil targets in Germany were struck that day, and fire and smoke blanketed city after city as they flew west toward England.[50]

Chapter 11

▼

Mission Three: Saved by the Silk

On Friday, August 25, on their third mission, Vic and Tom almost lost their lives. On a nine-hour, forty-minute mission to Politz, Germany, their combat-weary B-17 was shot full of holes. They barely made it back to England without injury.[51]

Tom's memorabilia from the war includes a piece of dingy white silk about the size of a woman's scarf, and torn at the edges. It was his share of a parachute used by the crew to slow their plane upon landing after a mission in which their brakes were shot out. "Flak almost got me," Vic wrote in his flight log, describing the end of the mission as a "parachute crash landing." He and the crew counted twenty flak holes in the plane. Tom kept a photograph showing a long, gaping hole just behind the flight control surface on one wing. The flak was bad, but no enemy fighters were spotted. They dropped twenty-five 250-pound bombs from 25,000 feet.

On that day, 169 Eighth Air Force B-17s attacked aircraft components factories, Luftwaffe experimental stations, and the synthetic oil industry. The Ninety-fifth lost four airplanes and a fifth was listed as missing in action in Sweden.[52]

It was a well-known fact among bomber crews that a convenient mechanical failure that forced a landing in neutral Sweden could put a crew out of harm's way for the rest of the war. The crews who landed in Sweden were consigned to captivity of sorts, one that kept them from leaving the country, but not one that threatened their lives or even their comfort. It was known that some crews deliberately put their planes down there to ensure they would not become casualties of war. As they flew over the North Sea and passed the Kiel Canal in Germany, Vic came on the radio and said, "Look down there. That's Sweden. You want to go down there and retire?" Everyone agreed they did not, that they wanted to go home. That meant taking their chances and finishing thirty-two more missions, but it was the right thing for these nine young Americans.[53]

Not everyone made that choice. Lt. David M. Taylor returned from a mission one day to learn that a crew from his barracks had declared an in-flight emergency and landed in Sweden, where the crew was interned. Taylor and the remaining residents began rounding up the missing crew's personal property to ship home to their next of kin. To their surprise, they found the missing crew had carried all their personal effects with them. They concluded that the crew had planned to land in Sweden and sit out the war.[54]

Tom watched as a close-by plane took a hit in the gas tank and was engulfed in flames. One crewman bailed out. Sam Clay said the crew of the stricken plane had arrived in England at the same time his crew did and bunked next door at Horham.

"We could see their plane as it was going down. They had to leave the formation. You could see a trail of smoke, see some of the guys leave the ship. One apparently waited too late, and you could see his chute caught on fire. It looked like a burning string as he went down. We all felt so bad, because we'd been kidding them that we were this seasoned crew with three missions under our belt, and they hadn't flown. It turned out to be a bad experience for us," Sam said.[55]

In their after-mission report, Vic's crew speculated that they had seen aircraft number 1992, piloted by Lt. A. M. Bussen, go down. But Bussen and his crew nursed the stricken plane to a crash landing in Sweden, where they all were detained by the neutral government. Vic's crew probably saw instead aircraft number 6085, commanded by Lt. A. B. Powell, which went down with its number three engine on fire. Powell's plane was observed in a steep dive before it leveled off, allowing the crew to bail out. Ball turret gunner Orlin E. Covel, tail gunner Melvin F. Wilhelm, and observer Berton E. Briley were killed by German flak guns.[56]

Tom's plane, nicknamed *Roarin' Bill*, a battle-weary B-17 with almost one hundred missions, was shot up so badly that Vic's crew was diverted to Woodbridge, an alternate field east of London that was 10,000 feet long, allowing the plane with no brakes to land safely. Sam recalled from his training that a parachute could sometimes slow a plane after landing. He helped Bill Galvin take Galvin's parachute, tie it to a spar in the rear of the plane, and throw it out the window to slow landing speed. Tom felt the crippled bomber touch down on the grass at one end of the field. It rolled the entire length of the paved runway, and its speed was not diminishing as fast as the crew would like. On and on it rolled, as their anxiety rose. Finally, the big bomber stopped on the grass at the other end, just short of the trees. Tom had a curious photograph that he shot of a gaping hole in the aircraft. Under it in his scrapbook, he labeled it "Third Mission." At first glance, it looks like the hole is in the fuselage, but closer examination reveals it to be a double exposure photo, and the hole is actually in the wing.[57]

In a letter to Callie on November 17, Tom wrote:

"Did you see the pictures that the folks got? The picture of the ship is the one that we flew on our third mission and it was by far the nearest we have yet come to getting shot down. We all sweat a lot that day."

Flak, the shattered pieces of anti-aircraft artillery shells, was the most feared hazard, more so late in the war than even the skilled German fighter pilots. Tom and Sam each preserved a piece of jagged steel from a German 88 artillery shell, both about the size of their thumbs, that they retrieved from their battle-damaged plane. Tom told the story many times about the shell exploding directly in front of his aircraft. The deadly shard pierced the metal strip between the Plexiglas windshields, struck and shattered the compass on the cockpit dashboard, and fell, spent, hot, and smoking, to the cockpit floor.

Their aircraft, a B-17G, number 42-31462, had been on the base for ten months, had chalked up ninety-seven landings, and would survive to be the last bomber on the base painted in the olive drab camouflage color. In 1944, factories began delivering B-17s with their shiny aluminum surface exposed. The paint not only added 250 pounds to the airplane's weight, but the destruction of the German air force had made the camouflage scheme unnecessary. *Roarin' Bill* would be repaired and survive until logged as missing in action over Strassburg on January 20, 1945.[58]

On Saturday and Sunday, August 26 and 27, Tom had his first glimpse of the favorite recreation site for American airmen—London. The young lieutenants received pay of $225, which would have the purchasing power of about $2,600 today. For Tom, it was a princely sum, considering he had been earning about forty-four dollars ($609) a month working in the textile mill.

"I was on pass in London over the weekend and I really had a good time down there. There are sure some beautiful old buildings around there and we had a lot of fun looking them over. Of course, we were there only a short time and did not get to see very much of the place. My main reason for going was to do some shopping that I'd been wanting to do for some time. You wouldn't know that there's a war going on by going to London. Every one goes about quite naturally and makes the best of everything. I think I'll go back down there on my next pass."[59]

Tom and Scotty spent the evening prowling the restaurants and bars of London. They marveled at Piccadilly Circus, wandered up Shaftesbury Avenue, and turned left on Charing Cross Road. At 1517 Old Compton Street, they found a menu to please the two young Americans' appetites. The Victory Restaurant specialized in tenderloin steak. And the owner, Sam Kalisperas, entertained American soldiers and airmen with his alcoholic concoctions. Tom asked for the recipe for one particularly tart drink, picked up one of the restaurant's cards, and wrote down the ingredients for a Windshift: three-quarters shot of brandy, one shot of lemon juice, one-quarter shot of crème de cocoa, and one-half shot crème de mint. He tucked the card into his wallet with an English ten-shilling note, upon which he had begun a list of his combat missions.

On Tuesday, August 29, Tom and Vic flew a practice mission lasting three hours, thirty minutes, in one of twenty-seven aircraft to fly the mission. They already had put in three combat missions, but they were beginning an intense, sixteen-day period of twelve practice and combat missions that would exhaust the strongest crew.[60]

Chapter 12

▼

Mission Four: The German Port of Bremen

Mother Nature began to give the Ninety-fifth Bomb Group a taste of the brutal winter ahead on Wednesday, August 30. Tom logged a six-hour, forty-five-minute mission to Bremen, four-and-a-half hours on instruments.[61] Wheels-up came a few minutes after noon, but into a low-hanging, solid overcast. Crews called such a start a "crash-and-burn" day. With planes taking off at fields just five or six miles away, the pilots of the Ninety-fifth had to fly a spiral pattern, climbing continuously in circles over the base. Planes too often became lost and wandered into the circular pattern of another base.

From bases throughout southeast England, the Eighth Air Force sent 327 B-17s to strike the ports of Kiel and Bremen. The Ninety-fifth fielded twenty-five Flying Fortresses for their assignment against Bremen.[62] The weather was terrible from takeoff. Solid clouds extended from 1,500 feet upward to 4,000 feet, with cumulus clouds intermittent up to 10,000 feet. They departed England at Great Yarmouth and made a long, sweeping turn to the east before crossing the German coast. They were flying above a 100 percent cloud cover that rose to 10,000 feet. About two hours after takeoff, the elements of the Ninety-fifth Bomb Group made a full-circle turn to climb above cloud cover over the North Sea. Soon after the turn they linked up with the One Hundredth Bomb Group to approach the target. A heavy bank of clouds towered over the German ports as high as 30,000 feet. At 4:05 PM, as they approached Bremen, there was 80 percent cloud cover below 10,000 feet, making accurate bombing all but impossible. At 26,000 feet over Bremen, the winds were blowing ninety knots, or 103 miles per hour, causing the Ninety-fifth B Group to forge ahead of the A group and creating an aerial traffic jam over the target. And fighting such a headwind could put the entire formation in great jeopardy from enemy gunners because it slowed their progress over the ground to the speed a horse could gallop.[63]

Vic's crew, flying another battle-weary fortress called *Able Mabel*, dropped forty-two 100-pound incendiary bombs from 25,000 feet. They were on their fourth combat mission in their fourth different airplane. New crews often were assigned the older, least desirable airplanes, while crews that made it to veteran status often would be assigned a plane they would fly again and again. But battle damage also could affect plane assignments, especially if a flak-damaged plane had to spend days or weeks in the hangar.

Cloud cover at the target was total, and the bomb run was directed by the lead bomber's radar operator. But at the last minute, the "Mickey" operator's radio connection broke down completely. Because of the cloud cover, the Ninety-fifth crews could not see where their bombs landed. Flak was heavy but inaccurate, and there were no enemy fighters. No planes were lost, and Vic's notes indicated no damage to their plane.[64]

Half their mission time was over the North Sea, about ninety minutes outbound and the same time returning. The Thirteenth Combat Wing dropped 457 100-pound incendiary bombs on the ports that day.

When they were not bombing Germany, they practiced flying. On Thursday, August 31, after a stressful, weather-hampered mission the previous day, Vic and Tom flew another practice mission. With twenty other aircraft, they flew in the relatively friendly skies over England for three hours, forty-five minutes. They got their first crack at the bomber that came the closest to being their own, number 42-102455, nicknamed *Screaming Eagle*. The airplane was delivered to the Air Forces March 4, 1944, at Cheyenne, Wyoming. It was ferried to Hunter Field at Savannah, Georgia, on April 18, where a combat crew picked it up for the trip across the Atlantic.[65] On May 8, it was assigned to the 335th Squadron of the Ninety-fifth Bomb Group.

Later that day, Tom wrote to Callie:

"We've been flying day in and day out and are usually pretty tired when we get back. I won't have time to write much tonight for I have to get up very early, for reasons you can probably guess."

And the sunny respite they had enjoyed earlier in the month ended:

"We've had some pretty bad weather over here lately and it really does get gloomy and dark on such occasions."

Chapter 13

▼

Mission Five: Forces
of Nature

The next morning, Friday, September 1, Tom ate breakfast prior to a pre-dawn briefing for a long mission to Mainz, in Germany's Rhine River heartland. They would be in the air seven hours and forty-five minutes, with four of those hours on instruments.[66] They got a tough lesson in European weather.

The Ninety-fifth began taking off from Horham at 6:41 AM into a cloudless, English sky. Over Bury St. Edmonds, after about a half-hour in assembly formation, Lt. Nelson Day aborted the mission after reporting his waist gunner, S.Sgt. E. Downing, complained about chest pain. At 8:15 AM, Downing was worse, and Day decided to return to base. His plane never exceeded the 11,000-foot assembly altitude. The weather remained clear over the English Channel, but built to 50 percent cloud over Paris, the French capital liberated by the Allied armies just a week earlier. Dense, persistent contrails streamed from the engines of the bombers in the cold, clear air above 15,000 feet, betraying the bombers' location to German gunners. At 10:01 AM, west of Paris at 18,000 feet, gathering clouds and the bombers' own contrails forced the group to make three full circles while lagging planes caught up.[67]

At 10:55 AM, now southeast of Paris, the Ninety-fifth A Group was still trying to break out of the clouds, and even higher clouds loomed ahead. With little likelihood that they would avoid the clouds, the mission was abandoned. Turning back, the group of twelve planes had to dodge and weave to avoid growing cloud formations and their bombers' own contrails, still hanging in the air near Paris from their flight into France. Back at Horham, they had the anxious task of landing with their bomb bay still loaded with explosives. At 1:50 PM, Vic set the explosives-laden bomber down at Horham without incident.[68]

Chapter 14

▼

Mission Six: Silencing Coastal Guns

After having Saturday to rest, Tom and Vic drew a mission on the French coast on Sunday, September 3. The seven-hour, fifteen-minute flight took them to Brest, on the peninsula that juts into the Atlantic Ocean south of Plymouth, England. Vic rolled the veteran airplane, *Able Mabel* painted on its nose, down the Horham main runway at 6:10 AM. Charles Wicker followed a minute later, with W. F. Curley bringing up the rear of the thirteen-bomber group at 6:23 AM. Takeoff intervals left little margin for error.[69]

Their flight path took them northeast of London, over Salisbury, and then a turn south over the English coast, two hours after takeoff. Assembly over their bases always took an hour or two. Another half-hour and they were over a 1,200-foot high ridge that resembled a spine on the Brest Peninsula. Their targets were gun emplacements around the port of Brest. At 12,000 feet, Tom's group started its bomb run. One hundred percent cloud cover frustrated their efforts to make a visual attack, and they did not have the necessary equipment to bomb by radar. They turned left, returned to the Initial Point, and descended to 8,500 feet in an effort to break out of the cloud cover. Again, the lead bombardier could not see the gun emplacements to make an accurate attack. The command pilot cut short the next return to the Initial Point. At 10:27 AM, still at 8,500 feet altitude, on a heading approximately northwest, the Ninety-fifth C Group dropped their bombs.[70]

In total, 404 B-17s attacked the gun batteries on the Brest coast.[71] The 452nd Bomb Group encountered flak over the Channel Islands. Vic and his crew dropped twelve 500-pound demolition bombs. Scotty said in his after-mission report that they scored a direct hit on their target, destroying the guns. There was no flak and no fighter opposition. No planes were lost, and there was no damage to their plane.[72]

But Vic's crew came near disaster because of vertigo, the disorientation pilots sometimes experience that prevents them from trusting their senses about their position relative to the earth. Tom was flying the plane in tight formation as they approached Brest for an attack. "All of a sudden, the plane was all over the sky," Scotty said. "I got on the phone to Vic and asked what the hell happened. 'Tommy got vertigo,' came the reply from the cockpit."[73]

Chapter 15

▼

Mission Seven: Smashing a Truck Factory

The Daimler-Benz plant in Stuttgart produced aircraft engines, military trucks, and utility vehicles. Previous attacks had inflicted severe damage on the factory. But the plant continued to roll out vehicles, about 5 percent of all the trucks going to the retreating German army. It was one of the three leading truck factories in Germany. As the German army retreated into the heartland, where roads were better and more abundant, trucks became high-value transportation for the German army—and high-value targets for the Americans. In addition, the aircraft engine plant conducted research on Daimler-Benz prototypes and initial production of new types of engines.[74]

On Tuesday, September 5, the Ninety-fifth Bomb Group targeted the Daimler-Benz plant. It would be a nine-and-a-half hour mission, fraught with danger and close calls. Starting at 6:15 AM, B-17s began rolling down the Horham runway. It took thirty-five minutes for all thirty-seven airplanes to take off.[75]

Formation over England took an inordinately long time. Almost three hours later, they crossed the French coast. Because of poor weather conditions, the Ninety-fifth aircraft were forced to make two full-circle turns. They did not break into clear air until 10:56 AM at 22,000 feet, east of Paris, near the city of Nancy.

At 11:42 AM, they crossed the Initial Point at 25,000 feet. Two groups dropped their bombs on the second run, while one group had to try a third time to sight the target. Lead bombardier Lt. D. W. Antonacci put his crosshairs on smoke in the target area because he could not identify the briefed aiming point due to smoke from previous bombing. Vic and his crew dropped five 1,000-pound demolition bombs from 25,000 feet. Their group dropped a total of fifty-five of the big, factory-busting weapons. Flak was bad, but there was no enemy fighter opposition.[76]

The Thirteenth Combat Wing became badly dispersed, and the wing was not reformed after the attack. Vic and Tom became separated from their group, and they were forced to fly back alone without protection. Scotty, plotting the course to the target, told Vic to turn right after the bombs had been dropped. But amid confusion over the target, Vic turned left. After clearing the target area, Vic's crew could not spot the rest of the formation. And Chuck, instead of dropping all five heavy bombs at once as planned, set the bomb release switch to drop them at intervals. Being the lead plane in the low squadron, Vic's plane carried the combat damage assessment camera. Scotty said the film later showed plumes from their five bombs stepping through Stuttgart's main business district like giant footprints.

Flying unescorted back to their base in England denied them the protective cover of their combat wing. And it exposed the lone Flying Fortress to every flak battery across southwest Germany and northern France. Somewhere over France, they were suddenly jolted by the concussion of a German 88 anti-aircraft blast just beneath them. Scotty yelled over the intercom for Vic to put the plane into a sharp evasive maneuver. They knew from bitter experience that the flak gunners would quickly fire another round, this time probably above their altitude. Having bracketed the aircraft, the third shot almost certainly would be fatal if they did not act swiftly. They put the plane into a sharp dive, and the tail gunner could see the third flak burst, right at the plane's previous cruising altitude.[77]

On Wednesday, September 6, Vic and Tom flew a three-hour, forty-five-minute practice mission in the *Spirit of New Mexico*. This started as a combat mission. Berlin was first aborted as a target, then Bremen. So they chalked it up as a training mission.[78]

On Thursday, September 7, Tom wrote to Callie:

"I've met several of my old buddies since I've been over here. That is, some of the boys that I've met since I've been in the Army. I met one fellow that joined the Army the same day that I did in Greenville."

Chapter 16

▼

Mission Eight: To Mainz, on the Rhine

On Friday, September 8, the target for the Ninety-fifth was the Maschinenfabrik Augsburg-Nuremberg A. G. at Gustavsburg near Mainz, a big ordnance depot. They flew eight hours, of which five hours, forty-five minutes were on instruments, in *Spirit of New Mexico*. Charles Wicker wrote in his debriefing report that contrails, clouds, and a backed-up bomber stream "became quite bothersome. Had to go up 2,000 feet to get above it." [79]

There was total cloud cover approaching the Initial Point for the bomb run, and 80 percent clouds inbound to the target. The Ninety-fifth B Group's lead bombardier sighted the target on its bombing run, but on instructions of the wing command pilot, did not bomb. The group made a turn and a radar run on the assigned radar target, the railroad marshalling yard at Mainz. Vic's crew dropped ten 500-pound incendiary bombs on the rail yard. J. C. Pipkin's bomb bay door froze shut in the cold air and his crew had to return to base with their bomb load still in the bay. J. C. Hofsaes and C. Lajeskie had five bombs apiece hang up in their bomb bays and returned to base with the weapons on board. [80]

The Eighth Air Force had 386 B-17 aircraft over targets at Ludwigshaven and Mainz. [81] Vic recorded that skies were overcast most of the day. No fighters appeared. "Light flak—not high enough," Scotty wrote after the mission. No planes were lost and Vic found no holes in his aircraft. [82]

Chapter 17

▼

Mission Nine: Dusseldorf

There was no rest for Tom's crew. They awoke on Saturday, September 9, for an early breakfast and a briefing for a six-hour, thirty-minute mission to Dusseldorf. They spent two hours on instruments, flying *Spirit of New Mexico*.[83]

The target was the light metal and armament works of Rheinmetall Borsig A. G. The Eighth Air Force sent 384 B-17s against munitions industry targets and lost sixty-three airmen missing in action, with two killed.[84] Vic and his crew dropped five 1,000-pound bombs from 26,000 feet above an overcast sky. Vic wrote in his logbook of watching two bombers go down on fire. In their debriefing, Scotty said one B-17 in the group following them blew up over the target, and he saw no parachutes. Then another bomber in the same group went down in a spiral with an engine on the right wing on fire. No chutes could be seen from it either. Flak around Dusseldorf was accurate, tracking, and moderate to intense. They also flew through flak bursts around Cologne and Aachen, both of which were poorly aimed at the bombers. Another feeble burst came from the area of Maastricht. The Ninety-fifth B Group was forced to track another group after flak hit the lead bomber's Plexiglas nose and showered bits of the plastic into the lead bombardier's eyes just before bombs away. The B and C groups made a left turn after bombs away as they were on a collision course with another combat wing.[85]

More than 210 bursts were seen in the factory, the northern half of the Dusseldorf marshalling yard and in adjoining industrial and business/residential areas. Hits were visible on seven of the eighteen major components of the armament works, starting a fire in a machine shop. Loading on the railroad sidings was light. A smoke screen pumped out a haze south and west of the target, but was largely ineffective.[86]

"Don't like Ruhr targets," Scotty wrote in the crew's debriefing report.

Pilot Billie B. Layl lost the number three engine in *Fireball* and returned early from the mission. He broke out of the clouds at 1,500 feet, leveling off as the crew discovered the tail wheel was not fully extended. Layl drifted over the grass beside the landing strip, five 1,000-pound bombs still in his bomb bay. Landing on wet grass, he slid beside the paved runway, and slammed into a pile of concrete rubble. The crew walked away, but the plane was destroyed.[87]

It turned out to be an unusually bad day for mechanical problems. Pilots J. C. Pipkin, Paul Fiess, Robert Harry, and William Hamilton all developed engine failure and aborted the mission. By the time they were over the target, just nine bombers were still in formation of the Ninety-fifth B Group.[88]

Saturday and Sunday were holidays for the Ninety-fifth Bomb Group. The unit had completed 200 combat missions since arriving in England, and this was a weekend of celebration. The highlight of the celebration was a dance featuring the Glenn Miller Orchestra. Lt. Eugene Fletcher flew a bomber, the *Zoot Suiter*, to Birmingham to pick up members of the orchestra. The weather was terrible, clouds were very low and visibility was just one mile. But they got away on instruments and completed their mission.[89]

Figure 5: Lt. Joseph Earle Johnston died on September 11, 1944 when his B-17 crashed in the Czech village of Kovarska. (Photo courtesy of Frances Goddard.)

Chapter 18

▼

Mission Ten: Tom Loses a Friend

On Monday, September 11, 384 B-17s were dispatched against oil targets in Ruhland, as well as a tire plant and a marshalling yard in Fulda. The mission had been planned as a major attack on synthetic oil plants and refineries, in a city on the extreme eastern border of Germany that American bomber crews had bombed previously. But for the first time since May 28, the Luftwaffe faced the bombers in force, putting aloft more than 500 fighters. In the face of such resistance, sixteen American aircraft and 153 airmen were listed as missing.[90]

But Tom's crew did not make it all the way to the target. Vic aborted the mission after the number four engine quit. They were loaded with ten 500-pound demolition bombs, flying at 22,000 feet. Vic wrote that they witnessed fighters hitting the group. "Dropped bombs on town," Vic wrote. The weight of 5,000 pounds of bombs was causing their bomber to lose altitude, so they aimed their bombs at the small German town of Hohenstein, at 11:21 AM. They did not observe the bombs hit anything of military or economic value.[91] Returning early due to equipment failure may have saved their lives. The mission proved to be deadly to many B-17 crews.

The Ninety-fifth Bomb Group mission report stated that Tom's bomber, aircraft number 1600, returned from map coordinates 5016N-0826E with its number four engine out. That put the crew within sight of Frankfurt, a few miles northwest of the big industrial city near the village of Oberreifenberg. They had flown well within enemy territory. After engineers inspected the plane and determined they were justified in turning back before they reached the target, they received credit for the mission toward their required thirty-five. A connecting rod in the number four engine had broken, and when mechanics inspected it at Horham, the engine was so thoroughly frozen that the propeller could not be turned.[92]

Despite being forced to return to base and missing a major air battle, the mission left Tom embittered in a way he would not soon forget. The war that had already claimed thousands of his fellow airmen claimed one of his best friends that day. He wrote to Callie: "One of my best friends that is from Atlanta, whom I became acquainted with in flying school, was stationed only a few miles from me. I went over to see him the other day and found out that he had been shot down on one of the same missions that I was on. I had met his family before I came over and they were swell people. I just can't figure out what to tell them when they write me, and I'm certain they will when they don't hear from him (I'm really sweating that out)."[93]

Tom later provided more detail.[94]

"I wrote two letters to cousins overseas, one to an aunt in Los Angeles and one to a Mr. Johnston in Atlanta. His son was a very good friend of mine. He's the one I told you about that was shot down over Germany. We called the boy Stoney because he is from Stone Mountain, Georgia. Mr. Johnston tells me that Stoney's navigator has been reported as a prisoner and is wounded. There may still be hope that Stoney is alive," Tom wrote from Goodfellow Field, San Angelo, Texas.

Lt. Joseph Earle Johnston's father, Joseph J. Johnston, lived near Stone Mountain, then a thinly populated suburb of Atlanta. His father was a bookkeeper for the Southern Railway in Atlanta, and had moved his family to the countryside in 1933. He had purchased about fourteen acres, part of a larger estate owned by the Holcombe family, who continued to surround the little family farm. He acquired chickens, and the family sold eggs. They grew corn to provide food for the chickens. Then came pigs, but only for a short while. After the pigs escaped their pen one rainy, cold winter day, and Mother Johnston and her sons had to chase them down, the pigs found new homes.[95]

Born in 1923, Earle (his family called him by his middle name to avoid confusion with his father) attended Avondale High School. A happy, outgoing young man, Earle showed an early passion for photography. He had grown up alongside the Holcombe children. Melba Holcombe, one year younger than Earle, thought he was one of the most intelligent young people she knew. She didn't think he was the best-looking boy around. His lips were a bit too large for her taste. But they were childhood friends and dated casually as teenagers. They usually met for a trip to the bowling alley on Ponce de Leon Boulevard, or hiked over Stone Mountain, with its wild trails and half-finished sculpture of Robert E. Lee, Jefferson Davis, and Stonewall Jackson.

Vance Percy, Earle's uncle and Mary Percy Johnston's brother, was a couple of years older than Earle, and would visit the Johnston farm from his home in Savannah. Vance liked the rural environment where his nephews Earle and Howard lived. The boys picked and ate wild plums and wild grapes. They worked together weeding the corn field and picking up Indian arrowheads near the creek. Earle was a smooth talker, and he had a Tom Sawyer style of avoiding his chores at his brother Howard's expense.

After graduation from high school in 1941, Earle pursued his education and developed career skills. He worked as a photographer for the public relations office of the National Youth Administration, a branch of the Depression-era Works Progress Administration. He also worked as a photographer for Norton Studio, a portrait studio in the Masonic building across the street from the county courthouse in Decatur. And he attended the Georgia Evening College at Atlanta in the 1940–41 and 1941–42 school years.[96]

On January 31, 1943, Earle enlisted as a private in the Army Air Forces.[97] He left behind Verda, his girlfriend. He also had a promise from the *Atlanta Constitution* of a job as a newspaper photographer when he returned from the war. His primary interest was photography. He took many pictures and developed and printed them with the enlarger in a darkroom he equipped in the Johnston family home. His subjects included swamps and other landscapes around Decatur and the heroic statue of Robert E. Lee and Stonewall Jackson that was then being carved on the side of nearby Stone Mountain. His father, in addition to working as an accountant for the railroad, had a greenhouse where he grew flowers for local florists.

When Earle left home to join the Army Air Forces, he left behind parents; Howard, a brother near his own age, who entered the Navy; and a five-year-old sister, Frances. He was especially fond of his little sister, a blonde, round-faced child who liked to sit in Earle's lap in the warm country home their parents had furnished with heavy oak furniture. A few special pieces were built by their grandfather, a master carpenter who specialized in repairs in the mansions of Palm Beach, Florida. The family took their meals in the large kitchen, except in the summer, when they moved the dining table to the screened porch. A large, spreading oak tree in the yard provided shade in the summer, when the family spent a lot of time outdoors to escape the indoor heat. Earle enjoyed sitting under the oak tree in one of the canvas chairs when he visited his family the last summer before he left to go to England with his crew.[98]

Earle's training to become an Air Corps pilot took place in Tennessee, Florida, and at Shaw Air Force Base in Sumter, South Carolina, where he met Tom Hammond. In the spring of 1944, while Tom was getting to know his new crew in Avon Park, Earle Johnston was training with his new crew at MacDill Army Air Forces base near Tampa.[99] Earle was assigned to a crew headed by Lt. Lawrence "Bill" Reigel, of Port Carbon, Pennsylvania. The navigator was George Prater of Millport, Alabama, the bombardier was Charles Dolby of Bridgeport, Pennsylvania. Enlisted crew members were Ralph Jacobson of Austin, Minnesota; Phil Mangan of Independence, Kansas; Edgar Herrick of Arlington, South Dakota; Jewell Spruell of Bellmont, Illinois; Nestor "Sully" Celleghin of South Euclid, Ohio; and Ray Deming of Teague, Texas. Together they logged more than one hundred hours of training flights around South Florida in April and May, learning to fly the B-17 bomber.[100]

Throughout their training at nearby Florida bases, Tom and Earle maintained contact. Tom drove his 1933 Ford to Earle's home near Decatur when he traveled between his South Carolina home and his Florida base.[101] When they received orders to go overseas, Tom and Earle did not go to the same bomb group or the same base, but their assignments were almost as good. Tom would be at the Ninety-fifth Bomb Group at Horham. Earle drew assignment to the One Hundredth Bomb Group at Thorpe-Abbot, just six miles from Horham. The two bomb groups, along with the 390th Bomb Group at Framlingham, formed the Thirteenth Combat Wing of the Third Division of the Eighth Air Force. The three groups flew missions together most days. Tom quickly learned that he could commandeer one of the ubiquitous bicycles on his base and in a half-hour be at the base that had come to dominate the Norfolk countryside around Thorpe-Abbott.

Earle's crew had their first taste of combat a month before Tom's crew flew their first mission. On July 17, they were part of a raid against a railroad bridge at Auxerre, France.[102] After one particularly ugly mission, they nursed their bomber back home with large chunks of its tail shot away.[103] Once they dropped material to French resistance fighters, a flight advertised by its planners as a "milk run." They came in low and slow, flying parallel to a railroad track, only to discover at the last minute that a train on that track was packed with German anti-aircraft batteries. The sides of rail cars dropped, anti-aircraft guns bristled from the platforms, and they flew through a hail of bullets to drop the supplies for the resistance.[104]

On September 11, 1944, the mission was against Ruhland, in former Polish territory, and one of the longest missions for the Suffolk-based bombers. It was Johnston's eighteenth mission and the tenth for Tom.

The night before the mission was Sunday. Navigator George Prater wrote to his mother that he had been to church that night, where he ran into Jewell Spruell, the tail gunner. Ray Deming wrote to his mother in Teague, Texas, on Sunday night as well. Sully Celleghin admired Deming, the radio operator, for his courage. Deming was plagued by air sickness that Celleghin knew had nothing to do with lack of courage. His body simply rebelled at the stresses of flight, causing debilitating vomiting and diarrhea. His crewmates understood and urged him to tell the flight surgeon; such ailments were perfectly legitimate reasons to be removed from flying duty. But Deming was determined to fulfill his commitment to his crew, and he flew every mission with them. Celleghin and Edgar Herrick took Holy Communion from the base chaplain on Monday morning before the crew began their mission. Their group was known to many as the Bloody Hundredth because it had experienced exceptionally high casualties in combat. And Ruhland was a very long mission, traversing the entire width of the German nation. They certainly knew the danger they would face the following day.[105]

Tom was in the air by 8:24 AM that Monday morning, assembling at 10,000 feet over Horham. They crossed the English coast at 10,000 feet at Felixstowe at 9:36 AM, then began climbing to bombing altitude. The One Hundredth Bomb Group was a few minutes ahead of the Ninety-fifth, which altered its course slightly to avoid the turbulence created by the dozens of propellers on the bombers ahead. At 10:03 AM, the Ninety-fifth was over Belgium. As they were flying northwest of Frankfurt, in the German heartland, Vic and Tom notified their leader that they had lost an engine, could not keep up with the formation, and were turning back.[106]

They would be alone, without the escort of American P-51 Mustang fighters. As Tom's crew announced over the radio they would turn back, one Mustang pilot listening was Charles S. Coe, who had soloed the same day as Tom a year earlier in Orangeburg. Coe was escorting the bombers to Ruhland with the 339th Fighter Group. He shot down a German Focke-Wulf 190 fighter later that day.

Meanwhile, the One Hundredth Bomb Group, flying as part of the same combat wing with the Ninety-fifth Bomb Group, was hit about noon by German fighters, about fifteen minutes before reaching the Initial Point for their bomb run. The initial attack by German fighters hit Prater's left leg. The bombardier, Charles Dolby, helped Prater out their escape hatch in the belly of the bomber, and then jumped after him. Prater was in free-fall for 22,000 feet before he opened his parachute, and he could see nothing of the continuing air battle as it slid eastward, off their briefed course and toward the German-Czech border.[107]

Luftwaffe fighter pilots assaulted the bombers in uncharacteristic strength, putting more than 500 fighters aloft.[108]

Sully Celleghin, Johnston's ball turret gunner, provided a vivid account of Johnston's death and his own survival:

"We lost our entire squadron within minutes. It was one of the biggest air battles ever," said Celleghin, who in 2005 lived in a suburb of Cleveland, Ohio, and was the only surviving member of Johnston's crew.

Records show the One Hundredth Bomb Group lost sixteen planes in minutes, including its entire low squadron.[109]

Celleghin's ball turret exploded when hit by German fighter cannon fire, and he was blown out into the sky. Celleghin, Prater, and Dolby were out of the doomed plane, but the six other crewmen remained in the bomber as it plunged toward Earth.[110]

Celleghin had learned an important lesson from a fellow gunner weeks earlier during a debriefing at Thorpe-Abbott. Standard procedure called for the ball turret gunner to remove his parachute before entering the confined space in the bomber's belly. Small men were usually selected for the tight space that still required them to squeeze accordion-style into the revolving gun platform. His parachute was stored in a rack within the aircraft. The gunner had to exit the swiveling ball turret and don the parachute before he could bail out. The complex machinery of the ball turret meant it sometimes jammed or otherwise failed and the gunner could not get back into the aircraft.

The other gunner, whom Celleghin did not know nor would he ever see again, advised that if the plane were hit, the ball turret gunner would never get to his parachute. He advised taking the chest-packed parachute into the turret, fastening it on one side, tucking it under one arm behind one machine gun.[111]

"'Try it. You'll see, it will fit,' he said. So I did try it, and it's a lucky thing I did, or I would never have survived that flight," Celleghin said. "I wasn't very large, only about 140 pounds, so it would fit. But I would never have tried it if that gunner hadn't told me about it."[112]

The last thing Celleghin remembered was the tail gunner, Jewell Spruell, shouting over the bomber's intercom that they were attacking from the rear and low. Celleghin hit the controls to spin his turret to the rear and aimed low. That was the last thing he remembered. He was in the turret one minute, and the next minute he was out, and the battle was gone. There was only silence as he was falling toward Earth from five miles high. The formation of bombers was flying at 27,000 feet, and Celleghin was expelled into the cold German skies without oxygen. He blacked out briefly. He did not know whether seconds or minutes passed before he became conscious of falling. Without thinking, he pulled the cord to open the parachute. But it was hooked only on one side, so he was hanging sideways from the parachute harness. There was nothing around him but the swirling winds. The battle had passed on. Then a fighter plane, German or American, he could not tell, soared close by and wiggled its wings. That's all he saw until the ground loomed towards him.[113]

Within minutes of landing on a hilltop in a mountainous region of eastern Germany, he was captured. "They were clearly watching the battle," he said. He quickly rolled up his parachute and stashed it in the undergrowth on the hill. He had acquired an English air force flying helmet, prized by ball turret gunners. He shed it as well, knowing that the Germans nursed a particular hatred of English fliers, who were regularly burning German cities with their night-time bombing raids. The Germans might just kill him on the spot if they thought he was English. He was soon accosted by two Germans in uniform, one of them an older man missing a hand. Celleghin guessed he had lost it in battle and had been sent home to join the Home Guard. Soon, Celleghin was sitting in the town jail in Oberwiesenthal.[114]

Reigel and Johnston were trapped in the damaged cockpit of their bomber, which was set ablaze by a German fighter's guns. The oxygen tanks under the cockpit were burning white-hot. Before he jumped, Prater knew the plane was riddled with holes from nose to tail by the fighter's cannons. Seeing his plane in flames, Prater did not wait for a command to jump. Reigel had given them standing orders that each crew member would make his own decision. Otherwise, battle damage might prevent them getting such an order and doom them while they still had the option to jump.[115]

The bomber's erratic death dive now took the direction of a mountain river that formed the border between Germany and German-occupied Czechoslovakia. Residents of Kovarska, a Czech mountain village, were witnessing one of the epic air battles of the Second World War. As the dueling German fighter planes and American bombers edged closer and closer to their village, battle-damaged airplanes began crashing in and around the village. From this clear, blue sky, they saw Reigel's and Johnston's plane in what appeared to be a controlled descent. Suddenly, the tortured airframe could no longer hold together. With just a few hundred feet remaining until they might hope for a survivable crash landing, the aircraft's tail section snapped loose from the rest of the fuselage. The tail glided on briefly and settled to earth without disintegrating. Local civilians found the tail section with gunner Jewell Spruell still in it, badly wounded but alive. He was put in an ambulance, but died later from his wounds. The main part of the fuselage, including the cockpit, pitched forward as it lost its tail, then flipped upside down just before it smashed into the ground outside Kovarska. It continued to burn intensely until only the metal parts of the plane remained. When the fire finally burned itself out, the blackened, grotesque metal skeleton rested with its cockpit compressed against the ground, and the metal hubs that had once held the big rubber tires reached for the sky.[116]

Other B-17s descended out of control upon Kovarska. The tail of another bomber, also separated from its main fuselage, crashed through the roof of the village school. Another crashed in a field just outside the village. Villagers described fields that glittered as if snow covered the ground because of the bits of shiny aluminum scattered around the village from shattered airplanes. Before the battle was finished, five bombers and two fighter planes crashed in and around Kovarska.[117]

Prater, Dolby, and Celleghin, who had parachuted from their plane immediately after the fighters riddled it with bullets, all landed in Germany. Prater, already suffering from a bullet wound in his left leg, broke his right leg when he hit the ground. A German family found him quickly and took him to their home for several hours. The woman of the home brought him a New Testament, a pocket notebook, a comb, and cigarette lighter and asked him if he knew who owned the personal items. Prater took them to be tail gunner Jewell Spruell's belongings. Spruell was, however, dying across the border where Czech and German rescuers had taken the mortally wounded man from the broken tail of his plane. Prater was looking at the belongings of some other dead airman who had come down near his own landing site. Prater wanted to go to the man's remains, but was unable to do so because of his wounds. Two days later, Prater was taken from a local German civilian hospital for transfer to a prison camp. As he was being transferred from one train to another, he looked up to see Sully Celleghin carrying one end of his stretcher. The brief encounter raised Prater's hopes that he would be imprisoned with his fellow crewman. But the Germans segregated officers and enlisted airmen into different camps, and Prater would not see Celleghin again until they were liberated at the end of the war.[118]

Celleghin surmised that the fighters he saw attacking his plane had gone for the cockpit, and that Reigel and Johnston had been killed instantly by the fighter planes' cannon fire. Subsequent investigations could not demonstrate conclusively whether they survived the first attack, only to die in the fiery crash in Kovarska.[119]

Spruell was buried in the German village of Hammerunterwiesenthal.

Frank Dimit, bombardier on a Ninety-fifth Bomb Group Flying Fortress, felt little but disgust for the conduct of the September 11 mission that was supposed to attack the oil refinery at Ruhland. "It was the most screwed up mess I have ever had the misfortune to encounter," Dimit wrote in his war diary. The Ninety-fifth formation failed to hit its primary target and steered instead toward its target of last resort. The lead bombardier aimed the group toward Fulda and a railroad marshalling yard, then inextricably at the last minute, ordered bomb-bay doors closed. He did it again at another rail yard near Frankfurt. The group returned to Horham with bombs still in the bomb bays. "I never thought I would see the day when we would bring back a full load from the middle of Germany. There was positively no excuse for not dropping them someplace," Dimit wrote. Dimit's pilot, Eugene Fletcher, wrote that it was the first and only time he ever saw an entire combat unit, the doomed squadron of the One Hundredth Bomb Group, destroyed.[120]

Despite the grievous losses over Kovarska, on the western frontier of Germany, American troops burst into German territory for the first time. It was the largest penetration of foreign troops onto German soil since Napoleon's forces charged across Germany more than a century earlier. The German army was on the run. The U. S. First Army plowed five miles into Germany territory near the frontier town of Trier, fifty-five miles from the critical Rhine River. Meanwhile, Gen. George Patton's Third Army captured a large portion of the old French Maginot Line, the German army's last major line of defense on French soil.[121]

Figure 6: The Ninety-fifth Bomb Group's high squadron during a mission over Germany.

Chapter 19

▼

Mission Eleven: No Rest for Tired Crews

On Tuesday, September 12, Tom's crew flew seven hours, forty-five minutes in *Doodle Bug*, part of a 348-bomber raid on Magdeburg and other targets.[122] Before they had left the assembly area over England, pilot G .L. Ferguson, flying ahead of Vic in formation, dropped out when his oil pressure in one engine failed. Vic eased *Doodle Bug* forward into Ferguson's position, behind and to the right of J.M. Miller's lead crew.[123]

They flew in over the North Sea and crossed the German coast, approaching the oil refinery from the northwest. Just after they crossed the enemy coast, at 10:20 AM, Scotty recorded seeing an out-of-place B-17 flying in parallel formation on the right of the Ninety-fifth Bomb Group, two to five miles distance. For about twenty-five minutes, the strange plane, possibly a captured bomber being operated by a German crew, maintained altitude with the Ninety-fifth, climbing whenever the American bombers climbed.[124]

Vic and Tom carried ten 500-pound bombs for an attack at 20,000 feet. After bombs away at 11:07 AM, they made the rally point at 11:12 AM. A brutal flight home loomed ahead of them. Twelve aircraft and 109 airmen were lost in action. It was a second straight day of heavy attacks on the German oil industry. The Ninety-fifth intelligence staff, S-2, estimated between twenty and thirty enemy fighters attacked the bombers as they left Magdeburg. They were met by friendly fighters, but not before the Germans inflicted grave damage. Suddenly, friendly airplanes were falling all around them. Lt. J. D. Taylor saw a bomber go down at 11:12 AM west of Magdeburg. At 11:15 AM, he saw another bomber going down, with five parachutes popping out of the stricken plane.[125]

At 11:28 AM, southwest of Wolfsburg, Tom saw a B-17 crash. He saw no parachutes. Two minutes later, in the direction of Kassel, they saw a fighter burning, falling, and lacking a parachute. At about the same time, north of the doomed fighter's position, another B-17 exploded. Tom's crew counted seven parachutes exit the bomber before it disappeared in a ball of fire and smoke. At 11:32 AM, just south of Hanover, another B-17 crashed. No parachutes. In just four minutes, Tom witnessed four airplanes and twenty-eight airmen lost from other formations.[126]

With unidentified American-made planes in the air around them, and friendly aircraft crashing in flames, the Ninety-fifth crews were more than a little nervous. Even friendly-looking planes could be controlled by German pilots. Pilot Kenneth Ringbloom's tail gunner, Sgt. L. R. James, reported an American-made P-51 Mustang, the most feared fighter airplane over Germany, headed straight for his B-17's tail, in a threatening pursuit. It was all they could do at such times to keep from firing their .50-caliber machine guns at such airplanes. Lt. J.D. Taylor wrote after the mission: "Keep friendly fighters from pointing nose at formation."

They crossed the Belgian coast at Ostende at 1:14 PM at 17,000 feet. Thirty minutes later, they were over their base.[127]

"Saw first dogfight, planes go down in flames," Vic wrote in his logbook. Vic's plane avoided damage, and no Ninety-fifth bombers were lost, despite the carnage they had witnessed around them in other groups.

Chapter 20

▼

Mission Twelve: Target, Sindelfingen

Wednesday, September 13, dawned cloudless over Horham Airfield, with visibility averaging one to two miles. But the relatively benign weather did not preclude a near disaster for the Ninety-fifth Bomb Group. Lt. Kenneth R. Ringbloom, taking off at 6:26 AM, one minute after the lead plane was airborne, was easing his plane into the air. As he crossed five hundred feet above the surrounding farmland, another B-17 suddenly loomed at his side and crossed in front of his plane. Ringbloom pulled back hard on his B-17's controls, jammed the throttles forward, and hoped the wings and four big propellers would bite the air and give him some emergency lift. Ringbloom's plane surged upward and forward and cleared the off-course bomber by only a few feet as the two planes barely escaped tragedy. Ringbloom believed the plane with which he almost collided was from a nearby airfield. Reserving his choicest remarks for the cockpit, Ringbloom, in his after-mission report, courteously urged base commanders to more carefully coordinate takeoffs in the future.[128]

The Ninety-fifth B Group assembled over the base at six thousand feet at 7:05 AM and climbed to 11,500 feet by the time they reached the English Channel coast, on a course that took them south. London's sprawling suburbs were on their right before they saw the beaches and the 140-foot lighthouse at Beachy Head, its brilliant light flashing every ten seconds and visible to ships for twenty-five miles. At Beachy Head, over its 500-foot high chalk cliffs, they turned southeast, and at 8:35 AM, they crossed the French coast south of Calais at 13,500 feet.

Pilot R. R. Harry's crew reported a jet-propelled aircraft flying 3,000 feet above the B-17 formation, in the same direction as the American bombers. They observed two gun barrels under its wings, but it did not attack them. At 11:07 AM, Harry's crew reported about fifty barges on the Rhine River at Worms, which they suspected were platforms for flak batteries. At Wiesbaden, they encountered both barrage and tracking flak, in bursts of three rounds, at least twenty-five times. Lt. P. E. Ristine's crew reported three bridges demolished as he flew over the Rhine at Mannheim. A dense smoke screen blanketed the town.[129]

By the time they reached the Initial Point of their bomb run at 10:35 AM, they were at 24,000 feet, just below a layer of cirrus clouds, with twenty-five miles of visibility. But ground haze obscured the target. Scotty Alexander observed a train of twenty-five to thirty-five cars head toward the target area from the east, then stop short in the woods east of town while the city was under attack. Lieutenant Ristine was forced to skid sideways out of formation as Lieutenant Metzinger crowded his position during the turn at the Initial Point.[130]

Lt. Bill Bramlett, flying his first combat mission, reported that the target was covered with smoke. The automatic flight control equipment (autopilot) was not functioning and Lieutenant Strachan, the lead bombardier, did not spot the target until a few seconds before bombs away. At 10:41 AM, they dropped 132 500-pound bombs on their target. Strachan noted afterward that the bubble on his bomb site was askew. By 3:34 PM all thirteen planes in B group had landed back at Horham. The intelligence analysis after the mission indicated that B group missed its target because of Strachan's aiming errors. The Ninety-fifth A Group bombed its target with good to excellent results.[131]

In their after-mission reports, officers used the crew comments and suggestions section to register a variety of complaints, some related to flying and some not. Ringbloom said his airplane's guns did not have proper sights, and some with sights were in bad shape. Maintenance of their .50-caliber machine guns was poor, he said. Lt. Eugene Payne reported his VHF radio was not operational. He also complained that the enlisted members of his crew had no hot water for bathing after their missions. Vic's crew penciled in: "Want some time off." With twelve missions under their belts, their commander took them seriously; they didn't fly again for two weeks.[132]

In total, the Eighth Air Force launched 376 B-17s against Stuttgart/Sindelfin-gen. Four aircraft and thirty-seven airmen were lost in the visual attacks on oil and industrial targets.[133]

Vic and Tom carried twelve 500-pound demolition bombs for an attack at twenty-four thousand feet. Vic reported no flak over the target and no fighters, but he also found seven new holes in his aircraft. They lost the number two engine when the supercharger went haywire. Lt. H. Griffin jettisoned part of his bomb load northeast of Karlsruhe after they hung up over the target. His gunners were forced to pry six of the 500-pound bombs out of the bomb bay. Once they were away, the bombardier was able to release the remaining six bombs. Lt. M. R. Scott was forced to land with all twelve of his 500-pound bombs still in his bomb bay due to a mechanical failure.[134]

For the first time, Vic and Tom flew aircraft number 42-102455, nicknamed *Screaming Eagle*, into battle. Previously, they had flown a variety of aircraft. They now were more or less assigned this aircraft, unless it was out of service because of mechanical problems or battle damage. *Screaming Eagle* would ultimately log eighty-five takeoffs and was marked for salvage on May 31, 1945.[135]

On September 17, Robert Hastie and Bill Lindley, 334th Squadron, flew Gen. Matthew Ridgeway on a special operation to watch his paratroopers jump from C-47s over The Netherlands to capture bridges held by the German Army. It was the beginning of Operation Market Garden, subject of the movie *A Bridge Too Far*. They flew in *Screaming Eagle*, the plane Tom's crew flew more than any other during their combat tour.[136]

On Friday, September 21, Tom wrote to Callie:

"I just got back from another pass to London. This time I had three days. I went down with my navigator, Scotty Alexander, and we did the town together."

"We had a very nice time down at London this time. We went around to see Buckingham Palace and Westminster Abbey. Wish that you could get to see them. I wanted to get to see London Bridge but our time soon ran out. London sure does cover a large area. I believe it would take me a year to learn how to get around there. The English cities are not built in orderly fashion like ours are. They are built very haphazardly and the streets run in every direction but the right one. There is also a very elaborate underground railway, but you almost need a guide in order to make use of it."

Tom didn't write about it in his letters, but Scotty showed Tom a side of life on their trips to London that the naive country boy might not have experienced on his own. On one such trip, they were carefully picking their way along a blackout-darkened street in London when a bolder-than-ordinary lady of the night approached Tom and took his genitals firmly in her hands to make clear her intentions. "What, who the hell is that?" a very surprised Tom exclaimed, and shoved the woman away.[137]

Another time, they met an English woman who seemed quite pleasant, and after making acquaintances over drinks, she invited the young American officers to "come over to my place." Her "place," rather than being the cozy London flat they had expected, turned out to be large hall, perhaps an old factory, with rows of not-so-comfortable cots and blankets hanging from clotheslines to screen the cots from one another. There were plenty of women to go with the cots. Scotty said that if anyone spent that night without a warm body beside him, "It was his own damned fault."

The Ninety-fifth Bomb Group historian composed a picture of base life each month for the group records. On August 1, he reflected upon the entertainment chosen by the 3,000 men on the base:[138]

"For three or four days after pay day, poker and the great American pastime 'craps' are in full sway, but soon the sheep are shorn of their wool and club activity settles back into its normal channels.

"Some of the more enterprising personnel have made the acquaintance of English families in some of the homes in the vicinity of the base. Nightly these sturdy fellows set off on their bicycles for a visit to their English friends. A few have become inveterate 'pub crawlers' and nightly adjourn to the nearest pub to swill their 'mild and bitters'.

"Almost every one takes advantage of their authorized passes. Some visit the historic landmarks, seats of learning and other edifying places. Some go to the small resort towns and pass their time getting as far away from the military routine as possible. Women are the greatest factor in regard to men going on pass. Almost without exception, everyone has some 'doll' he goes to see when on pass."

When 3,000 to 4,000 men, most in their twenties, are set down amid countryside and villages with little more than a few dozen inhabitants, people are going to look for every way possible to separate them from their paychecks. The Eighth Air Force did what it could to avoid unwanted parental responsibilities or sexually transmitted disease. This notice was included in the base Orders of the Day on August 23, 1944:[139]

"This headquarters is advised that the contents of old type prophylactic kits, known as 'V-Packette,' is subject to deterioration and is harmful to the individual if used in such condition. It is therefore requested that all stations in your command be instructed to turn in all 'V-Packette' (prophylactics) now in possession of units to the nearest Quartermaster Depot and draw authorized allowances of new type 'Pro Kits' from the same depot."

Saturday nights were reserved for parties on the base at Horham, with officers and enlisted men having their events on alternate Saturdays. The base historian noted in his August report that "this is the night looked forward to with much anticipation. It was a night of revelry and acts more or less as an escape valve for the shut-up emotions of the soldiers.[140]

"Girls are brought from nearby towns in GI trucks. Some of them don't look so good but all and one they appeal to the soldiers who are starved for feminine companionship. Occasionally a romance flowers but usually it is only good fellowship and mutual though temporal enjoyment that prevails," the group historian wrote.[141]

It fell to Tom, the Southern Baptist from a tee-totaling family, to get Scotty back to the barracks after a round of the village or London bars. Tom never acquired a taste for English beer, a claim seemingly confirmed by his distaste for beer throughout his life. Scotty often resorted to liquor after surviving another flight into hell over Germany. Once, after having several drinks, he got into a poker game on the base. After a lengthy game, he looked down at the table and realized there was no money left in front of him. Assuming in his alcohol-induced haze that he had lost it all, he got up and started back to the barracks. Sticking his hand in a pocket, he drew out a wad of cash. Checking his other pockets, he found more cash, eventually totaling more than $2,000 ($23,125). "I said, 'come on, we're going to London and have a party'," Scotty said. In wartime London, it was relatively easy to organize such a party. He rented a suite of rooms, bought all the liquor he and his comrades could drink, and put out the word that women were welcome. "We had a great time until the money ran out," he said.[142]

Not all encounters between American airmen and English women were for short-term gratification. Sgt. Ed Smith met Olga at a dance at Horham, and he stayed beyond his combat tour to marry her. Her ambulance group, a women's auxiliary of the British military, was invited to a weekend dance, and as senior non-commissioned officer, Olga had to go in order for the others to attend. Ed courted Olga, a native of nearby Felixstowe, for several months while he continued to fly combat missions. Her family welcomed Ed and made him feel at home. Ed could often be found visiting Olga's family, even when duty kept her on the job. When they could not see each other, they corresponded by mail.[143]

In 1944, between 12,000 and 15,000 British women applied for visas to the United States after they married American soldiers and airmen. *Good Housekeep-*

ing published the "Bride's Guide to the U. S. A.," in conjunction with the Office of War Information.[144]

In his September letters to Callie, Tom had changed his tune on the weather:

"Boy! Have we been having some miserable weather over here. It doesn't rain quite all of the time, but it is cloudy practically all the time and makes everything very dismal indeed. We had some nice weather for a few weeks after we got here but I guess that is gone for the coming winter."

On Tuesday, September 26, Tom flew a local training mission. "Made three landings," Vic wrote in his log. The night training mission took one hour, thirty minutes.[145]

Chapter 21

▼

Mission Thirteen: Return to Mainz

On Wednesday, September 27, Tom and Vic flew *Spirit of New Mexico* for six hours and thirty minutes, of which five hours, thirty minutes were on instruments.[146]

The Eighth Air Force sent 171 B-17s to attack industrial and transportation targets in western Germany. The Third Bomb Division lost two aircraft and twenty-two airmen, compared with the Second Bomb Division, which attacked the Kassel/Henschel/Gottingen area and lost twenty-six planes and 265 airmen.[147]

Vic and Tom carried twelve 500-pound bombs and attacked Mainz at 27,000 feet. Photo reconnaissance showed the group's bombs exploded in fields southeast of Gonselsheim, west of Mainz.

Vic wrote that flak was light and there were no fighters. But flak nonetheless knocked out their tail wheel and the hydraulics quit working.

The mission aimed to knock out railroad switching equipment that was being used to channel German troop re-enforcements for the Siegfried Line, a porcupine-like defensive corridor along the Belgian-German border. Because the lead Pathfinder aircraft was not armed with smoke bombs, the Ninety-fifth bombardiers did not know where to drop their bomb loads. The Thirteenth Combat

Wing was the last into Germany and the last out that day, and the crews endured prop wash all day.[148]

Charles Wicker noted the impact of the approaching winter on operations. "Sun glare off ships (is) hell. Tail windows frost over all the time," Wicker reported. The glare from the polished aluminum of the bombers was a new phenomenon. The old airplane *Roarin' Bill* that Vic and Tom flew in September was the last one on the base with the olive drab paint common early in the war. The Army decided the camouflage was not needed; the paint added weight and cost.[149]

On October 1, Vic logged a practice mission, but Tom did not list it in his logbook.

Chapter 22

▼

Mission Fourteen: Targeting German Ordnance

On Monday, October, 2, Tom flew an eight-hour, fifteen-minute mission against Kassel aboard *Puddles*.[150]

The Eighth Air Force launched 305 B-17s against Kassel, Bettenhausen and Fritzlar with no losses.[151] Among the industrial and military targets was the Bettenhausen Ordnance Depot. Vic's crew dropped five 500-pound bombs from 24,000 feet. Photo analysis showed 130 bursts across the depot and in adjacent fields. The buildings continued to burn throughout the day and one large ordnance building was completely destroyed. The combat wing lead navigator did not fly the briefed course, and failed to rendezvous the entire wing until well beyond the rendezvous point. The Ninety-fifth lead navigator, Lt. E. J. Murray, complained after the mission that the wing lead was poor, due to deviation from flight plan in course and air speed. He also said the low group command pilot showed poor judgment. Vic's crew sustained no injuries, but the plane had three holes in an engine and the fuselage.[152]

After the mission, thoughts returned to the airmen's favorite complaint: "Crew had only a slice of bread for breakfast," Charles Wicker's crew wrote. Eugene Payne's crew wrote: "£10 for eggs a month, and no eggs for a hell of a long time. Mess attendants are extremely discourteous. One told an officer, 'I'll be fucked if I'll feed you'."[153]

On October 5, Tom flew a practice mission for two hours, forty-five minutes in *Spirit of New Mexico*. "Abort target was Munster; No. 2 engine burning," Vic wrote in his logbook.

Enroute back to Horham, an engine caught fire. They had heard about crews, faced with burning engines that threaten to burn through a wing, put their plane into a steep dive until the wind put out the fire. Tom watched the flames lick around the engine cowling, felt the gathering speed of his diving bomber press him against his seat, and watched anxiously as the slip stream pushed back the oil-fed flames. Finally, the flames flickered out, and Vic gradually pulled the plunging airplane into level flight. Their gambit had saved their lives, and they were able to get the damaged aircraft back to Horham.[154]

Tom and his buddies settled in to a wartime routine focused on the weather, food, American music, and trips to London.

On Thursday, October 5, Tom wrote to Callie:

"Well, it rained again today. Darned if I don't believe it rains every day just to keep the record going. It was during the morning that it rained but there isn't a cloud in the sky tonight and the old moon really looks pretty, even from England.

"We had popcorn again tonight and it shore wuz good. One of the boys got some from home and we figured that we had better use it before it spoiled or the rats got it. There are more darn rats around here. We have to keep everything in boxes to keep them out.

"I had another pass to London the other day and had a good time too. I'll tell you about it when I get back, and you can't imagine how much I'm looking forward to that day. In fact, all the boys over here are looking forward to it.

"I told you we had a phonograph didn't I? Well we must have worked it a little too hard for the spring broke. I took it to town to get a new one put in but haven't had a chance to go after it. Guess I'll have to go tomorrow. We've really got a swell collection of records too. I guess we have more than seventy in all. The only trouble is that they are pretty expensive over here. One of the crews in my barracks has just finished up their missions and is leaving for home. Boy! Would I like to be going with them, the lucky boys.

"I haven't been to a movie now in over three weeks. I'm usually too tired to go so I just go to bed. That's something else that I'll have to catch up on when I get back. Did you ever see the show, *Make Your Own Bed*, with Jack Carson and Jane Wyman? It is really a scream and see it if you can.

"I haven't been lucky enough to see Bing since he has been here but we did have Glenn Miller's band here to play for us about a month ago. What do you think of his band? I always did think that they were about the best and now I'm sure of it. We have several of his records too. The best one of his I think is '*Under Blue Canadian Skies*.' You should hear it if you haven't."

Chapter 23

▼

Mission Fifteen: Confronting Flak Alley

On Friday, October 6, the Thirteenth Combat Wing targeted the Spandau Military and Ordnance Depot in Berlin. The airmen feared the German capital's flak batteries. Vic's crew reported seeing twenty-five to thirty guns "right in where our bombs hit—circled target area." It was the most anti-aircraft fire Tom had experienced. He watched as an aircraft went down right in front of his group, but because of the fog of battle, he could not tell whether it was an American escort fighter or a B-17. They could not see any parachutes from the plane.[155]

"Flak hit between seats," Vic wrote in his logbook after the eight-hour mission. "One plane burnt up; group head." Flak was light, and there were no fighters, but *Screaming Eagle* came home with seven new holes from enemy fire.

Scotty said the tension of being over Berlin would sometimes elicit strange outbursts from the crew. "It was really hot in there. Suddenly, someone keyed the microphone and said 'Oh baby it's hot out here. Put your belly close to mine.' Vic was furious. 'Who the hell did that; I'll kill the SOB.' I said, 'Vic, slow down, he's just letting off a little steam.' It wasn't me. It was either Nutt or Galvin. Nutt's down there in the ball turret, doesn't have a friend on Earth. Galvin's back in the tail, nine months from anybody."[156]

Records show 418 B-17s flew into thick flak shrouding the German capital. Seventeen aircraft crashed, 234 were damaged, and 157 airmen were lost.[157]

Across Berlin, bombs fell on munitions dumps, aircraft industry plants, and armored fighting vehicle factories. At the ordnance depot, aerial photography showed at least 130 high-explosive bursts blanketing the Standard Ordnance Buildings and spilling over some 1,800 yards into residential areas and open fields. Analysts rated bombing that day fair to good, with many scattered bombs, probably due to late drops or planes out of formation. The photo interpretation report stated "numerous incidents of business/residential damage is seen just northeast of the target and several of the buildings are still smoking."[158]

Vic wrote in the after-mission report that his crew had "creamed target." They dropped five 1,000-pound bombs from 26,000 feet, blockbuster explosives that could peel open hardened structures such as ammunition bunkers and cause even larger explosions. The Ninety-fifth A Squadron dropped fifty of the giant bombs. The Ninety-fifth B Squadron followed up the 1,000-pounders with 456 fire-starting, 100-pound M47A1 white phosphorous bombs that set the rubble ablaze and created a firestorm.[159]

The fighter escort took a beating. S. Sgt. Gerald Hoefert watched four P-51 Mustang fighters explode over the target, and no parachutes. There were about 200 Mustangs escorting the bombers. Hoefert's heated suit was turned off, but the sweat poured off his head. He had never been so scared before, in the face of the 800–900 flak guns around the German capital.[160]

On Tuesday, October 17, Tom wrote to Callie:

"I've been on flak leave for the past week and just got back Sunday. We went to a nice seaside town (Bournemouth, in Dorset, on the south coast of England) where everything was nice and quiet and had a swell rest. We went horseback riding one day and got wet as luck would have it. We rode for over an hour and most of the time in the rain. It rained every single day we were down there and every day since. This is the darnedest place I ever saw for rain. When it isn't raining there is usually a nice gloomy fog obscuring the landscape. Sounds great doesn't it?

"Remember I told you about my friend being shot down. Well, I got a real nice letter from his family today. He has a swell family; I met them once when I was on my way to Florida after I graduated. They told me that they had a wire from the War Department to the effect that he was missing in action. I think I'll have to go and see them when I get home.

"Speaking of London, it sure is a large place but I won't vouch too much for the beautiful part. There are a few parts of the town that are beautiful such as Buckingham Palace and some of the Cathedrals. As a whole it is mostly an industrial city and you know how ugly and dirty some of the factory districts can get.

One of the most interesting things about the cities and towns over here is their age. Most of the buildings that you see are aged in the hundreds. You wouldn't think to look at them that they were so old but I guess they are just put together well. A week or so ago, I was in a small inn and got to talking to one of the natives. He informed me that it had been built way back before 1700, and it didn't look to be more than ten or fifteen years old.

"One of the things that confuses me most in London is the subways. I've been there several times now and am just about to get used to them but at first I was at a complete loss.

"You would really get a big kick out of the taxis in London. They look like old 1925 Model T Fords but the majority of them are Austins and are really quite the thing even if they do look funny. I'll try to get a picture of one and send it to you. That brings something else to mind, do you have a picture that you could send me?"

Chapter 24

▼

Mission Sixteen: Setting a City Ablaze

On Thursday, October 19, Tom and Vic drew a mission officially aimed at armored vehicle plants on the Rhine River. But the practical effect of the munitions loaded that day would be to burn a city.[161]

They took off at 9:10 AM in a veteran airplane named *Paisano* and assembled over the base at 13,000 feet. At 11:40 AM, they crossed the English Channel, ninety minutes ahead of schedule. But their quick assembly dogged them, as they had to fly S patterns to avoid over-running the formations that took off ahead of the Ninety-fifth.

It was a relatively direct route, over the Belgian coast west of Ostende, south of Brussels, and across the Ardennes Mountains, to Mannheim, on the Rhine River south of Frankfurt. But the weather was lousy, and six-and-a-half hours of the six-hour, forty-five-minute flight was on instruments. Stratocumulus cloud cover was 100 percent below 10,000 feet as they flew toward the target. At times the big stratocumulus clouds reached above 25,000 feet. Above 25,000 feet, hundreds of bombers crisscrossing the continent created dense and persistent contrails in the cold air, making flying conditions even worse. Over the target at 1:10 PM, the cloud cover was 80 percent and reached to 20,000 feet.[162]

More than 600 B-17s attacked Mannheim targets, led by Pathfinder aircraft.[163] "New radar used seems 100 percent," Vic wrote in his log. Meager and inaccurate barrages of flak did not interfere with the attack. The Ninety-fifth Bomb Group's lead bombardier, Ray Davis, was flying in clouds and haze, but he was able to trigger the formation's bombs by targeting the lead squadron's smoke bombs. He could not see the results of their bombing because of the smoke and haze.[164]

At least fifty-six high explosive bursts were visible in the center of Mannheim's business district, extending from the bridge crossing the Rhine River northwest for three-fourths of a mile. The bridge took one direct hit, and there were at least fifteen probable hits on buildings. The Ninety-fifth squadron of thirteen bombers dropped 182 M-57 250-pound bombs and thirty-nine M-17 incendiary explosives. The latter were particularly nasty weapons. Each of the 500-pound units was a shell holding a cluster of 110 four-pound magnesium fire-starting chemical bombs. The shell was fused to open at 5,000 feet, allowing its small but deadly munitions to scatter over a wide area. That meant 4,290 potentially blazing structures as the fire-starters scattered to the winds. The tiny bomblets were almost impossible to extinguish. Incendiary bursts were evident in the business district for at least a half-mile.[165]

Maintaining formation became almost impossible as fierce winds at different altitudes split up the bombers. The lead squadron outran the low squadron, which despite maintaining airspeed of 165 miles per hour, could not overtake the lead squadron. Bill Bramlett's crew wrapped up their debriefing that afternoon with their minds on food: "Need rations on long trips," they wrote.[166]

On October 24, Tom flew a two-hour practice mission to "the Wash," Vic wrote in his flight log. The Wash was a bay north of their base where the bomber crews often flew practice missions. "Buzz job, calibrated air speed, swung compass." They flew *Screaming Eagle*.

Chapter 25

▼

Mission Seventeen: Hamburg

On Wednesday, October 25, Tom and Vic flew seven hours. For five hours, they were on instruments and most of the day over the North Sea. Their target was Hamburg; 455 B-17s were sent against targets of opportunity and an oil refinery.[167] All planes were away from the base at 9:23 AM. The wing leader approached the assembly point from the opposite direction as briefed, and confusion ensued until formation was achieved. The wing continued to wander, flying the first leg over the North Sea about ten miles off course before returning to the briefed route. By the time the wing was back on course, the undercast of clouds was total. Over the target, Tom and Vic dropped nineteen 250-pound bombs through the cloud cover. They were flying with the Ninety-fifth A Squadron. The B squadron leader developed engine trouble on the bomb run and lowered the formation 3,000 feet in an attempt to keep up with the A squadron. After bombs away, the leader aborted and returned to base, while the deputy leader took the formation into its former position soon after the bombers reached the rally point.[168]

Group command took the opportunity to make an example of a pilot whose failure to observe standard procedures kept him from joining his squadron or dropping his bombs. Lt. Gregory L'Ecuyer was late taking off because the interphone system on the first plane he was assigned did not work, and an engine was running rough. After about thirty minutes, he requested a backup airplane. He took off about seventy minutes behind his squadron, but he never visually contacted his formation. They followed the bomber stream headed for Germany, but after flying about seventy-five miles, they still could not find their formation, and they joined the nearest group they could see. The group they joined was recalled, so they returned to base. His squadron commander criticized L'Ecuyer's failure to join his group in an after-mission memorandum, citing his failure to use his radio to aid rendezvous over the English coast, despite arriving at the control point several minutes before his formation was due there. "He milled around from formation to formation instead of making a decision to keep in close to the division line on a time that would eventually bring him to his group," the squadron commander wrote. In addition to ordering a general briefing for all pilots on rendezvous procedures, the squadron commander ordered L'Ecuyer's next pass delayed by one week.[169]

A B-17 of the 486th Group taking off from Sudbury radioed that a corporal from the ground crew had stowed away in the aircraft. After the pilot received instructions to proceed to the target, at 19,000 feet, the corporal panicked, opened an aircraft door, and jumped out without a parachute.[170]

The Ninety-fifth was guided by the radar-carrying Pathfinder airplanes. Lt. Frank Dimit, bombardier on Eugene Fletcher's crew, could not see his target, but he guessed they hit something of consequence because they saw black smoke boiling up through the clouds as they flew away from the target. They got a good lesson in the value of anti-radar devices. Their previous mission to Hamburg cost the Ninety-fifth dearly in battle damage. This trip, the anti-radar devices so thoroughly confused the German gunners that they fired blindly into the clouds. As a consequence the American bombers sustained relatively little damage. Fletcher's crew could not find a single flak hole in their airplane after landing at Horham.[171]

"Radar is 100 percent. German R. O. with us," Vic wrote in his log. (Vic's passenger was S. Sgt. D. B. Pearl, a German-speaking radio operator who would monitor any German radio transmissions and perhaps even try to create mischief by responding to German signals.) Flying their old standby, *Screaming Eagle*, they encountered heavy flak but no fighter opposition.

Scotty remained focused on the important stuff: "Bad eggs at breakfast," he wrote on the after-mission report.[172]

Chapter 26

▼

Mission Eighteen: Mid-Air Collision

The next day, Thursday, October 26, Tom and Vic only had to spend one hour of their six-hour mission in *Screaming Eagle* on instruments as they attacked communications targets at Hanover. They were joined by 431 other bombers.[173]

"Saw mid-air collision over base. German R. O. with us," Vic wrote in his logbook. (Their passenger was S. Sgt. A. F. Piunti, a German-speaking radioman.) Other crews witnessed the mid-air accident as well. "Two blew up over England this a.m.," wrote Lt. W. C. Shaw.[174]

Bill Bramlett feathered the number one engine when oil pressure dropped to zero, and returned to base. Maintenance crews discovered the malfunction was in the oil gauge, not the engine.[175]

Chapter   27

▼

Mission Nineteen:
Chaos over Hamm

After one day off, on Saturday, October 28, Vic's crew flew five hours, fifteen minutes, most of it on instruments in *Screaming Eagle*, to attack Hamm. There were 192 aircraft bombing marshalling yards at Hamm and Munster.[176] Attacking at 25,000 feet with fourteen 250-pound bombs, Vic still found five new holes in his airplane. Other bombers dropped M-17 magnesium cluster bombs to sow fires amid the rubble. "German R. O. with us. Lead plane on fire. B. T. (ball turret) bailed out," Vic wrote in his logbook. (Their passenger was S. Sgt. B. W. Kneupper.)

For the Ninety-fifth C Group, there were harrowing moments over the target. Bombs were released at 12:20 PM at 25,000 feet. After passing the target, the squadron entered thick clouds, and the lead squadron was lost from view. As they let down through the clouds, intense flak erupted from the ground. The aircraft flown by formation leader Lt. Gordon Braund was hit and set ablaze, forcing him to give up lead to the deputy leader. Vic and Tom were flying behind and to the right of Braund. Lieutenant Kroos was on their wing to the left. When Kroos attempted to let loose his bomb load, four 250-pound general purpose bombs and two M-17 magnesium firebombs failed to drop. In the confusion, Tom thought he saw a parachute, but assumed it to be from Braund's burning bomber.

Meanwhile, *Screaming Eagle* was suffering damage. The leading edge of the right wing outside Tom's window was hit by flak. Then the number two propeller on Vic's side of the plane was struck. Frank Nutt reported the ball turret also was hit by a flak burst. While Vic and Tom temporarily lost sight of the rest of the Ninety-fifth C Group, they maintained radio contact. They plotted a course to try to intercept the rest of the group as they crossed the Belgian coast. At 1:22 PM, at 18,500 feet, they crossed the Dutch coast north of Amsterdam, but soon had to deviate further north to avoid towering cumulus clouds. At 2:30 PM, Vic set *Screaming Eagle* down at Horham. Lieutenant Kroos, his wingman, followed four minutes later, the six stuck bombs still in his bomb bay. After Kroos landed, squadron leaders searched the skies for the group leader. Twenty minutes after Vic was on the ground, Lieutenant Braund, who Tom thought had been lost over the target, landed at Horham. The plane was damaged, but the crew was still alive. They were the last to land, a full fifty minutes after the first of the C Group's thirteen bombers returned to base.[177]

Lt. Richard W. Ellsworth aborted the mission while still circling the airfield, blaming low oil pressure, and left the formation over the North Sea, returning to base with all his bombs still loaded on the plane. Sometimes squadron commanders would make an example of a pilot who too casually decided to abort a mission. Maj. Jack Beckelman, commander of the 336th Squadron, noted in the mission record "Action taken," and added, "Lt. Ellsworth will present a lecture, at the next Squadron meeting for pilots, on the subject, 'When to Feather an Engine'."[178]

On Sunday, October 29, Tom flew a three-hour practice mission in *Screaming Eagle*. On Monday, October 30, the crew flew another one-hour, fifteen-minute practice hop. "Shot landings; Hammond in pilot's seat," Vic wrote in his flight log.

On Tuesday, October 31, Tom wrote to Callie:

"I received a very nice letter from you two days ago and I hope that you will not think too hard of me for not answering immediately. After all there's a war on, and no matter how much I wanted to answer your letter, why they just insisted that I go along with the boys to bomb the Reich.

"Speaking of fires, we've had to have one for the past two months. In fact, we had a pretty heavy frost here the other night. While I'm still on the subject of weather we still have our daily rain. Honest, I have never seen so much water without being on the open seas.

"The old moon is full now and it really looks swell when the clouds occasionally open up and let it pop through.

"Sure wish I was there to go to the county fair. Do you realize that it's been three years since I've had a chance to go to one of those. I hope you'll have a good time for me too. If things keep going as well as they have so far, I may possibly be on my way home by X'mas. Here's hoping anyway.

"You know, our phonograph has kinda taken a back seat recently for we managed to pick up a good radio and we get some pretty good programs on it. We've just been listening to Tommy Dorsey and his band. He really has a swell outfit. How do you like him?

"Oh yes, in case you hadn't heard, Glenn Miller is a major now. As for Sinatra, I think that he has a very good voice and as you say, I like him on the radio, but he doesn't impress me very much in pictures. Bing rates first with me too.

"I haven't had a pass for some time now and am about to get all set for one.

"Reckon you're getting bored with all this, so I'll call it a day and hit the hay. Probably be a big day tomorrow."

Chapter 28

▼

Mission Twenty: Flak and Near-Miss Stories

Thursday, November 2, was a costly day for the Eighth Air Force. Twelve aircraft and 104 airmen were lost in a seven-hour mission against Merseburg by 616 aircraft attacking oil industry targets. Merseberg was the site of Leuna, the world's largest synthetic oil refinery. In 1944, it was the principle source of oil for Nazi Germany. Merseberg was encircled by hundreds of flak guns and protected by many squadrons of Luftwaffe aircraft.[179]

"Oxygen went out. German R. O. along. R. O. hit in wrist, broke his watch," Vic wrote in his log. (The passenger was S. Sgt. A. E. Piunti, a German-speaking radio operator.) A piece of flak had pierced the fuselage of *Paisano* beside radio operator Joe Hagerty's station, cut the watch band off Hagerty's wrist, and left the startled Pennsylvanian without even a scratch where his watch had been. Tom and Sam remembered and told the story, and Vic confirmed it in his logbook notes. It was one of the more fantastic near-miss stories from the crew.

Everyone had a near-miss flak story. Scotty's flak jacket saved his life. An 88mm shell burst directly in front of their plane, its characteristic *frump* concussion accompanying the black ball of smoke with a brief orange glow at its core where the shell exploded. A jagged piece of steel pierced the Plexiglas nose of the plane, and hit Scotty in the chest. It didn't take long to figure out that his flak jacket had stopped the projectile and saved his life. But when he returned to base and took off his shirt, he had a deep purple bruise radiating outward from where the flak had impacted his chest and protective vest.[180]

They attacked with ten 500-pound bombs at 28,000 feet. There were no enemy fighters, but flak was bad, and Vic counted twenty holes at the end of the mission. After-mission photography showed bombs scattered for miles around Merseberg, in open fields, on highways, and in villages, but few hit the oil refinery itself.[181]

Tough missions made the air crews think of creature comforts: "K rations on missions; lower tour to 30 missions; *hot water* for showers after missions," wrote Fletcher's crew after returning from Merseberg.[182]

Merseberg was a meat grinder for the Eighth Air Force. But the fuels it produced for the German war machine kept it at the top of the target list. In September 1945, the Army issued the United States Strategic Bombing Survey, which said this about Merseberg's importance:

"From the first attack to the end, production at Leuna averaged 9 percent of capacity. There were 22 attacks on Leuna, 20 by the Eighth Air Force and 2 by the RAF. Due to the urgency of keeping this plant out of production, many of these missions were dispatched in difficult bombing weather. Consequently, the order of bombing accuracy on Leuna was not high as compared with other targets. To win the battle with Leuna a total of 6,552 bomber sorties were flown against the plant, 18,328 tons of bombs were dropped and an entire year was required."

Chapter 29

▼

Mission Twenty-one: Mauling the Rails

On Saturday, November 4, Tom flew a seven-hour mission to Neunkirchen, about fifteen miles north of Saarbrucken. A total of 228 bombers of the Eighth Air Force attacked oil manufacturing plants and marshalling yards.[183]

Vic's crew dropped ten 500-pound bombs in two runs at 25,500 feet. A coking plant of Neunkirchen Eisenwerk A. G., a target of the bombers, was untouched. But the Otto Wolf Group plant was severely damaged. Railroad spurs were blocked by debris from a blasted gas holder. The roof and walls of the locomotive depot were blasted away. Slight, scattered damage could be seen in the town.[184]

Figure 7: Lt. Vic Radke with Roarin' Bill, a B-17 his crew flew on their third mission. Their hydraulic system was shot out, and they made a hair-raising landing at Woodbridge, on the English coast. (Photo from Tom Hammond's collection.)

Figure 8: Lt. Scott Alexander was the crew's navigator and Tom's best friend during their combat tour in 1944. (Photo from Tom Hammond's collection.)

Figure 9: Tom Hammond (left) and Scott Alexander were frequent companions on weekend excursions in England. (Photo from Tom Hammond's collection.)

Figure 10: Tom Hammond (right) and Bill Galvin kill time on the runway at Horham awaiting orders to begin a mission. (Photo from Tom Hammond's collection.)

C h a p t e r   30

▼

Mission Twenty-two:
The Rhine River
Maelstrom

Sunday, November 5, was scheduled to be a relatively short mission, just six and one-half hours. But Tom knew the target, the I.G. Farban-Industrie A.G. chemical and synthetic oil plant at Ludwigshaven on the Rhine River, was one of the most fiercely protected industrial sites in Germany. It had a reputation among airmen of the Ninety-fifth Bomb Group as one of the worst missions to fly. They knew it well. Eighth Air Force bombers had rained death on its 150,000 inhabitants forty-five times already. Today, they would do it again. Vic and Tom carried six 1,000-pound bombs to the target. Scotty Alexander reported the target "burned furiously" as they passed over the refinery.[185]

The Eighth Air Force sent 454 B-17s against Ludwigshafen and Kaiserslautern marshalling yards and oil industry targets; eleven aircraft and 104 airmen were missing when it was over.[186]

Scotty reported reddish bursts in the target area flak barrage. At 11:25 AM, over the target, Scotty watched one B-17 slip down to just above the cloud layer before it broke into flames. He could see two parachutes leave the burning airplane. They encountered a smoke screen over Worms. Then they caught a glimpse of the space age for the first time.[187]

At 12:28 PM, as they flew toward England northeast of Reims, France: "Feathered No. 4 engine. Saw V-2 vapor trail go up to 40,000 feet," Vic wrote in his flight log. Later, in debriefing, he said the vapor trail shot up at an angle of eighty-five degrees, vectoring 270 degrees beginning at about 5,000 feet. Vic estimated the rocket was traveling 300–400 miles per hour up to 30,000–35,000 feet altitude. Scotty estimated the position of the launch site for the rocket somewhere east of Malmedy, Belgium, near the German border.[188]

Tom's plane had fifty holes when they returned to base, the most of any of their missions. They described battle damage as "major." Frank Nutt, the ball turret gunner, was absent on this mission, replaced by R.W. Quick. Tech. Sgt. E. Cremer flew as an observer. They were flying aircraft number 42-102455, *Screaming Eagle*, which had become their regular ride. Mechanics and sheet metal benders back at Horham patched it up, and it continued to fly missions until May 31, 1945, long after Vic and Tom had returned home.[189]

Lt. R. H. Wright's crew illustrated how bad the flak was over Ludwigshaven. The number one engine was knocked out by flak, a gas line punctured. The number two engine had a runaway propeller and the nose section blew off. Number two began burning, but then the fire went out. The hydraulic system was shot out and the pilot's and navigator's oxygen shut down. The right flaps were damaged. Wright ordered the crew to bail out 100 miles northeast of Nancy, France. Fifteen minutes later, the plane had closed to within seventy miles of Nancy, still heading west. Lt. W. L. Olson, the navigator, had a slight flak injury on his right arm. Most of the crew jumped between Saarbrucken and Mannheim, and cleared the plane successfully at 22,000 feet. Wright and his bombardier, Lt. I. H. Levin, stayed in the aircraft and crash-landed it at an airfield ten miles southeast of Nancy. The left flap and wheel collapsed upon landing. There were extensive flak holes throughout the aircraft. Two P-51 Mustang fighters flew formation with Wright's crippled B-17 until he touched down on the friendly field.[190]

Airmen coming back from a tough mission frequently needed to vent their frustration, anger or fear. Often they blew off that emotion over things that had little to do with combat. The crew of Lt. H. C. Rose came back from this mission reporting accurate and intense flak tracking the bombers over Ludwigshaven. They saw at least one plane go down, the fate of the crew unknown. By the time they returned for after-mission interrogation, their crew comments were limited to: "Let's get this God-damned Orange Marmalade off the tables. No one eats it." Bill Bramlett's crew wrote: "Crew wants K-rations." Charles Wicker's crew groused: "Lead ship did not use lamp in tail on take off."[191]

In just a week, it began to look as if November might be a record month for air combat. In five days, 8,700 heavy bomber sorties dropped 25,000 tons of bombs on twenty-five German cities. Another 15,000 medium bombers and fighters struck airfields, rail lines and trains with rockets, bombs and gunfire.[192]

On Tuesday, November 7, President Franklin Roosevelt won an unprecedented fourth term in office. The war president and those who returned him to office could look with satisfaction at the progress of the war to defeat Hitler. American troops were within thirty miles of Cologne, the first major German city to be threatened by Allied troops pushing east from Belgium and France. Cologne sat astride the Rhine River, a hurdle the infantry and armor must cross to threaten the German heartland. American troops southeast of Aachen in the Ardennes Forest shivered in the bitter cold, while others fought German troops house-to-house in the town of Schmidt, and special units used dynamite to blast away German concrete defenses at Vossenack, thirteen miles southeast of Aachen. German troops who had overrun countries from the Atlantic to the Ural Mountains were now forced to defend their homeland.[193]

A twenty-four-year-old German who had been in the city of Cologne in early November told a United Press reporter with U. S. forces in Holland that during October, American and British bombers had destroyed 80 percent of the city. The allies had dropped 11,500 tons of bombs on the communications and rail center on the Rhine. Many Italian, Russian, and French people forced into slavery by the Germans remained in the city, living in cellars and wood shacks outside the city. But the pre-war population of 750,000 had been reduced to between 300,000 and 400,000 people.[194]

On November 7, Callie wrote to Tom:

"I surely was glad to get your letter today. It has been sometime since I had heard from you. It took this letter a little longer than usual to get here. But it's here and that's what counts.

"I'm sure glad to hear you have had a rest. From the accounts the papers have been giving, I know you fellows have been kept busy for the past few weeks. But I surely hope that it won't be very long until you will be home and take a long rest.

"Last week and the week before I was sick with a cold, but I am about to recover. I didn't loose any time from work but several days I could hardly make it. A few days I had such a sore throat I could hardly talk above a whisper, which sure bothers me. But I am feeling much better this week.

"The weather here is cold. Today there was ice out of doors, the first we've had I think. But it really hasn't been so cold for the time of year. We haven't had any rain in quiet awhile. I like rain once in a while, but darn it everyday.

"Today is election day, so all I can hear over the radio tonight is election returns. I will be glad when this is all over; it's all you can hear for the past few weeks.

"Last week I met Helen in town and we had lunch together. It's the first time we've been together in ages. Since she is going to school, it's hard for us to get off the same time. I think we'll try having lunch again soon, even if we only have such a short time.

"One of our high school teachers is married. Betty Pollard, remember her? She was married a couple weeks ago, to Cranford Bradley. His home is over near hers. He is now in the Navy. They are living in Richmond. I thought about the most of Betty, of any of my eleventh grade teachers.

"And do you remember Ruth Paris? She too is married, to George Morrow. You probably remember him as one of the twins that played on the Jordan basketball team.

"I don't know what kind a ball team Mt. View is going to have this year. It can't be much as all the kids are so small. But time will tell. By the way, our families are planning an oyster supper through Christmas and I'll be counting on you being here. The different hours we all have, we can't ever get together, so we thought maybe we would have some time together then. We haven't had any since that snowy night last winter.

"Tom, I am very sorry that I don't have a picture I can send you now. I haven't had any made in a long time. But I'll try to get some made sometime soon. I would like very much to have one of you. And those pictures of London. Can you get picture postcards of the city?

"I had better close this since it's about bed time. Hope it won't be so long until I'll be hearing from you again."

Chapter 31

▼

Mission Twenty-three: Supporting Ground Troops

On his twenty-third mission on Thursday, November 9, Tom flew a necessary make-up mission with another crew to catch up with his crewmates for the mission he missed at the beginning of their tour of duty. He flew co-pilot with Lt. P. A. Kroos against a target vital to defending the American troops locked in battle in the Ardennes.[195]

It was a long trip for a relatively nearby target—seven hours, fifteen minutes. Takeoff was at 6:30 AM, still dark in the cold, short days of winter in northern Europe. They spent more than two hours forming up over East Anglia, finally crossing the English coast at 8:58 AM. Ten minutes later, they crossed the Normandy beaches east of Calais. They flew southeast for thirty minutes, and then turned east toward Luxembourg. When they got a glimpse through the 80 percent cloud cover, they could see the mountains of the Ardennes rising beneath them; they could also see the lines of American trucks winding around the narrow roads with gasoline to fuel American tanks and food for the troops. An airman's odds of returning from a mission were worse than the survival rate for an infantryman, but at least the bomber crews that returned would have a warm bed to sleep in instead of a freezing foxhole. Visibility at 20,000 feet was unlimited, so long as the cockpit crew did not have to follow the dense, fluffy contrails of the bombers' Wright radial engines. Despite all the preparations to attack the German forts, cloud cover was 100 percent when the Third Division arrived over their primary targets at 9:57 AM.[196]

The Third Bomb Division sent 459 B-17s to attack German-occupied fortresses confronting American ground troops near Thionville.[197] Of this force, 345 bombers actually attacked primary or secondary targets, dropping 1,067.5 tons of high explosives. Just thirty-seven aircraft attacked the forts. Because they were under orders to attack only if they had visual contact with the primary target, 271 of the planes attacked the secondary target, the railroad marshalling yards at Saarbrucken. The junction funneled supplies, ammunition, and reinforcements to the German troops trying to hold the Americans at Germany's western frontier. Tom's aircraft was among those that helped smash the railroad assembly yard. In total, the Eighth Air Force launched 1,120 heavy bombers against the Thionville forts threatening the American troops, and the thirty-seven Third Division planes were the only aircraft to bomb the fortifications.[198]

An eleven-page tactical mission report issued by Eighth Air Force Headquarters reveals at least one first for this mission. American troops were within sight, and cannon range, of the Thionville forts defending the German homeland. Sending hundreds of heavy bombers against enemy targets within sight of American troops was risky at best. In the early days after American troops landed at Normandy, there had been tragic episodes of American bombs falling on friendly troops. Close air support was a new idea, and the risks still poorly understood. But the Air Force and the Army were trying to find ways to protect their own troops, while laying down a deadly barrage of bombs on the enemy.[199]

On this November 9 mission, several aids were employed to "minimize the danger of bombs falling within friendly lines."[200]

For the first time in a bombing operation, friendly lines were marked with SCS 51 Localizer transmitters and friendly anti-aircraft bursts. The SCS Localizer transmitters, operating on different frequencies, were set to show yellow indications on the approach to the warning line and blue indications after crossing the line. The friendly anti-aircraft bursts were coordinated with the localizers to create black smoke at 500-yard intervals, for one mile on either side of the localizer transmitters. Anti-aircraft gunners were to start the warning bursts ten minutes before the arrival of the bombers and continue for ten minutes after the attack was scheduled to end. Air crews were briefed on the warning system, and drilled on the fact that the warning line was not a bomb release line. Lead bomb crews were to use flare signals to alert their formations that the warning lines had been sighted. Pilots who failed to see the appropriate flare signals were told they were not obliged to drop their bombs. Each bomb division sent a single aircraft over the target area twenty minutes ahead of the main formation to ensure that the SCS 51 stations were operating. And each division sent a ten-bomber flight ahead of the main group to drop metal chaff to confuse German radar operators and protect American air crews. No one wanted American blood on his hands in this operation.[201]

Four bombers, all from the Third Division, failed to return from the mission. Eight other aircraft sustained serious enough damage to be scrapped upon their return to base. Brig. Gen. Walter Todd, in his comments in the Tactical Report, described the initial use of the SCS 51 Localizer transmitters as "highly effective." Just one airplane out of hundreds flying over the American lines dropped its bombs on the wrong side of the line, and no casualties were reported from that incident. The attack caught the German army in the process of exchanging gun crews, and American infantry troops were able to occupy many of the German gun sites. "Not only did the aerial bombardment lower the morale of enemy troops but it afforded an excellent morale stimulant for our forces," Todd wrote.[202]

No sooner had Tom caught up with the crew in his number of missions than an accident in the barracks cost him another trip to the Third Reich with Vic and the boys.

On November 11, Vic and the crew flew without Tom. "Scott flew co-pilot. (Records show Lt. C. G. Scott flew co-pilot.) Hammond burnt face. 1 bomb hung up," Vic wrote in his logbook.

Bombs lodging in their bays was not uncommon, but they posed a serious threat to the lives of the crew. The bombs hung by two attachments that were designed to release at the same time and allow the bombs to fall free. But in this case, one of the attachments did not fully release. The bomb hung precariously from one attachment point, the little propeller on the front was spinning, arming the detonator, and the bomb bay could not be closed. Landing with the bomb still in the bay would surely cause it to explode, destroying the plane and killing the crew. They were ordered to a pre-arranged set of coordinates over the English Channel where surplus bombs were supposed to be dropped. The pilots put the plane through a series of maneuvers to try to shake it loose. Finally, Vic put the plane into an arch, like a car traveling fast over a hilltop that briefly separates the passengers from their seats. The momentary weightlessness floated the bomb off its malfunctioning attachment point and allowed it to drop away from the plane and fall harmlessly into the sea.[203]

Tom's burns that kept him from the mission resulted from a housekeeping chore in the barracks. The crews lived in quarters warmed by crude heaters. One morning, Tom opened the stove door, and flames leapt out, burning his facial hair and reddening his skin. He spent several days in the hospital recovering and missed the November 11 mission with his crew. He could not wear the abrasive mask and other cold weather gear until his skin healed.[204]

On November 12, Lt. Gen. Carl A. Spaatz's U. S. Strategic Air Forces in London gave American journalists a balance sheet for the cost of the air war in Europe for the first two years. Enemy aircraft destroyed: 15,210; bombs dropped on the Third Reich: 638,880 tons; American airmen lost: 8,157; American bombers destroyed: 5,708; American fighter aircraft shot down: 2,449.[205]

On Friday, November 17, Tom wrote to Callie:

"As usual it has been raining all day long and the ceiling is down so low that even the birds think twice before coming out of their nests. It's only 5 PM and it's so dark out that you need a light to walk by. You know, it is days like this that makes us homesick. When we are flying and have something to do it isn't so bad, but when we sit around and have plenty of time to think of these things it gets pretty blue.

"Oh yes, I want to thank you for the package. That was darn nice. I got it two days ago.

"The mail situation is sure in a sad state of affairs over here now. Yesterday I received five letters and every one of them dated back from two to three weeks. It was the first I'd received in two weeks with the exception of two packages.

"Scotty and I went into town last night to see a show and almost froze to death. There is something funny about the cold over here; it seems to go right through you no matter how many clothes you wear. I suppose it's just the dampness in the air.

"The mail just came in and still I didn't get a letter from you. Disappointed? Yes!

"We finally have a plane of our own now. The name of it is *Screaming Eagle*. However, we didn't name it. The name was already on it when we got it, so we just let it stick. For the last couple of missions we had to fly another ship as we got shot up so bad one day that it took them about a week to get it back in shape again. Did you see the pictures that the folks got? The picture of the ship is the one that we flew on our third mission and it was by far the nearest we have yet come to getting shot down. We all sweat a lot that day.

"Just took time out for chow; hope it stops raining for a while so some of this water can get a chance to drain off.

"Sometimes we hear a German radio program that comes on about 12 o'clock at night. On it there is a girl named Midge who is supposed to have come from Pittsburgh before the war. It's really amusing to listen to them carry on. You should have heard them knocking Roosevelt the other night. They were really raking him over the coals. They play a lot of good American swing music though so we tune in just to hear that."

Chapter 32

▼

Mission Twenty-four: Familiar Plane Goes Down

On Tuesday, November 21, Vic's crew flew seven hours and thirty minutes, joining seventy-six other bombers to attack a railroad marshalling yard at Geissen.[206]

Their original target had been Merseberg, but the clouds were too high to attack. "Saw lots of flak," Vic noted in his logbook, adding that aircraft number 1600, which he had flown several times into battle, was lost on this day. At 11:40 AM, the aircraft was observed with two engines shut down. It left the formation under control of its crew and jettisoned its ball turret. It remained in radio contact until 12:54 PM and was accompanied by friendly fighters until 1:20 PM. The plane was last observed by a P-51 pilot five miles south of Munster with three engines feathered, flying at 500 feet. The entire crew, under the command of pilot Roy R. Shoaf Jr., became prisoners of war.[207]

At 11:37 AM, eight P-51 fighters chased a German jet fighter over Giessen. Near Koblenz, a B-17 went down in a spin. Then a fighter fell from the sky, and the pilot parachuted out. At 11:55 AM, two V-2 rockets soared high above Amsterdam.[208]

Vic's crew dropped twelve 500-pound bombs on the Geissen railroads, their target of last resort. Chuck Delcroix reported their bombs hit on and near the tracks. By 3:34 PM, all but one of the Ninety-fifth planes that had bombed Geissen was back on the ground at Horham.[209]

> *U. S. Fliers Executed?*
> ZURICH (Nov. 23) U.P.—Frontier reports said today that five American airmen who parachuted to earth during the last U. S. air attack on Friedrichshafen were rounded up and shot by SS men. The local population, according to reports, protested the executions, fearing American retaliation.[210]

Certainly, the editors of the *Greenville News* in 1944 did not know they had a local angle when they put this brief item in their "News from Everywhere" column. But the pilot of the B-17 Flying Fortress alluded to in the Zurich report was Lt. Peter Franklin Cureton Jr. of Greenville, South Carolina.[211]

His name and the names of his crew appear on the same orders that sent Tom overseas from Hunter Field, Georgia, in June 1944. They did not know each other, but their paths were parallel. They were both from Greenville, they were both assigned to B-17 combat crews, and to combat duty in the Eighth Air Force in England.

Frank Cureton was born June 4, 1919, and grew up a block from the Furman University campus in downtown Greenville, about two blocks from South Main Street. His father was a real estate broker. In high school, Frank showed the traits of a scholar. He participated in the Modern Problems Club, as well as the Latin, Drama, and Science clubs. Frank graduated from Greenville High School in 1936, and enrolled at The Citadel, South Carolina's military college. He was a member of the Calliopean Literary Society, a club organized to encourage cadets to improve their ability as public speakers. His demeanor and fondness for talking earned him a nickname, "The Reverend," from his fellow cadets. He was also a member of the riding club and he majored in business administration. Pictured on the same page in the college yearbook, *The Bulldog*, with Cureton was Horace E. "Sally" Crouch, who became a navigator on one of Jimmy Doolittle's Tokyo Raiders in 1942. Crouch knew Cureton as a well-liked cadet. Crouch said there was a sense among his graduating class of 1940 that while some would begin preparing for careers, they were also being prepared for war. Their eyes were on the war already under way in Europe, and few had any idea that America would be attacked first in the Pacific by the Japanese.[212]

After graduating from The Citadel, Frank enrolled in graduate school at the University of the South, a college supported by the Episcopal Church at Sewanee, Tennessee. He was doing all the things necessary to become an influential member of Greenville society. He was a member of the Southern Kappa Alpha fraternity, he earned the rank of 32nd degree Mason and he was a Shriner. Frank was living up to his Citadel nickname, "The Reverend." He was a member of Christ Episcopal Church, Greenville's largest Episcopal congregation and one of the largest in the nation. He asked Bishop Gravatt of the Diocese of Upper South Carolina to allow him to become a postulant for Holy Orders in the Episcopal Church and won the Bishop's support and approval to study for the ministry.[213]

When the war broke out, Frank was called to active duty in the Army. After serving 14 months in the Coast Artillery, and a year in the balloon barrage, Frank chaffed at such duty. Eager to win a place in a fighting unit, he transferred to the Army Air Forces. He was commissioned lieutenant on April 30, 1943. He was assigned as chief pilot of a B-17 bomber crew, which in June 1944 was assigned to the 303rd Bomb Group based at Molesworth, northeast of Cambridge.[214]

Tom and Frank were among the crews that attacked Germany on November 21. Frank was further along toward completing his required thirty-five missions; this Tuesday mission was number twenty-eight for him. He had flown his first combat mission on July 29, also against Merseburg, the original target of the November 21 mission.

The formation was flying at about 18,000 feet, heading south, when at 11:43 AM, Cureton's plane was hit by "intense and accurate anti-aircraft fire," according to the Missing Air Crew Report. According to an airman who witnessed Cureton's final moments at the helm of his Flying Fortress, the number three engine was burning, with flames streaming back to the tail. Soon the number two engine began to burn, then the entire aircraft. The bomber was slipping to the right, away from the formation and losing altitude. As it drifted away from the combat formation, Cureton's plane salvoed its bombs, according to Lt. William D. Russo, who witnessed Cureton's plane disappearing into a dense haze. Crewman James Ellis was blown out of the stricken aircraft, and knocked unconscious by the concussion. He had only managed to get one chute strap connected before blacking out, but it saved his life. At about 5,000 feet, he became aware that he was falling amid debris from his plane, and he could see eight parachutes.[215]

Various reports indicated members of two crews from the 303rd Bomb Group were murdered on the ground after surviving the bailout from their aircraft. One aircraft had two crew members killed by local SS troops. Cureton and two of his crew were rounded up by local farmers and killed with pitchforks. When German intelligence agents recovered Cureton's body. The only item they found among his personal belongings besides his Army-issued flight certificates was his membership card in the Association of Citadel Men.[216]

Co-pilot Paul Nally missed the fateful flight that took his pilot and crewmates because he was in the base hospital recovering from an earlier bullet wound.[217]

As Eighth Air Force bombers continued to pummel the Reich, and Allied soldiers advanced eastward in Europe, America began to see the truly barbaric nature of the Nazi government in Germany. A presidential commission concluded that the Nazis had killed at least 1.5 million Jews, citing two eyewitness accounts from Auschwitz and Birkenau in southwest Poland. "The board has every reason to believe that these reports present a true picture of the frightful happenings in these camps," reported Secretary of State Cordell Hull, Treasury Secretary Henry Morgenthau Jr., and Secretary of War Henry Stimson to President Franklin Roosevelt.[218]

On November 27, in one twenty-four-hour period, the Eighth Air Force destroyed 239 German fighter airplanes. In a single furious battle, almost unprecedented in scope, 500 American Mustang fighters shot down ninety-eight German interceptors. The epic confrontation developed over Magdeburg, Munster, and Brunswick and was the first time the Luftwaffe sought to stop the highly effective ground strafing by the Mustang pilots. In a separate action over the oil refinery at Misburg, 130 German planes went down in a savage exchange with American pilots. The German army was fast losing its air cover.[219]

On November 27, Callie wrote to Tom:

"Now I am the one to ask to be excused for being so long about answering your very sweet letter. I received it the last of the week, and it seemed that I just couldn't get around to writing. As for you, I think you do well to write often as you do, doing the job you are. I am always glad to hear from you at any time. Maybe there won't be so many more letters until I'll be seeing you in person. I hope it won't be so long.

"Today has been one of those old long blue Mondays. It rained all day yesterday and today. I hate weather like this. It is so lonesome. Mondays are always long and today has been exceptionally long. Last weekend was just about as bad, but this is about the first bad weather we've had this winter. And we haven't had too much cold, either.

"Did you get a nice Thanksgiving dinner? I hope so, anyway. Maybe and I hope you will get to eat Xmas dinner with your folks. If not that soon, maybe by soon in the New Year. I had a rather nice time Thanksgiving. Spent Wednesday night and Thursday in Greenville with a couple of girl friends. We slept until about noon, and went to a movie in the late afternoon, then had a nice dinner. Just the three of us had lots of fun, we always do. If it wasn't for them, I don't know what I would do. There just isn't any one or any place around here to go.

"I am trying to write on the kitchen table. John is popping popcorn and the two Collins children are in here talking at full speed, so if this (supposed to be) letter makes any sense at all it will surprise me. I am eating John's popcorn about as fast as he gets it popped.

"You knew Hilliard Bridgeman didn't you? His wife (Barbara Millard) has received word that he has been killed in action. I didn't know him very well, but have seen him several times. He and Barbara were married only this summer, they were together but about two weeks.

"Carroll Bomar is in France now. So I hear. I don't think he has been gone so long. Gary Tate is in Montana now. He is married too. I don't think I know his wife. She is from around Taylors. Whelchel Hollifield is in Georgia and James Albert Neves is in Texas. I guess that is about all the news of boys I know right now.

"From the news I gather now and then in the news, you aren't doing so bad yourself. I am indeed proud to know someone like you and I hope you will be very careful so that you will be on your way home by Xmas.

"Guess you are about fed up with all this corn, so I'll be signing off and get to bed. Good night and I'll be seeing you."

Always,

Callie

"P. S. I almost forgot to tell you that I received a nice Xmas card from you, too, last week."

Chapter 33

▼

Mission Twenty-five:
Return to Hamm

"My first runaway prop," Vic wrote in his logbook following a harrowing mission to Hamm, the nerve center of German railroad traffic, on Wednesday, November 29.[220]

A runaway propeller was one of an aircrew's worst fears realized. In order to stop a damaged engine from turning, the pilots and flight engineer had to be able to turn the variable-pitch propeller on that engine so that the edge of the propeller was parallel to the wind. Otherwise, the forward motion of the airplane in the wind would keep the engine turning. If the engine was damaged, the force of the 155 mile-per-hour slipstream could cause the spinning crankshaft and propeller to spin so fast it could fly apart. The cold temperatures at 25,000 feet could turn oil in the engine to jelly, further diminishing the ability of metal parts to withstand the stress. In the worst case, the propeller might separate from the airplane, crashing into another engine, the wing, or the fuselage of the bomber. Or it might fall away and strike another airplane. A runaway propeller could cause the airplane to vibrate violently, telegraphing to crew members outside the cockpit they might have to bail out. Such an event could be a terrifying moment, as the cockpit crew rushed to feather the prop, or turn its edges into the wind. Failure to feather the four spinning blades could doom an aircraft. Fortunately, that day,

Vic, Tom, and Sam brought the renegade engine under control and nursed *Screaming Eagle* back to base.[221]

Almost three hundred bombers attacked rail lines and oil refineries around Hamm.[222] But the primary target was the railroad marshalling yard, one of the busiest in Germany and regarded by many Allied analysts as the heart of the German rail system. It could hold 10,000 rail cars and was the largest yard in the country for general traffic. It was a vital intersection between the industrial Ruhr region and north and central Germany. The long, narrow mass of rails stretched for three miles and was up to 630 yards wide.[223]

Weather over England was ideal, with only about 10 percent cloud cover. The Ninety-fifth A Group led the Thirteenth Combat Wing. Radio operators experienced German jamming of their radio channels from takeoff until they crossed the Dutch coast. But the skies became increasingly troublesome as they crossed the English Channel and gathered to 90 percent clouds over the target. In addition, the lead navigator of the Thirteenth Combat Wing experienced malfunctions of his navigational instruments. They crossed the enemy coast just after noon. Electronic problems caused the lead to be passed to the high squadron, then to the low squadron's Pathfinder aircraft, which also began having navigational equipment problems about five miles from the target. Finally, the clouds opened enough for the bombardier to toggle his bombs visually, targeting smoke markers dropped by the 390th Group, flying ahead of the Ninety-fifth. Other mechanical failures diminished the outcome of the bombing. One bomber crew was forced to hand-crank its bomb bay doors open, while a second airplane crew saw its bomb load freefall because of a bad electrical circuit when bay doors opened. The group's bombs fell around Westtunnen, about three miles from the rail yards.[224]

The Ninety-fifth Bomb Group dropped 385 general-purpose, 500-pound bombs on the rail yard, as well as sixty-one M-17 incendiary cluster bombs. Each M-17 weapon would open above the target and scatter 110 four-pound, magnesium, fire-starting bombs into the debris created by the high-explosive bombs. The tiny magnesium bombs were difficult to extinguish. The Ninety-fifth bombs fell mainly in the city. The target had been extensively bombed by the Allies. Little additional damage occurred in the rail yards on this mission, except for one locomotive shed that was about 50 percent destroyed. Moderate damage was inflicted upon the already heavily damaged town east of the main passenger rail station.[225]

Vic wrote cryptically in his logbook: "Chewed out element leader," after a relatively short six-hour mission. But he made no mention in his after-mission report of the cause of his displeasure. The crew interrogation report contained only the usual complaint about the thirty-five-mission requirement, or Doolittle's missions, in reference to Gen. Jimmy Doolittle, the Eighth Air Force commander. "DFC (Distinguished Flying Cross) and 30 missions," the crew noted at the end of the debriefing paper.[226]

Chapter 34

▼

Mission Twenty-six:
Watching Friends Go
Down

Thursday, November 30, was a particularly tough day for the Eighth Air Force. Seventeen bombers were lost on the seven-hour, forty-five-minute attack on the I. G. Farben-Industrie A. G. synthetic fuel plant at Merseberg, one of the most heavily defended industrial sites in Germany. The Third Division sent 539 B-17s against the oil industry targets. In addition to the seventeen aircraft lost, 325 were damaged, and 312 airmen were lost.[227]

"Saw three blow up. Payne and Wicker went down. Rough," Vic wrote in his logbook. "Flak was bad," he wrote, and their plane *Screaming Eagle* came home with nine holes in it.

Vic and Tom watched as planes carrying officers from two crews who lived in their barracks go down, hit by anti-aircraft artillery. Almost simultaneously, bombers piloted by Eugene A. Payne and Charles C. Wicker were hit.[228]

Wicker was killed. At 1:20 PM, a flak burst in the bomb bay caused the *Thomper*, aircraft number 2102560, to leave formation engulfed in flames. The aircraft rolled upside down and began its plummet toward the ground. It quickly split apart at the radio compartment. Other crews reported seeing two chutes. Tom and Vic saw their friend's plane in the squadron above them burst into flames. One wing broke away from the plane, and it was doomed. Also killed was the co-pilot A. Rivas; navigator F. D. Johnson; bombardier W. E. Briggs; top turret gunner J. F. Robinson; and radio operator K. G. Bryce. Crewmembers J. E. Knighton, D. C. Dale, and E. J. Kobley survived and became prisoners of war. German intelligence troops recovered Wicker's remains, identified by his metal military identification tag, near a railway station five kilometers north of Merseburg.[229]

The Thirteenth Combat Wing lost its group leader over the target. The wing overshot the Initial Point, taking it over a particularly deadly flak zone at the town of Zeitz. An excessive number of S-turns over the continent had made it difficult to follow the briefed course. Being off course was the primary reason the formation blundered into the flak defenses at Zeitz.[230]

Ray Davis, the Ninety-fifth A Group's lead bombardier, mistook the oil refinery at Zeitz for the primary target, which was completely covered with a smoke screen. Trying to recover, he tried to realign his bombsights and release bombs into the smoke on the Zeitz refinery. The bombs fell in fields two to three miles east of Treglitz, missing the main refinery. Two of the Ninety-fifth bombers jettisoned their bombs somewhere other than over the target, one because of a gas leak, and the other because of an engine failure.[231]

As they watched Wicker's plane go down, Tom and Vic also spotted an American fighter escort plane hit and destroyed over the target and a B-17 from another group disintegrated over the target. Lieutenant Gillen's crew reported the stricken plane was from the One Hundredth Bomb Group, flames streaking the length of the left side of the plane, as it began a wide, flat spin. No parachutes were spotted leaving the bomber. Lt. W. C. Shaw's crew reported seeing two P-51 fighters blow up over the target amid thunderous flak.[232]

At 1:21 PM, Tom and Vic watched Eugene A. Payne's aircraft, number 297383, leave the formation just before arriving at the target, its number one engine smoking. The aircraft jettisoned its bombs, and began a controlled dive and disappeared from sight. Payne, the chief pilot, was hit by flak in the wrist, and bailed out.[233] Co-pilot R. H. Schmolke remained at the controls of the airplane, despite orders to bail out. His remains were recovered from the wreckage of the airplane. Navigator J. F. Baer and bombardier T. G. Salavos were POWs, as were crewmen Elias Schwartz, C. L. Mussehl, J. T. Crevitt Jr., and E. Bukrim. Top turret gunner and engineer Hershel R. Greshman was last seen in the nose of the plane and was killed. Several hours after they bailed out, all the surviving crew members were assembled by their German captors in a police station. Schwartz had a flak wound in his thigh. Navigator Baer had been beaten about the head. Payne was taken to a hospital at Obermassfeld.[234]

Losing friends became much too commonplace. Wicker, Payne, and their officers had bunked with Tom's crew. The two crews represented half the occupants of the Nissen hut. The young men tended to bond with those on their crew and in their barracks. But more often than not, they did not make long-standing acquaintances with many others of the thousands of airmen around them. Eugene Fletcher, in his war memoir *The Lucky Bastard Club*, described the phenomenon: "We remained close friends with our roommates and the crews who joined the 95th with us. We visited with others and worked with them, but we did not come to know them or to associate with them socially.... Unconsciously they were blocked out. If they did not return the hurt would be less."

Soon after Wicker and Payne and their crews' officers disappeared from Tom's barracks, replacement crews began to arrive and take over their Spartan quarters. Among them was Robert Vernon Mercer, a red-haired farmer's son from eastern North Carolina. Despite the pain of losing crews they had come to know, Tom liked Mercer immediately. His warm and outgoing personality helped the survivors of the November 30 mission think about the future instead of the past. The two young men had much in common, from their rural farming backgrounds to their southern heritage and their fiery tempers. They were both short of stature. Hubert Fackrell, Mercer's bombardier, liked the red-haired kid from Bladenboro. Mercer had a reddish complexion and was "full of hell," whether he was cursing a crew member who fell down on the job, or celebrating life in the barracks, or hanging out on leave in some English city. Mercer's wit and thick eastern North Carolina drawl had a way of brightening up the dark English winter and barracks that Fackrell found to be cold all the time.

It was not the first time Tom and Scotty had to cope with combat losses in their barracks. Scotty knew distraught crew members could usually go to the flight surgeon and get a bitter potion of grapefruit juice and medicinal grain alcohol. That medicine was usually followed by a visit to the officers' club and more drinks. On this particularly bitter occasion, Scotty got it in his head that if his crew were assigned to be lead crew, they could save their fellow airmen from future casualties. It was a drunken urge, and it made no sense, but Scotty was a big fellow, and he was determined to be heard. When the group commander, Col. Karl Truesdell Jr., came in for drinks, Scotty tried to make his point. Failing to get the commanding officer's attention, Scotty grabbed him and pinned him against the wall. Tom, at least six inches shorter than Scotty and a good bit lighter, was left to pull Scotty off the colonel and get him back to the barracks and out of harm's way. Assaulting a senior officer, particularly the group commander, could have landed Scotty in the stockade, cost him his commission, or worse. But nothing was said about the incident the next morning or ever.[235]

"We didn't like the SOB anyway," Scotty said of Colonel Truesdell. "He had issued orders that all personnel were to salute him, regardless of the place or the circumstances. Well, one day, a bunch of us were walking along a path, all strung out, when the colonel approached us on a bicycle. We all saluted him, as he had ordered, and he had to return the salute. It wasn't long before he fell off the bicycle and was on his ass."[236]

Chapter 35

▼

Mission Twenty-seven: Blasting the Rail Yards

The railroad marshalling yard at Koblenz, at the confluence of the Rhine and Mosel rivers, could move 2,600 rail cars through every day to nearby battle lines in the Ardennes and around Luxembourg. Analysts concluded that if the rail junction were disrupted, Koblenz could become a serious bottleneck when the battle flared on the German-Belgian frontier. Trains leaving Koblenz were on the heavily traveled, double-track route that paralleled the Rhine from Mannheim to Koln. Any damage to these tracks could relieve pressure on the American forces pushing into the Ardennes. There would be no passes this weekend for Vic's crew. On Saturday, December 2, they drew a five-hour, forty-five-minute mission to attack the rail yard at Koblenz.[237]

The Third Bomb Division, including the Ninety-fifth Bomb Group, had no problem assembling over their assigned radio beacon, after takeoff around 9:30 AM. They crossed the Belgian coast at Ostende at 12:06 PM at 22,000 feet. As they crossed Belgium, they encountered stronger winds than expected. Soon after crossing the Initial Point, they ran into high clouds. Northeast of Luxembourg, the group leader abandoned the mission, and the group turned back because of suddenly deteriorating weather.[238]

"Contrails bad," Vic wrote in his logbook. They turned *Big Casino* around when the mission had been aborted because clouds were too high for the formation to fly over. The thirteen bombers of the Ninety-fifth B Group came home with all 152 ANM-64 bombs in their bays.[239]

Chapter 36

▼

Tom Celebrates a Birthday

On Sunday, December 3, Tom wrote to Callie:

"Every day this week I've been hoping to get a letter from you. But no luck. Today, though, it came and on my birthday, too, my 22nd. I was very glad to hear from you too. If you find time to do so, please don't wait until you hear from me to write, for it takes so long now for the mail to get back and forth. I'll do likewise.

"It's another bad day today. We've had a terrific wind all day long that is very cold and it's been raining to boot. We got up to fly this morning, but couldn't take off due to the weather. As we didn't fly, the whole crew went to church this morning. Very unusual. The rest of the day we spent inside where it was warm.

"Sorry to hear that you haven't been feeling well but I hope that you are better now. It's bad enough when you aren't feeling up to par but to work at the same time is pretty bad. Several times I've flown when I could hardly make it just because I didn't want to get behind with my missions.

"We heard the Army-Navy Football game last night. I was backing Army and even went so far as to bet a pound (four dollars) on it. I'm a pound to the good now. I'd sure like to see a good basketball game also.

"Well, I reckon I had better say 'cheerio,' as the witches probably have something vicious brewed up for tomorrow."

On December 4, Callie wrote to Tom:

"Received your very nice letter today. I was a little surprised hearing so soon. But I'll assure you it was quite a pleasant one. I am always glad to hear from you, so write often as you can. And you can always be sure I'll answer as soon as I can.

"Again tonight we have company, or should I say Daddy does. So don't be surprised what might be here. I am listening and writing all at the same time.

"There's really not so much to write about from here. The weather is plenty cold, ice, but no snow yet. I sure hope we have some snow this winter. Speaking of rain, last weekend and the first of the week was very cold and lonesome. I'll agree with you that weather like this will give you the blues. Even at home and I know it would be still worse to be away from home.

"But really, Tom, I am earnestly hoping that it won't be so long until you can be home again. You undoubtedly have been through some tough times, lately. May Lady Luck be with you and the time swiftly pass until you can be back with all the folks.

"No, I haven't seen the pictures you sent the folks, in fact, I haven't seen any of them in a month, I guess. I think we all are to get together one night through Christmas. And that's not far off. I sure wish it was possible for you to be here.

"Speaking of mail being uncertain, it is rather that way here. Some times I get your letters in a week, some times three weeks. I guess there is so much that it is hard to keep it all straight. The day after Thanksgiving I received a Xmas card from you. And your letter of the 17th tells me of you receiving the gift I sent you for Xmas. And by the way, did they fit? As you know, it was a guess. I hope you can find use for them. After all I haven't seen you so many times.[240]

"I saw a real cute picture last week. *Dough Girls,* Ann Sheridan, and Alexis Smith. It was real comical. And about a couple weeks ago I saw *Rainbow Island,* Dorothy Lamour; and Eddie Bracken, it was a comedy. I don't go to very many movies. But I do listen to the radio about every night. I have a special program two or three nights a week, I always listen to.

"It's getting late and I still have to crawl out early these cold mornings. So guess I had better get a little shuteye.

"Good night and pleasant dreams."

C h a p t e r   37

▼

Mission Twenty-eight: Giessen

The "witches" had targeted the rail yards at Giessen for Monday, December 4. The seven-hour mission instead ended up at Friedburg for the Ninety-fifth. High winds forced two groups onto a collision course, and the Ninety-fifth broke off and bombed a rail yard at Friedburg instead of Giessen. Of approximately 400 500-pound bombs dropped among the rail tracks, all but about twenty hit their target: in the center of the marshalling yard, on the choke point on sidings filled with loaded rail cars and on two round houses.[241]

"Hit target of opportunity," Vic wrote in his logbook. "Brakes out at end of runway."

Chapter 38

▼

Mission Twenty-nine: Destroying the Will to Resist

The official target on Tuesday, December 5, was Berliner Stadtische Gaswerks A. C., in the northwest suburbs of Berlin, about six miles from the city center. This largest gas works in Berlin produced a variety of products on a large scale, and it was a number one priority target for the bombers of the Eighth Air Force.[242]

But the young officers and enlisted men of the Ninety-fifth Bomb Group knew this mission had a darker objective than just slowing the production of gas and other war materials; it had been calculated to strike fear into the hearts of ordinary Germans—children, grandparents, mothers, and fathers trapped in the suburbs that hemmed in the giant gas works. For the first time, it struck Bill Bramlett that his crew would be dropping bombs on a heavily populated civilian area with the primary aim of killing a lot of innocent people. They had been told that these attacks would help shorten the war, but Bramlett had his doubts. Instead of the big 500- and 1,000-pound bombs they often dropped on fortifications or industrial plants, they would be carrying twenty of the smaller 250-pound bombs that were nevertheless lethal against unprotected homes. In their larger numbers, they would scatter and possibly destroy even more houses, schools, shops, or public buildings. The thirty-five planes of the Ninety-fifth

Bomb Group would drop a total of 700 such bombs on the Berliner Gaswerks—if their aim was good that day. And the weather over Europe was growing worse and worse as winter loomed, dramatically lowering the likelihood that they would have visual sighting of their target in early December. The bombers of the One Hundredth Bomb Group would double that number, putting tens of thousands of Berlin residents at risk.[243]

Bramlett knew that the group navigator, when he learned of the nature of the mission, pleaded with the group's senior officers to relieve him of a mission so clearly aimed at a civilian population. But he was told that he had no choice.

The official Ninety-fifth Bomb Group records do not reflect it, but Bramlett said the bombing strategy was calculated to cause the maximum chaos in the German capital. The first group of planes over the target would drop bombs with their fuses set to explode on impact. The second wave of bombers would drop bombs with their fuses set to explode two hours after bombs away. And the third hail of bombs would be set with six-hour delays. After German families emerged from air raid shelters, bombs would continue exploding across the city all day. It would also cause firefighters to pause before plunging into Gaswerks to extinguish fires caused by the initial bombing.[244]

Bramlett doubted what amounted to terror bombing would accomplish the stated goal of the high command that such raids would shorten the war. But participation was not optional; he and others who had doubts would fly the missions and drop the bombs, or be court-martialed.[245]

Others who flew that day had no qualms. David M. Taylor, another crew leader and pilot, had seen his fellow American airmen shot down by the dozens, and he believed it was a necessary tool to defeat an evil regime. He kept a log of his missions and their purposes, and beside one he had penciled in "to kill women and children."[246]

On the heels of the death of his friend Earle Johnston, Tom Hammond also hardened himself to the rain of death on German civilians. In a December 17 letter to Callie about the reported death of a soldier from his home community, Tom wrote:

"I'm sorry to hear about Hilliard Bridgeman. I remember him but don't believe that I know his wife. There are a lot of boys that won't be going back after this is over. There were thirteen crews that came over with us from Avon Park and only five left. I didn't think that I could get to hate anyone so much as I do the Germans. According to the rules we are not supposed to drop bombs on anything but military targets, but at times we have dropped them on the civilian population due to error and it really suits me for I'd like to see them all wiped out. I don't know how I got off on such a subject, I didn't mean to."

After the mission, the intelligence report estimated that the A squadron dropped its bombs in woods about two miles from the target; the B squadron's bombs fell in woods or near a fully built-up residential area three miles north of the target; and C squadron dropped its explosives about three-and-one-quarter miles north of the gas works in a fully built-up residential area. The One Hundredth Bomb Group followed with another 689 bombs that fell in fields and a sparsely built-up residential area three-and-one-half to four miles northeast of the target.[247]

Whether by design or by accident, the mission had missed the gas works completely. All the destruction that was accomplished was to some trees and the homes surrounding the target. Navigation was fouled up as the group approached the target. As they neared the Initial Point for their bomb run, Major Cumbaa, the lead navigator, was forced to hand over control to the high squadron navigator because his compass, radar, and other navigational equipment failed. Cumbaa's plane had experienced similar failures on previous missions. When he returned to base, group leaders grounded the plane until the necessary repairs could be accomplished.[248]

The Eighth Air Force launched 229 B-17s of the Third Division that day, many against munitions and tank works. Three planes were shot down, 105 damaged, and thirty airmen lost.[249] It was a night takeoff and rendezvous, using only instruments to fly, after briefing at 4:00 AM—a nerve-wracking experience for all the crews. It was just good luck if they did not collide with another bomber in the assembly points over East Anglia. It was an extremely cold day. Planes took off at thirty-second intervals and flew circles around the airfield, constantly climbing to assembly altitude. Climbing in the fog and the dark, pilots kept a sharp vigil for the red-and-green wing lights of other bombers, hoping desperately to avoid a collision. Pilots were dodging and ducking above airfields all over East Anglia that morning to avoid hitting each other. It would be eight hours before they returned to the airfield, and they had nothing but dismal flying weather ahead. There was a 100 percent cloud cover over most of Europe. Winds over the target area would be clocked at sixty-five knots, which could reduce a B-17's ground speed to that of a 1930s truck or sedan.[250]

"Flak came up under me," Vic wrote in his logbook. The plane had one new hole when they arrived back at base.

The newspapers back home were full of reports of the progress of the war, but they also reflected the contrasts and changes taking place in society in great part because of the war and its impact on the young men and women being pummeled by change. On the one hand, South Carolina still had living veterans of the Civil War. The *Greenville News* reported the death at age one hundred of Marcus Lafayette Martin of Spartanburg County, the oldest known Confederate veteran in South Carolina at the time of his death. The newspaper reported that Martin had participated in numerous battles in the Civil War. The old man must have marveled at the advent of tanks, airplanes, and other modern weapons that evolved in his lifetime.[251]

Meanwhile, the newspaper reported from Washington the "hiring of the first negro girl as a switchboard operator by the New York Telephone Company was announced by the President's Committee on Fair Employment Practices." America was still trying to process the social changes that began with the defeat of the Confederacy and the end of slavery eight decades earlier.[252]

Women had begun to shoulder much more responsibility for the nation's economy, and they were less and less likely to stand still for second-class citizenship. And many men agreed. Eighteen-year-old Gloria Jeanne Heller was expelled from Louisiana State University amid charges she advocated "free love" on campus. The LSU president kicked her out of school for protesting reprimands of several other young women for giving good-night kisses to their boyfriends at the dormitory door. Among those coming to Miss Heller's defense were 130 ex-GIs attending college under the new GI Bill of Rights.[253]

Chapter 39

▼

Mission Thirty: Rockets
over Maastricht

On Tuesday, December 12, Vic's crew pulled a seven-hour, thirty-minute mission to Darmstadt, with four hours, thirty minutes on instruments, flying *Screaming Eagle* over Ostende, Brussels, and the Ardennes. Along the way, they watched a virtual fireworks display of German rocketry. Scotty Alexander estimated the V-2 contrail they witnessed about 12:10 PM to have risen into the cold winter sky from near Maastricht, in the Netherlands. Scotty watched as the contrails began about 10,000 feet and rose as high as 50,000 feet. Bill Bramlett's crew reported rockets launched from Aachen, Darmstadt, Frankfurt, and Maastricht. They bombed the railroad marshalling yard. The Ninety-fifth A Squadron's bombs fell two-and-one-half miles northeast of the railroad, in a field. But the other two squadrons hit the marshalling yard, the roundhouses, and locomotive shops, and damaged a choke point where several tracks merged. Bramlett's crew reported their bombs fell in the south end of the marshalling yard. The Ninety-fifth bombers carried a mix of high-explosive 500-pound bombs and the M-17 magnesium incendiary cluster weapons to ensure fires engulfed the rubble created by the big bombs.[254]

"One bomb hung up. Milk run. No flak. No fighters," Vic wrote in his logbook. Vic's hung bomb was one of the M-17 magnesium fire-starter weapons, lead bombardier Lt. Leon Sheweloff noted in his report. The failure of the bomb rack to release the cluster bomb canister caused the crew to hold their breath as they touched down back at Horham. They had tried to shake it loose over the English Channel. Frank Nutt, the ball turret gunner and primary armorer on the crew, even tried to kick it loose as they flew back toward the safety of the English coast. They could have all bailed out of the airplane over the English countryside or their base. But their efforts to dislodge the dangerous payload convinced Vic their odds of survival were at least as good to land the plane as to jump out of it.

On December 15, Tom and Vic flew a two-hour, fifteen-minute practice mission in *Screaming Eagle*.

Chapter 40

▼

Mission Thirty-one: Nazis Use Captured Aircraft

Railroads remained a priority target for American bombers throughout the war. In mid-December, as American infantry and armor pressed toward the German frontier in northeast France, Luxembourg and Belgium, the railroad targets were especially important. Mangled rail marshalling yards and twisted locomotives meant fewer supplies would reach German soldiers facing the advancing Americans. The marshalling yard at Kornwestheim, a village six miles north of Stuttgart, was one of the most important in Germany. It could handle 4,800 rail wagons per day, one of the largest and busiest yards in southwest Germany. It was astride the line between Munich and Karlsruhe, and also served branch lines to the Black Forest and Lake Constance to the south.[255]

On Saturday, December 16, a seven-hour, twenty-minute mission to Stuttgart was a nerve-wracking experience for Vic's crew, because of foul weather and an unorthodox threat by the Luftwaffe. They spent six hours of the mission on instruments, a tense task for the pilots. Over the base at takeoff, clouds were solid up to 18,000 feet. Their target was the railroad marshalling yard at Kornwestheim. Extremely poor weather meant only the Ninety-fifth, 486th, and 490th bomb groups attacked from the Third Division. The First Bomb Division abandoned the mission over England. Upon return to Horham, the Ninety-fifth found a ceiling of only 500–1,000 feet, making landing very difficult. At mission altitude of 21,000 feet, clouds and contrails made formation dangerous and difficult. To make matters worse, seven aircraft had radio, radar, or navigation equipment failure. And the lead and deputy lead aircraft aborted, causing the low squadron to have to move into lead position. "Overcast up to 18,000 feet. Rough weather," Vic wrote in his logbook.[256]

Five aircraft turned back because of mechanical problems, including one carrying Col. Jack Shuck, the new commander of the Ninety-fifth Bomb Group. Two bombers from the 412th Squadron went missing. The Ninety-fifth made its bomb run at 1:01 PM, twenty-one minutes behind schedule. The A squadron's bombs fell in fields and on a road; the B squadron's bombs missed the primary target by almost five miles, and the C squadron's bombs were scattered across fields 2,400 feet from the rail marshalling yard.[257]

At 1:13 PM, Scotty Alexander noted a large four-engine airplane sitting on the taxiway of a long runway of an airdrome northeast of Schwabisch Hall as the Ninety-fifth departed the target area. He was pretty sure it was a B-17. That's why it caught his eye, sitting on a long runway in the heart of Germany. It just didn't fit. Air crews had been warned that the Luftwaffe had several dozen captured American Flying Fortresses, operated by a special unit, KG-200. It made the hair stand up on the back of Scotty's neck to think that one of their own planes might infiltrate their formation. He had observed a similar out-of-place B-17 tracking the Ninety-fifth formation at a distance of about five miles for about twenty-five minutes on the September 12 mission to Magdeburg. Today, Scotty had noticed as they neared the Initial Point for their bomb run, an out-of-place B-17 flying alone about ten to fifteen miles to the left of the Ninety-fifth formation, and not obviously associated with any other formation. The B-17 bombers typically flew in groups, wingtip-to-wingtip, so the group bristled with hundreds of .50-caliber machine guns for maximum protection. A single Flying Fortress would only have a maximum of about ten guns, and not all of them could be brought to bear on a target at once. The out-of-place bomber did not cross over the target with the American formation, maneuvering instead to bypass the flak bursts over the target and rejoining the American formation at the return point following the bomb run. Scotty was convinced he had seen a German scout crew flying a captured B-17. It appeared the plane that shadowed their formation around the target was the same one he saw on the runway of the German airdrome, and he reported it as such in their after-mission debriefing.[258]

Scotty's observations were not paranoia, but healthy, informed skepticism. American gunners had orders to shoot down any airplane, no matter what model airplane or unit insignia it displayed, if the airplane behaved strangely and could not produce the daily codes designed to prevent the infiltration of enemy aircraft. Bomber pilots complained in their debriefing sessions about apparently friendly fighter aircraft that pointed their noses at American bomber formations. Over and over again, the bomber pilots asked that orders be passed through high command for American fighters to avoid putting their airplanes into positions that made the bomber crews feel threatened. Lt. J. D. Taylor, after the September 12 mission, told the group interrogator to "keep friendly fighters from pointing nose at formation." Lt. Kenneth Ringbloom's crew reported the same day that a "P-51 headed straight for tail and came within 100 yards in a pursuit."

With knowledge that the German squadron KG-200 also had captured P-51 Mustang fighters, such encounters made American bomber crews jumpy. On April 4 and 5, 1945, Lt. David M. Taylor's crew flew back-to-back missions against the port of Kiel, in Germany. On one of those missions, Taylor's B-17 was shot up and severely damaged. He had to shut down an engine, and was incapable of keeping up with the formation. A wounded bomber flying alone was a sitting duck for German fighter planes, and Taylor knew it. He also knew that combat-damaged bombers often would seek the company of other similarly wounded planes so that they might mass their guns against any potential enemy. So Taylor did not think it odd when he saw another B-17 flying alone and approaching his aircraft. It was a long, lonely flight back to base over the North Sea, and he welcomed the company. As the other B-17 began sliding into position alongside his own, Taylor suddenly saw an American P-51 Mustang dive from above, its machine guns blazing, and streak past him toward the approaching bomber. The B-17 Taylor had welcomed for protection burst into flames and careened into the sea. It had not been able to give the fighter pilot the daily code because it was being flown by a German crew. And it was just seconds away from shooting down Taylor's bomber when the American fighter pilot intervened.[259]

Other Ninety-fifth crews also became wary of lone-wolf bombers in their midst. Bill Bramlett's crew noted their sentiments in their after-mission report on December 12: "Single B-17s that fly along beside formation on the way to target should be challenged."[260]

Aircraft came into the possession of the Germans in a variety of ways, most by straightforward result of combat. One of the more bizarre examples of an aircraft falling into the hands of the Luftwaffe occurred in the Ninety-fifth Bomb Group on the night of Monday, November 6, 1944. Seven B-17s took off at 7:25 PM for

a night navigation practice flight over friendly territory. At 8:23 PM, radio operator Gilbert Frazer radioed the base ground station for a bearing. It was the last
contact between the base at Horham and Fortress number 42-31760 piloted by
Lt. George Birch McVay. At 8:30 PM, the weather officer declared a weather
emergency and all seven aircraft were recalled. The base received no acknowledg-
ment from McVay's bomber. As the other six aircraft landed, 42-31760 could
not be located in the local traffic pattern and staff of the Ninety-fifth called in an
overdue aircraft message to the Third Bomb Division Flying Control.[261]

Eugene Fletcher, also assigned to the night navigation mission, knew something odd was afoot. The Eighth Air Force did not fly night combat missions. Its
entire raison d'etre was to prove that daylight precision bombing was the superior
method of attacking German targets. And for crews unschooled in the mysteries
of night flight, it could be terrifying, particularly over war-time England, which
was completely blacked out at night. Not a light shone on the ground anywhere.
Fletcher had never seen a country so dark. "You could fly over airfields, towns,
and water and it would all look the same. Totally, utterly black. Immediately
after takeoff, the lights on their airfield were shut off and were not turned on
again until the weather recall order came."[262]

On Sunday, November 5, Fletcher's crew had flown in formation with
McVay's crew on a combat mission. On Monday, seven pilots including Fletcher
and McVay, and five other crews, were summoned to the group operations office,
and briefed that they would fly a practice navigation mission that evening. They
kept their mouths shut at briefing, but once they were on their own they shared
their anger that, after flying a tough combat mission, now they were ordered to
do this unusual night mission. Since the Eighth Air Force did not fly night missions, they knew something unusual was in the planning stage because all of the
pilots on this practice mission were experienced combat pilots. There were no
newcomers in this group.[263]

After Fletcher and five other crews landed, concern began to grow about
McVay's crew. The pilot and his crew were lost in the dark and murky weather of
East Anglia and the Channel coast. McVay had reason to hope he could sort out
his dilemma. He had 2,700 gallons of high-octane gasoline in his tanks when he
took off from Horham. He could remain aloft until dawn if necessary. And there
were scores of military airfields across this part of rural England, one about every
five or six miles in every direction. If he couldn't find his home base at Horham,
surely he could locate one of the others. One especially large field at Woodbridge,
right on the Channel Coast, had been built expressly for bombers returning from
combat missions in trouble of one sort or the other. It even had special equip-

ment that could burn off ground fog. But ground control at Horham knew McVay was in trouble. It would not be the first time one or more bomber crews had flown off into the night over this island nation and were never seen again. At 11:30 PM, four hours after wheels up, the English Royal Observer Corps reported an unidentified American four-engine bomber over Norwich, well north of the Horham base. Ten minutes later, a similar report came in from Thetford. By 12:30 AM, November 7, a four-engine bomber was heard flying over London. The plane had been aloft for five hours. It still had enough fuel to fly at least that much longer, but the fatigue of night flying and the anxiety of being lost was taking its toll. As far as ground control at Horham was concerned, McVay had flown his bomber into a black hole. In fact, they had crossed the English Channel without ever knowing it, a crossing that opposite East Anglia, would have taken only minutes to cover the twenty-odd miles over water.[264]

Somewhere over the continent, Cpl. Edward Fetherston, a student navigator on the flight, thought it was over Holland—the plane blundered into a flak battery and was damaged. Two of the crew, radioman Gilbert Frazer and tail gunner Vincent Blazquez, donned their parachutes and bailed out of the plane. The plane flew on until about 6 AM when the pilots spotted an airfield. By the time they touched down, they had been aloft eleven hours. After flying in circles over England for about four hours, they had begun an odyssey that took them 750 miles east of London. They were on the ground in Cottbus, Germany, southeast of Berlin, near the Polish border. As the realization became clear that they were in enemy territory, they sought to finish the destruction of the bomber that the earlier flak attack had started. They smashed equipment, burned maps and other documents, and set the airplane itself on fire. By the time they were captured on the airfield by personnel of a pilot training school, they had at least accomplished 80 percent destruction of the ill-fated bomber. McVay, co-pilot Charles O'Brien, navigator David Kile, engineer Carl Slivinski, and Fetherston, all of whom had stayed in the airplane until it landed at Cottbus, became prisoners of war. Whatever its purpose, Fletcher knew nothing ever came of the night exercise, except the loss of one crew.[265]

On December 17, Tom and Vic flew a one-hour, fifteen-minute practice mission in their regular ride, *Screaming Eagle*. It would be a week before they could fly again as a gray winter blanket of clouds settled over the continent.

Chapter 41

▼

The View from the Ground

In Luxemburg, a small principality nestled between Belgium, Germany, and France, Private First Class Robert Huff of Greenville, South Carolina, had only recently arrived to join the 565th Anti-Aircraft Artillery Battery. The unit, equipped with batteries of .50-caliber machine guns, was assigned to provide cover for Gen. George Patton's Third Army tanks. In the early morning of December 16, 1944, the Germans launched their Ardennes Offensive, taking advantage of a prolonged cloud cover that kept the Eighth Air Force bombers grounded in England. But on December 24, Christmas Eve, "the clouds parted," Robert Huff said. "I never saw so many planes. They filled the sky as far as the eye could see." Records show that the entire flight of 2,046 Eighth Air Force bombers was deliberately routed over American troop positions at the unusually low altitude of 15,000 feet to boost the spirits of the American troops, then under attack by the German army.[266]

Soon after Christmas, a large formation of B-17 bombers appeared over Luxemburg. Robert watched as the German 88s, the big cannon that pumped deadly shrapnel into the air around the American bombers, struck one of the B-17s. As they watched flak burst near one American bomber, the B-17 began billowing smoke. Robert and his gun crew watched as the B-17 reversed course and came in their direction. It settled lower and lower and finally skidded into a snow-covered field right before their eyes. When the bomber stopped plowing through snow and farm field soil, the crew emerged and all of them ran for the surrounding trees. Robert's unit raced in their direction. Once the crew realized they had landed amid American troops, they came out of the trees. With uncharacteristic good fortune, they had survived the mangled bomber's crash landing with only one small cut on one airman.[267]

The bombers whose massive destructive power was needed to blunt the German offensive had been grounded by the worst winter of the war.

On December 18, Tom wrote to Callie:

"Today is our blue Monday, too, only it didn't rain for a change. It's one of the few days that we haven't had rain all during this fall and winter. It sure helps to see the sun shine occasionally.

"Speaking of Thanksgiving, I really had a swell dinner that day. The turkey was done up in fine style, with all the trimmings, by the cooks. It really surprised me that it was so good. Right after dinner that day I took off for London on pass and had a very good time. I've had another pass since then but didn't go to London. Chuck and I, he's my bombardier, went up to Birmingham to see an uncle of his who was in the hospital from wounds received in France. It took us an entire day to get there and one to get back, so we only spent one day there. We sure were tired after all of that time on the train. It isn't very far over there but the trains are so darned slow.

"I sure hope that I'll be on my way home by the time this reaches you. All I ask is a few days of good weather and everything will be dandy."

Vic and Tom still had four more missions to complete, but they were not so lucky when it came to the weather. Nor was the Eighth Air Force, nor the American Army slogging its way through the forests of Belgium and France.

The crews of the Ninety-fifth Bomb Group knew their fellow Americans holding out stubbornly against the Germans in the cold, snow-covered Ardennes Forest were suffering and dying. The young airmen wanted desperately to fight, to use their bombs to disrupt airfields, roads, and rails behind the German lines.

For Bill Bramlett, that meant more than a week of early morning briefings, sitting in his aircraft on the taxiway at Horham, his Flying Fortress fully fueled and loaded with bombs, waiting for the clouds to break and unleash the bombers against the German army.

And for more than a week, they would return to the barracks at the end of the day without flying. The weather was the worst in a generation in Europe. Ice coated the wings. Frost covering the windshields obscured their vision.

Fletcher, his crew also nearing the end of their tour, shared Bramlett's frustration. On December 19, they arose at 4:00 AM, slogged through the cold to the mess hall, then to a pre-dawn briefing. Fletcher was happy to finally be scheduled for a mission to support the ground troops. But by 9:30 AM, their mission was scrubbed because of bad weather. It was cold, and fog hung thick over the English countryside.[268]

Chapter 42

▼

Mission Thirty-two:
Airmen Fight Back

When the clouds parted on Sunday, December 24—Christmas Eve—the Eighth Air Force unleashed every plane it could put in the air, a total of 2,046 bombers.[269] The Ninety-fifth Bomb Group alone launched sixty-three airplanes and crews, a maximum effort. Everything that would fly, including war-weary hangar queens with more than one hundred missions, was launched that day. Horham also had as guests a group of planes from other bomb groups that had landed at base 119 because they could not land at their home fields for one reason or another. Those too were readied by the ground crews of the Ninety-fifth for the all-out Christmas Eve mission. In total, the ground crews at Horham repaired, fueled, and armed eighty-nine bombers for action and launched them with 146 tons of explosives.[270]

It was the biggest bomber attack the western Allies had ever mounted. Airfields and rail marshalling yards were targeted throughout western Germany. A high-pressure weather system extending across western Europe broke up the clouds enough for the first attacks on airfields and communications centers in more than a week. The Third Division alone sent 858 B-17 aircraft into the skies. The Third Division led the assault, and when their bombs were falling, bombers of the First and Second divisions were still taking off in England. The mission commander, Brig. Gen. Frederick Castle, was awarded the Medal of Honor posthumously for taking over the controls of a doomed B-17 to give the crew the chance of parachuting to safety. South of Liege, Belgium, a flight of German fighters attacked Castle's bomber, which was running fifteen minutes late. Six bombers, including the one piloted by Castle, were destroyed by the relentless waves of German fighters.[271]

"P. F. F. ship. 60 ships. Most ever put up. Saw one spin in," Vic wrote in his logbook. They were flying a relatively new aircraft, number 44-8364, with just twenty-one takeoffs on its log that had been assigned Horham on October 12. PFF was shorthand for Pathfinder, the radar-equipped aircraft that carried the new H2X radar where the ball turret guns would ordinarily be attached in the belly of the B-17. When visual targeting with the Norden visual bombsight was not possible, the H2X radar could achieve 50 percent accuracy despite clouds obscuring the target.[272]

The Ninety-fifth D Squadron took off around 9:00 AM and assembled over the field. The group had not flown in more than a week, and from the start, the operation was ragged. They crossed the Belgian coast at the beach resort of Ostende, proceeded south of Brussels, and turned left toward their targets over the Ardennes. Lt. W. C. Shaw, trailing the lead squadron, complained that Lieutenant Pearson, flying lead in the low squadron, was flying too high and dangerously close to the lead squadron flying above them. Lieutenant Greer, in the middle of the lead squadron, flew back too far from the planes ahead of him. And Vic's crew complained that Lieutenant Owen, the lead pilot, provided poor leadership that day. At 1:28 PM, they were forced off their briefed course when the stream of traffic carried them north over Koblenz, Giessen, and Fulda.[273]

The original target for Tom's formation was an airfield at Biblis, in the vicinity of Frankfurt. The 100-pound bombs, thirty-eight to a plane, were calculated to put as many "post holes" in the airfield's surface as possible. But poor weather made it impossible for the lead bombardier to locate the primary target. So the formation commander diverted his thirty-four bombers carrying eighty-seven tons of explosives to a railroad marshalling yard at Kaiserslautern. Vic wrote in his logbook that they attacked at 25,000 feet. "Flak heavy, fighters, 0 lost, 1 hole," Vic wrote.[274]

Even over the secondary target, haze and flying directly into the winter sun made visibility poor. Lead bombardier Marshall J. Thixton had only seconds to confirm his group was in the right place. The Mickey, a code name for ground-targeting radar, guided the planes toward their target. Thixton spotted the edge of the railway workshops. But just before bombs away, the high squadron was directly above the low squadron, delaying the release of their bombs.

Thixton had just ten seconds to put the crosshairs of his bombsight on the target and make one correction. After bombs away at 2:38 PM, Thixton thought he saw explosions left and short of the railway workshops. After-mission analysis showed their 422 bombs, each with 100 pounds of explosives, missed the railway shops completely, landing in a forest. Loosed from the bomb bays with an intervalometer rather than in a single salvo, the bombs would have walked through the site, spreading destruction over as wide an area as possible.[275]

The huge number of bombers crisscrossing Europe caused a traffic jam in the sky. Because of the necessary sharp left turn, the high squadron lost contact with the lead squadron and proceeded back toward England alone. The lead and low squadrons went west of Kaiserslautern and later resumed the briefed course. At 3:45 PM, Lt. Bob Mercer reported seeing a B-17 "on the deck, heading west, and under control." It had been hit over the target and began lagging behind and trying to hold altitude. Near Agincourt, France, Mercer got on his radio and called for fighter support for the stricken bomber. Fighter pilots responded that they had spotted the damaged aircraft in the bomber stream. Mercer noted on his after-mission report: "think he might have made it OK." Their departure from the target had carried them south, across the Rhine River, and into France, near the American forces pressing the Germans back toward the border. The stricken plane, number 338760 and nicknamed *Lucky Lady* by pilot G. T. Purdy and his crew, were indeed lucky that day. They were logged as *loc*, meaning landed on the continent, within Allied occupied territory.[276]

The Ninety-fifth Bomb Group attack on Christmas Eve was just one of dozens of targets across western Germany aimed at disrupting transportation, communications and air defense operations of the German army that were attacking American forces in the Ardennes.

Chapter 43

▼

Mission Thirty-three: Christmas over Germany

There was no let-up on Monday—Christmas Day. A six-hour, forty-five-minute flight to Badmunster turned into a comedy of errors. The target of the Ninety-fifth was a rail bridge. The day's orders sent numerous small flights of Fortresses against communications centers and rail bridges west of the Rhine. Allied troops were approaching the Rhine and beginning to probe the German homeland.[277]

"Clear target. Primary not hit," Vic wrote in his logbook.

The weather had cleared enough to launch a mission, but not enough to guarantee clear skies for all of the dozens of targets marked on mission maps. Vic's crew arrived over Germany to find a massive cloud formation blocking the path to their target. Vic put the airplane into a steep climb to clear the obstacle and find their primary target. Others in the formation could not keep up as he pushed his bomber above 32,000 feet. Bomb-laden B-17s usually were limited to about 27,000 feet. When Vic pushed the plane over the top of the cloud formation into clear air, the crew found they were all alone. The plane had left its formation behind. "So, we said, bomb something. We picked out a village with railroad tracks and bombed the rail yard," Scotty said.

The operations officer's report stated that due to a bombing malfunction in the lead aircraft, the formation became disorganized and only seven aircraft were over the target. All eleven aircraft, however, were in the target area, and were credited with a completed combat mission. Lt. Donald Van Patten, the lead navigator, said in his report that when he opened the bomb bay doors, the bombs fell out. Vic's report stated that once the lead navigator's bombs fell out prematurely, the formation broke up, "and I was alone in the elements," he wrote. They observed their combination of high explosive and magnesium fire bombs hitting a highway instead of the railroad targets.[278]

It was their last flight in the airplane they flew more times than any other, B-17G, number 42-102455, *Screaming Eagle*. The bomber had been assigned to Horham and the Ninety-fifth Bomb Group on May 8, 1944, and survived eighty-five takeoffs before being scrapped for parts on May 31, 1945.[279]

Chapter 44

▼

Mission Thirty-four:
Two More to Go

On Wednesday, December 27, the target was the railway storage siding yard just south of Fulda. The recent attacks on Hanau and Giessen resulted in disruption of rail traffic on the two main lines between Frankfurt and Kassel, causing freight to back up into the yards on both sides of the breaks in the lines. Fulda was the focus of much loading activity, with rail cars backed up waiting for cargo. The Ninety-fifth aimed to destroy as much of that cargo as possible. If they could not attack the primary target, they would go for the passenger station in the marshalling yard south of Hanau. Weather for the seven-hour, thirty-minute mission was terrible, bitter cold. Two Ninety-fifth pilots, Robert Dillon and William Dunwoody, aborted the mission when frost and ice became so dense on their windshields that they could not see through them at mission altitude. Dillon abandoned the mission at 13,000 feet, before even reaching formation assembly. Failing to remove the frost, they descended to 2,000 feet and circled the field, managing to clear a large enough portion of the windscreen to land. Squadron commander Maj. John F. Losee cited Dillon for failure to observe procedures. Losee wrote in his report that the frost typically would evaporate in the sun and dry air at higher altitudes.[280]

Dunwoody also was written up because he ignored control tower instructions to continue on the mission as briefed. Squadron commanders took a dim view of pilots who they thought too quickly abandoned a mission after takeoff, and they noted those incidents in mission records.[281]

Vic had flown a mission with another crew before the rest of his crew saw combat. Tom needed a make-up flight with another crew in order to be able to finish his thirty-five missions with Vic. Others needed make-ups as well. So Tom, Chuck, Joe, Sam, Frank, Smitty, and Bill flew this mission with chief pilot G. K. Painter, and 117 other bomber crews.[282]

Chaos descended upon the target area as, half-way between the Initial Point of the bomb run and the target, two formations from the 390th Bomb Group interfered, forcing the planes of the Ninety-fifth to make S-turns to avoid a collision. Trying to recover, the bombardier resynchronized and released his bombs. Photo intelligence showed the bombs of the Ninety-fifth fell on top of a portion of the pattern laid down by the 390th B Squadron, blanketing a built-up residential area. There were four or five strikes on repair sheds in the rail sidings, but that was well short of the almost one hundred bombs dropped by the Ninety-fifth. Less than 1 percent of bombs fell within 1,000 feet of the target.[283]

Because four Ninety-fifth bombers aborted the mission, Tom's plane was one of just two in the lead squadron over the target, and just two planes made up the low squadron.

Back at the base, crews focused on their favorite complaints. Robert Mercer's crew wrote in their mission report: "Rags to clean guns—need them badly. Mess hall chow getting steadily worse. Several of us sick today. Too much K ration hash."[284]

Painter had more serious concerns: "Screwed up at target again. J group (J was the tail marking for the 390th Bomb Group) passed right under at about bombs away. Security at briefing very poor," he wrote.[285]

Chapter 45

▼

Number Thirty-five:
The Last Mission

Tom, Vic, and the crew awoke Thursday, December 28, knowing they would be flying their last mission, no matter how it ended. Their Doolittle's Missions, the thirty-five necessary to go home, would be finished. At takeoff about 9:00 AM, there was 30 percent cloud cover up to 10,000 feet. Visibility was so poor they could only see halfway down the runway at Horham. They were aloft at 9:27 AM with the C group, and they completed assembly over Felixstowe two hours later. They crossed the Belgian coast at Ostende. Enroute the formations bunched up, forcing a lot of S-turns to avoid overrunning the Fourth Combat Wing. Approaching Koblenz, they learned cloud cover was 100 percent over the primary target, communications centers in Koblenz. The lead pilot decided to go for their target of last resort, the rail sidings in the marshalling yard. The C group leader aborted prior to the target run, but Vic's crew dropped their bombs anyway. They were ready to go home, and they were not taking another bomb load back to base. They dropped twenty 250-pound bombs, but were unable to see where their bombs fell because of the cloud cover. Their final mission lasted seven hours, fifteen minutes. It was the 253rd mission for the Ninety-fifth Bomb Group and the 766th mission for the Eighth Air Force.[286]

A total of 399 B-17 aircraft attacked the Koblenz/Mosel rail marshalling yard. One airman was killed and no aircraft were lost.[287]

Their wings had badly iced in the cold winter air. But there were no fighters and no flak. Their plane returned without damage. The plane they flew that day, B-17G number 43-38469 (no name), was relatively new, having been assigned to Horham on September 5, 1944. It endured eighty-two takeoffs before being returned to Kingman, Arizona, and scrapped on December 10, 1945.[288]

Vic wrote, "Last Mission" in his log following the final mission, then added this:

"When I landed and plane settled on runway the boys made so much noise that engines could not be heard. Nutt finished up with 34 missions. All the rest had 35. The boys said if they had to go into combat once more they wanted to go with me. A great compliment for me. Now all I'll think of is getting home to the sweetest, dearest wife in the whole wide world, wish she were here now."

Tom waited a couple of months before putting his feelings about surviving the war on paper. On March 2, he wrote to Callie:

"The war news sounds good tonight doesn't it? I sure do want to see the end of this war, but quick. No matter how good it sounds, though, I can't bring myself to be all optimistic about it. Maybe it's because I came so close to not getting back myself and know too that there's still a lot to do yet. Believe me, honey, I know that I wouldn't be sitting here writing you now if God hadn't watched over me and brought us back. It's such a rare thing for a crew to fly a tour without someone getting hurt and that's what makes me so sure."

Just barely twenty-two, Tom had finished his part in the greatest concentration of air forces the world had ever known. In September 1945, the Air Force issued the United States Strategic Bombing Survey (European Theater), which summarized the breadth and scope of the bombing campaign:

"In the attack by Allied air power, almost 2,700,000 tons of bombs were dropped; more than 1,440,000 bomber sorties and 2,680,000 fighter sorties were flown. The number of combat planes reached a peak of about 28,000; at maximum strength, 1,300,000 men were in combat commands. The number of men lost in air action was 79,265 Americans and 79,281 British. More than 18,000 American and 22,000 British planes were lost or damaged beyond repair. In the wake of these attacks there are great paths of destruction. In Germany, 3,600,000 dwelling units, approximately 20 percent of the total, were destroyed or heavily damaged. Survey estimates show some 300,000 civilians killed and 780,000 wounded. The number made homeless aggregates 7,500,000. The principal German cities have been largely reduced to hollow walls and piles of rubble. German industry is bruised and temporarily paralyzed. These are the scars across the face of the enemy, the preface to the victory that followed."

Tom's unit, the Ninety-fifth Bombardment Group (Heavy) lost more than 1,700 men and 192 bombers in battle during the war.[289]

Figure 11: In the fall and winter of 1944, Tom Hammond carried this English ten-shilling note in his wallet and recorded on it the missions he flew.

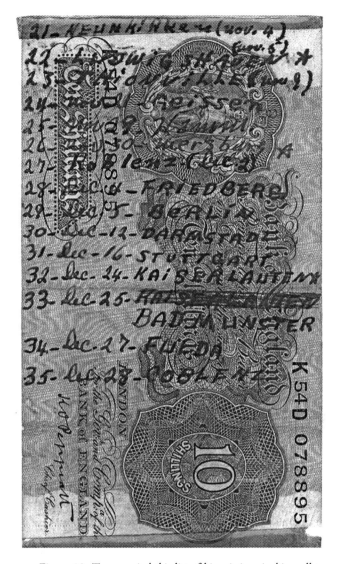

Figure 12: Tom carried this list of his missions in his wallet.

Chapter 46

▼

Departing England

Tom and his fellow crew members spent the next couple of days with Army housekeeping chores, as the Army made sure these airmen, who had risked their lives thirty-five times over Germany, did not return home with any unauthorized equipment. On December 31, Tom dutifully turned in his B-3 flying bag, flying sun glasses, B-8 flying goggles, A-11 winter flying gloves, rayon glove inserts, A-9 summer flying helmet, and his A-9 winter flying trousers. Air Corps Capt. M. M. Helm signed the receipt certifying the return of Tom's gear. On January 3, 1945, Tom signed a routine statement that he understood the security regulations for Army Air Forces personnel returning to the United States and certifying that he did not have in his possession "any uncensored photographic prints, undeveloped exposed negatives, diaries, operational maps, prohibited classified documents, prohibited operational data, unauthorized captured enemy material or prohibited items, including letters to be transmitted for other personnel."[290]

Tom was fortunate to be going home. On January 1, 1945, the U. S. Eighth Air Force reported that during 1944, some 29,000 American airmen had been shot down and were killed or missing in action. Many of them were dead, and others would remain in German POW camps until the war ended. Meanwhile, the Eighth Air Force used nearly 450,000 tons of bombs during 1944 to pulverize German industrial might. In December alone, some 42,000 tons of bombs were dropped on the Nazi regime. Most of that total was dropped in the nine days late in the month to repel the German push into Belgium, known today as The Battle of the Bulge.[291]

On New Year's Eve, Callie sat in her parents' farmhouse in South Carolina, worrying that she had not heard from Tom in three weeks, and hoping that he would be home soon.

"I hope nothing serious is wrong. Let me hear from you soon. This will be the last letter from me this year. The New Year has already rolled in over there I guess.

"This has been a terrible day. The fog is so thick you can hardly see your hand before you. If the sun doesn't shine soon, I think I'll go completely crazy (or should I say crazier?) Saturday and Sunday of last week were pretty, but they were the only pretty days we've had in about a month.

"Did you have a nice time Christmas? I hope you did. I had a very nice time. We only got Monday off from work. Sunday Night we ate oysters up at your folks. Sure had a swell time. Then Monday we had company for dinner. It was swell just being home with the folks.

"Last Thursday was John's fifteenth birthday. Friday night I slipped a little surprise party on him. It was so rough that there wasn't but a few here. But I think they all enjoyed it. You should see that kid, he is almost grown. His is five, nine and weighs around a hundred thirty. He certainly has out-grown me.

"Your folks tell me that you have made first lieutenant. You certainly are doing well. I have noticed in the paper all along about those oak leaf clusters you have been receiving. They are all so proud of you, and I too feel proud to know someone like you. And I hope that their hunch that you are coming home soon is true. We'll sure have to kill the fatted calf when you get here."

The next morning, she finished the letter, and her mood had brightened with the weather.

"Well, the sun is shining today, hurrah! The wind is blowing worse than March. But I can put up with it so long as the sun still shines.

"I did sleep this year in, and have just been fooling around the house all day. It will be back to work tomorrow. But one thing good, I didn't have to start the year off, working, at any rate down at the plant."

Tom's certificate of service states that he left Europe on January 4, 1945, and arrived in the United States on January 9. The enlisted members of the crew came home on the Queen Elizabeth liner. The voyage from Glasgow, Scotland, lasted six days. The officers flew home, via Casablanca, the Azores, Bermuda, and New York. Tom had orders to report to the Washington National Airport Army Air Base, 503rd AAF Base Unit, at 8:00 AM on January 10, 1945. Tom took the train home to Greenville, stopping off briefly in Greensboro, North Carolina, to visit a wartime pen pal.[292]

When their plane landed in Washington, and they had checked in at the Pentagon, Tom, Scotty, Chuck, and Vic went their separate ways.

When he returned home to Orange, Massachusetts, Scotty found that Gloria, whom he had married the night before he shipped out to Europe, had relocated to his hometown and moved in with his parents. But the union sealed in the passion of men departing for war did not long survive. When Scott was reassigned to San Marcos, Texas, in 1945, Gloria did not follow him there, and they later were divorced.[293]

Figure 13: Lt. Tom Hammond had this photo made in Miami Beach in 1945 to send to his sweetheart, Callie Barnette.

Chapter 47

▼

The Homecoming

Tom's sister Helen already had begun the vigil for her big brother. Someone had given her a diary for 1945, and she noted on January 1 that "Aunt Leila got a V-mail letter from Tom. Hadn't heard from him in a month." Leila was Tom's father's sister, married to Ed Hill. They lived on Lloyd Street, near where Tom Sr., Leila, and their many brothers and sisters had lived in the early part of the century with their parents, Herbert and Ella Hammond. Herbert was an engineer with the Southern Railroad, and Lloyd Street was just a few blocks' walking distance from the Washington Street train depot. During the war, Helen and her sister Nancy attended business school in Greenville and worked the late shift in the Dunean textile mill along with their parents. Their father carried passengers from the rural northern part of Greenville County who also worked in the mill, to earn a few extra dollars. Helen and Nancy stayed with Leila during the week and went home to the farm on the weekends.

Sadness and fear for their son and brother, Tom, had permeated the Hammond farmhouse that Christmas. Many boys from the community had not come home, and they never would. Tom's father hung a pair of his son's britches from the fireplace mantel, hoping it would make a good omen and bring the boy, only recently twenty-two, home from the war. Pauline often stood at the kitchen sink, preparing supper for the rest of her family, with tears rolling down her cheeks as she silently prayed for his safe return.

On January 2, Helen wrote: "What a day. Got a cablegram from Tom. He says, Kill the fatted calf, folks, I'm on my way. We're tickled to death. Also received an answer to telegram to Vic's wife. She says the boys have completed their missions and are on the way home. What a day."

Communication was largely written for the struggling families of wartime Greenville. Helen wrote in her January 6 diary entry: "I used a telephone today! Imagine that!!"

On Sunday, January 7, after writing a long entry about the day's church service, she added: "Looked for Tom." Again on Tuesday, "We looked for Tom all day but he didn't come." On January 10, "Got a letter from Vic's wife Erna Radke. She seems to be a swell girl and oh, yes, she is a secretary!! (Helen was taking secretarial courses at business school.) Said she is walking on air and just trying to be calm."

An anxious week passed, and on Monday, January 15, Tom's father drove the girls to Greenville for school. They went to work at the mill at 3:30 PM. "Had an odd feeling all night, wishing there would be a light on at Aunt Leila's porch. Sure enough there was!

"They tried to hide Tom from us, but we found him in the pantry!! Gee, were we happy?? We talked for a while, then Dad brought the passengers home in the A-mobile and Ralph and Ethel brought Thomas, Mom, Nancy and I home. Then we watched Tom wake all the kids. That was fun. We sat up and talked until 4:30 AM."

The next day, Tom and his father carried the girls to town for school and then went on a search for a car for Tom. He had left his previous car in Florida when he shipped out for England because he had blown a tire and could not buy a replacement. "They bought a Grey '36 Ford. Looks swell; has a radio, heater and everything," Helen wrote.

Lieutenant Hammond's first mission in his new car was a reconnaissance trip a half-mile down the Groce Meadow Road, to the Barnette farm to call on Callie. They had been acquaintances before he shipped out to Europe, but he had thought about her a lot while he was in England, and he wanted to see her. He pulled the grey Ford into the Barnettes' semi-circle driveway, killed the engine, got out, and straightened his immaculate uniform, complete with waist-length Eisenhower jacket and pilot's wings. He walked up the four steps to the door. He shivered a little in the winter air as he knocked gently on the door. Callie was happy to see the handsome young airman. She had thought a lot about him while he was overseas, even though there were other young men coming and going between the war and their Greenville County homes. They chatted, two painfully shy young people breaking the ice. They barely knew each other. Callie asked Tom why he had come to see her so soon after arriving home to his large family. "Helen told me it would be a good idea," he replied.

The Hammond girls skipped work for the day on Wednesday and went home to the farm to visit with their brother. The next day, they skipped school. "Gee, is it swell to have Tom home again. Dad and him have a jolly time; they fight the war every day," Helen wrote. On Friday, January 19, Helen bemoaned her brother's busy social life. "Tom is still at home they say. We never get to see him much. We went to school, then to work." On Saturday, the Hammond family joined Callie Barnette's family at the Barnette farm for an oyster supper, a favorite social event for these rural farming families. The next day, Sunday, Tom attended Locust Hill Baptist Church with his family. "Sure looked swell to see Tom riding around with us again. Everyone wanted to know who that good-looking lieutenant was. I proudly replied, why that's my big brother, didn't you know?" Helen wrote.

Helen Hammond and Callie Barnette were close friends. Their families lived on farms a half-mile apart and they had attended high school together, doubled-dated, and even wrote letters to each other when Helen was staying at Leila's home in Greenville. Helen had encouraged Callie to write to her brother Tom when he was overseas. When he returned home, she prodded Tom to call on Callie. Her match-making began to catch fire. "Tom and Callie came down late in the afternoon. They stayed 'til about 11:30 PM," Helen wrote that Sunday evening.

In fact, Tom and Callie were almost inseparable while Tom was at home. They went to basketball games at Mountain View High School where they had first met. Despite the winter weather, they drove into the nearby foothills of the Blue Ridge for picnics beside the clear mountain streams. They went bowling, and to the movies. And they spent time with their families. But they were engaged in an intense courtship, trying to learn as much as possible about each other before he had to return to military duty.

"Dad stayed home and helped work on Tom's car," Helen wrote on Friday, January 26. Tom's "new" car was not new at all. No cars were built during World War II because the big, midwestern industrial plants were all engaged in making guns, tanks, airplanes, and the other material of war. The Ford needed attention, and the two Toms were just the ones to do it. Repairing cars and farm machinery was in their blood. Tom Sr. had been driving a Ford T-model pickup since about 1925, one he had bought new when he worked in the gypsum mines in upstate

New York. And he had purchased an A-Model car for the family. The next day, Helen wrote: "Tom got his new motor in today and the car runs grand."

On Friday, February 2, the Hammond and Barnette families gathered at the Hammond farm, for another oyster supper. "Seems as though we like those animals! Mom had supper served and it was delicious. After supper we sang for quite a while. We played games after games. What a time. Mr. Butler even tore his shirt," Helen wrote. And she was happy with her matchmaking. "Tom and Callie look cute together," she wrote.

The next day, the family drove Tom to Greenville to catch the bus for Miami, Florida. "We tried not to think of his leaving, but those last hours were tough. We got to the bus station about 6:30 and his bus was already in. We decided it would be best if we left then so he would be sure to get a seat. Goodbyes over with and we left Tom rushing into the station with a cigarette in his mouth," Helen wrote. On Monday, Helen observed that "it feels mighty lonesome at home since Tom has gone."

Chapter 48

▼

Tom Returns to Duty, and the Hospital

During his training, Tom had his nose broken in a softball game when the ball smashed into his face. The injury caused him headaches when he flew at high altitudes. When he returned home from his combat tour and finished his twenty-one days of furlough, he was assigned to an Army medical center in Miami, Florida, for surgery.

Tom had been home about two weeks following his combat tour. He returned to the red hills of Greenville County that he had missed so desperately, and his romance with Callie Barnette shifted into high gear. What had been a tentative correspondence, encouraged by his sister Helen, had blossomed during the days he was home.

South Florida had been taken over by the military. The money spent in the region by the federal government helped offset the losses in the tourism business caused by the war. The Army set up the replacement training center, the officer candidate school, and the officer training school on Miami Beach. The Army spent more than $3 million ($41.5 million) there in 1942, and by 1944 the schools occupied almost 400 hotels on the beach, plus the Nautilus and Biltmore hotels, which had been converted into hospitals. Tom would be assigned to the Biltmore Hotel at Coral Gables, or the Army Air Forces Regional Hospital, as it was known during the war. Built in 1926 at a cost of $10 million ($138.5 million), the Biltmore was an opulent resort with pools, a golf course, and other luxuries Tom had never before experienced.[294]

The drumbeat of his letters to Callie increased dramatically, as he wrote almost daily and implored her to come to Florida to see him. She never did. Callie, meanwhile, was contributing to the war effort on her job at Piedmont Shirt Company in Greenville: "I buttoned up Army shirts, and thought of you, all day. My fingers are sore from buttoning about a dozen buttons per shirt on ten dozen shirts," she wrote to Tom. And the tone of Tom's letters changed from friendly to lovesick.

Tom had spent two weeks at home with his family, but most important of all, he spent a lot of that time with Callie, and their relationship changed rapidly as Tom decompressed from combat. Callie was smitten by this young airman with his pilot's wings pinned on the chest of his olive green Eisenhower uniform jacket. Now, as he waited in a Miami beachfront hotel for a bed to open in the Coral Gables Army Hospital, he could hardly contain his blossoming love for Callie. His letters also reflect a sense of awe in a farm boy thrust into an alien urban world by the war. On Monday, February 5, Tom wrote to Callie:

"I got into Miami yesterday about eleven, and got a good night's rest too, but I've been going to lectures all day long and am just about ready to drop. My hotel is right on the beach and the water looks mighty inviting but guess I'll have to wait until I can find me a bathing suit. I had two of them overseas but I sent them back in my footlocker and I probably won't get it for sometime yet.

"I sure wish you were down here. I'll bet you would really like it and we sure could have a good time. West Palm Beach is mostly made up of hotels and they line the beach for some three to five miles. All the hotels are made of white stone and all have palm trees and nice lawns around them. The ocean here is about the bluest I have ever seen. It looks as if someone poured coloring in it. The picture postcards don't exaggerate it a bit as they do most places. All in all, it's about the most beautiful place I was ever in. I'd like to stay here for the duration, only it costs too much money.

"This is nice down here and I shouldn't complain but I just seem kinda lost, not knowing anyone. I don't know what to do hardly in my spare time. I wish I was home again for I had a better time there than I believe I've ever had. I'm just sorry that it didn't last longer.

"I'd better say 'Au Revoir' for now as it is supper time."

Miami was a rest and relaxation base for crews returning from combat. Tom had time to swim, go to movies and concerts, and play golf. His basic Army pay of $150 ($1,695) a month gave him plenty of resources to take advantage of the tourist mecca. He saw Vic and Erna Radke and Chuck Delcroix while he was there. But he had fallen in love, and he was missing the object of his affection. On Wednesday, February 7, Tom wrote to Callie:

"I was admitted into the hospital out here at Coral Cables today to get that nose operation I've been wanting to get for so long. The doc took one look at my nose and wanted to know how I'd been flying for so long in that condition. They are also going to make x-rays to find out if I have sinusitis trouble. He seems to think that's the reason for all the headaches I've been having.

"Coral Gables is the home of a lot of rich people who have built homes out here to come to in the winter. It's about ten miles out from Miami. The name of the hospital I'm in is the Biltmore. It's sure a big affair and there are a lot of patients here.

"I'm in a room with a colonel, who, incidentally, is a doctor. He was in India and caught some disease and was sent back here. He is from Atlanta.

"I think they are going to keep me here for some time. At least that's what I've been able to gather from idle rumors that I've heard. One good thing is that I can get a pass to go into town once in a while to see a movie if I like.

"This hospital used to be a big hotel and my room is a small one with just two of us. We have a radio to help relieve the monotony, a private bath and all the modern comforts. The only thing is that it's kinda lonesome."

Tom continued to cool his heels in the Coral Gables hospital for several days, writing to Callie and sending her postcards. On Monday, February 12, Tom wrote to Callie:

"Here it is another day and they haven't operated on me yet. The actual operation, so they tell me, isn't bad at all, but this suspense is killing me.

"I got a pass for a few hours last night and went into Miami to see a show. I just had to get out for a little while. The show I saw was "Mrs. Parkington," with Greer Garson and Walter Pidgeon! I thought it was very good and would like to see it again.

"I have a very nice view from my window. There's a big swimming pool right below and a big golf course beyond that. This must have been a swanky hotel before the Army took it over; it sure has all the trimmings.

"Be sweet, don't work too hard, and write as often as you can. Don't forget the picture you promised to send me."

Callie was impatient as well to see Tom again. It had been two weeks since he left. On Monday, February 12, Callie wrote to Tom:

"I was somewhat surprised to hear from you today! But boy, I sure was glad. I have written, but I doubt if you will get it, since your address is changed. Now that it is changed, I think I should hear from you quiet often, for you really will have a lot of spare time. And that will be a grand way for you to spend it.

"Today has really been a blue Monday. Right now, it is raining at full speed. You having to leave was bad enough, but the sun to stop shining makes it worse. Yesterday it shined a bit, but that is all since you left. I walked up to see Helen, but she wasn't home. The exercise was good for me though.

"I guess you really feel like a big shot, laying up resting in a big hotel. I am glad, for you really deserve every minute of it. And I'm glad too, that you are getting your nose all fixed up. I sure hope it won't hurt too bad.

"It really is a beautiful building you are at. I know you are glad it's down there instead of being in a colder climate this winter. Only wish it was near home so I might visit you now and then. But anyway, maybe you'll get to come home again soon, I hope.

"I'm just back from church, imagine that, church on a Monday night??

"I haven't been to a single movie since *Here Comes the Waves*. I wanted to see *Marriage Is a Private Affair*, but did not make it. *30 Seconds over Tokyo*, is on in Greer this week and Daddy has promised to carry us one night. Don't know if he will or not. I'm not any too eager to see it.

"Basketball tournament is this week. John and Genelle are trying to get me to stay from work and go with them Thursday to see them play. But from the looks of things at Piedmont, guess I'll be working.

"That rain is really pouring down it most puts me to sleep, listening. So guess I had better stop and get to bed, everybody but me is already there now."

Tom had been in the hospital for a week when he finally was scheduled for his nasal surgery. On Thursday, February 15, Tom wrote to Callie:

"I had a very nice letter from you two days ago and you can bet that I was very glad to get it. It was the one that you wrote to me while I was over at Miami Beach. I got a pass from the hospital and went over there as I was hoping there would be some mail there for me, and there was. I haven't had a letter from you since I've been here but am looking forward to the afternoon mail in hopes that I will get one then.

"I found out this morning that I'm to get my new nose tomorrow. I just can't bring myself to worry about it for I've seen some of the work that the colonel (yes, a colonel) has done. He's supposed to be about the best in the country.

"Oh yes, they made me change rooms again last night. That makes three times now and it's just about to get tiresome. You just get to know one of the boys, and bingo, off you go. I'll probably be here some time now, though, at least until my nose gets in shape again.

"I went out to the beach a few days ago, and guess who I ran into. It was Chuck, my bombardier. We talked a while, and lay around on the beach in the sun. He's going to take pilot training and is being sent to Texas. I think he left last night. I don't have the slightest idea that he will ever get through, but I didn't tell him this. I didn't want to discourage him too much. I don't like to see him even try it for I'm afraid he's liable to kill himself in a plane.

"I found out that I will probably be sent to an advanced flying school to instruct cadets. Can't you just picture me taking those poor guys up to teach them how to fly? I haven't flown for so long that I'll probably have to start all over again. It will probably be two more months before I get to fly again."

Tom had splints and gauze in his nose, but it didn't keep him from writing almost daily. On Friday, February 16, Tom wrote to Callie:

"You know, Honey, I'd sure hate for you to see me now. I'm just about the most horrible looking sight that you would ever expect to see. One look and you would disown me for good. The doc put some kind of brace on my nose to hold it in place until it heals and it makes me look like some fantastic character out of one of these funny books. He also put a lot of packing in there to keep it from bleeding too much and I can't taste a darn thing with it stopped up. It sure is a funny feeling to eat a whole meal and not be able to taste a bit of it.

"My eyes are just about swollen shut and I can't see very well so I'll make this one short. I'll be thinking of you so be sure and write often.

"Love,

Tom (Sad Sack) if you don't believe it come and see."

Tom continued to recover for several days, and to think about Callie. On Monday, February 19, Tom wrote to Callie:

"I sho wuz a happy little boy when I got your letter in the morning's mail. I hadn't had one in several days and was wondering if you had run out of stationery, or something. I hope you can read this for I am in very poor shape to even try to write, much less make it look good. I have two of the blackest eyes that any white person could ever have, I imagine. I look as if I got hit by an east-bound freight.

"I got operated on right after dinner on Friday, only they wouldn't let me eat. They didn't put me to sleep but just gave me a few shots to kill the pain. It sure was a funny feeling to hear them cutting away and not feel a bit of pain. The only time that it hurt at all was when he was sewing it up. I guess some of the dope had worn off by that time.

"Thanks for sending the clipping. I knew the boy very well."

The *Greenville News* clipping Tom referred to was about a young man from Taylors with whom Tom had attended school, Sgt. George L. Hammett. He had been a gunner and assistant engineer on a B-24 bomber of the 489th Bomb Group that was returning to base at Halesworth, England, with one engine shut down and the hydraulics and radio systems shot out. The landing gear would have to be cranked into landing position by hand, a task that fell to Sergeant Hammett. Descending below the flight deck, Hammett managed to get the main landing gear cranked into position, but the nose wheel stubbornly refused to budge. After a Herculean effort, Hammett got the nose wheel into landing position. But just about that time, two more engines suddenly stopped running, leaving the stricken plane with just one operating engine. It was not enough to save the plane. It was just a few seconds by crew accounts before the plane slammed into an English pasture, sliding some distance before coming to rest against a dyke. It took a few minutes for the rest of the stunned crew to realize that Hammett, because of his position below the flight deck, was crushed to death instantly when the plane crashed into the pasture. The crew told Hammett's family in letters that they credited his heroic efforts to lower the landing gear for saving their lives.[295]

The next day, Tuesday, February 20, Tom found his outlook improving, and he wrote to Callie:

"Here I am again and today I feel a hundred percent better than I did yesterday. The doc took the packing out this morning and it sure was a relief to be able to breathe out of it again.

"It's really been hot down here for the past few days but today there is a nice cool breeze and that makes it just pleasant. It hasn't rained once since I've been down here. I don't mind that, though, for I had enough of that in England to last me a lifetime.

"They won't let me go outside the ward until I get this darn brace off my nose and that sure does make me mad to see all this nice sunshine outside and just going to waste.

"I have a sneaking idea that I'm liable to end up out in Texas some place after I leave here. I don't know for sure but some of the boys, who were in about the same position as I, have been sent out there. As much as I would like to stay in the southeast, I'll take just about anything as long as it's on this side of either of the oceans."

On Wednesday, February 21, Tom wrote to Callie:

"Still wishing for it to snow, are you? Well, I sure hope it does for your sake. And I challenge you to snowballs at thirty paces. Really, I would like to see some snow also.

"So you met Jim Holcombe. I've often wondered where he got to and here he turns up at home. I'd sure like to see the old boy. It's too bad he didn't get home while I was there. We used to work together down at Taylors. I like the old boy a lot and I hope you gave him my address.

"The doc took the braces off my nose this morning, and was I glad of that. It sure was a relief to get my old beak out in the air again. The doc sure did a nice job on it. It's just as straight as if it had grown that way. It's still a bit swollen but should look a little better after a few more days.

"Just think, only five days ago I was operated on and today I was out playing golf again. That's really a quick recovery isn't it?

"You could have knocked me over with a feather when I got word that Vic and his wife dropped by home to see the folks. He is about the most unpredictable guy that I ever knew. I'm glad he did stop by, though, and I think a lot more of him for it. I met him and his wife one afternoon down here and talked to them for a few minutes.

"I'm so glad that you and Helen went to church together and I hope you can make it more often.

"Sammy Kaye is down here in Miami now. I sure would like to go in and see and hear him. Tell you what, you come down and we'll go see him together. I'd enjoy it a hundred times more that way."

Figure 14: Lt. Robert Vernon Mercer died January 28, 1945 at the controls of his B-17 bomber, near Tournai, Belgium. (Photo provided by his sister, Nolie Lennon.)

Chapter 49

▼

Memories from the
Attic in a Bread Tin

February 25, 1945. The war losses followed Tom back home. Tom wrote in a letter to Callie:

"I had some bad news the other day. One of the crews that was in my barracks in England was shot down just after I left. I wrote his (the pilot's) family when I got back in the states and told them that he was doing fine over there. They live in North Carolina. I sure did hate that after I had told them how well he was doing. Bob Mercer was the boy's name and he was one of the nicest fellows that I ever ran across. I hate those damned Nazis more every day. Pardon those hard words but I really mean it."

Today, Robert Vernon Mercer's remains lie beside those of his father and mother in the Butters-Singletary Cemetery, near Big Swamp, outside Bladenboro, North Carolina. His final resting place is marked only by the one by three foot Veterans Administration granite marker. It is inscribed with his name, rank, branch of service, and World War II. The centipede grass surrounding the flat stone tries to grow over and hide it. With no children to preserve his memory, the sons and daughters of his seven siblings try to keep the stone from disappearing. On a warm December day, Myrtle Jolly and Beverly Bryant helped me brush away the invading grass and soil so that we could see their uncle's grave stone. They both have warm memories of Bob as a teenager and a young man going off to war. He was the youngest of his parents' eight children, ambitious and a natural leader. His classmates in his 1941 graduating class at Bladenboro High School elected him to seven of the twenty-four Senior Superlative listings in their yearbook, including Most Dignified, Best Personality, Most Versatile, Most Conceited, Most Likely to Succeed, Most Courteous, and Most Original. Like his older brother Gerald, Bob stood out among the Mercer children because of his red hair and fiery blue eyes. He was vice president of his senior class and clearly marked by his peers as a leader.

Myrtle Jolly, who was just eight years younger than her uncle, described his spirit and mischief with a story. Once he found a corn husk being used by a mouse as a nest, containing a handful of hairless, blind baby mice. He shut Myrtle up in a room in the barn with the toothless and harmless critters while she pleaded for him to let her out. "I'm still terrified of mice," she said with a smile, clearly more endeared to her dead uncle than scared from the childhood prank.

Nolie Mercer Lennon, now past ninety years old, but with crystal clear memories of her brother Bob, recalls that he built himself a house trailer in his parents back yard, complete with a bed and kitchen, and he entertained his friends in it. "He was ambitious. He wanted to do something for himself," Nolie said about Bob. After he finished high school, Bob worked as an electrician in nearby Wilmington at the North Carolina Shipbuilding Company, a wartime enterprise on the Cape Fear River that built Liberty Ships. His brother was a supervisor at the shipyard. Bob took electronics courses as well.

Louise, Bob's sister, who was five years older than he was, was working for the USO in Wilmington at the time, and lived near Wrightsville Beach. She said Bob's experience in electronics school and at the shipyard, convinced him he wanted to enter the Army Air Forces and become a pilot.

"He applied to go to flying school, but he flunked the medical exam because his blood pressure was too high. He went to a local doctor, a family friend in Bladenboro who helped him get his blood pressure down. He reapplied and was accepted for pilot training," Louise said.

Bob's Army service started with basic military training in Florida, where he was in the same company with Hollywood actor Clark Gable. On January 28, 1943, exactly two years before his death in a plane crash in Belgium, Bob entered the U. S. Army Air Forces Cadet Training Corps to begin training as a pilot. Bob received additional training at Marysville, Tennessee, and entered basic flight training at Malden, Missouri. On April 15, 1944, he graduated from advanced pilot training and received his commission as a second lieutenant at Stuttgart, Arkansas. He also received training at Columbus, Ohio, where he met Susan

Greer, a medical laboratory technician, who he told his family he intended to marry when he returned from the war. He ended his training at Avon Park, Florida, and was dispatched overseas in November 1944.

In one of his letters, Bob described the urgency and haste with which the Army Air Force was giving young pilots the bare minimum of training, then shipping them into combat. The air war to bring the Nazi regime to its knees had become a meat-grinder for air crews and pilots. One of every thirteen people who served in the Eighth Air Force would die in combat or other service-related incidents.

"John, I seriously doubt I'll get a furlough any time soon. They are needing pilots mighty bad and shooting them through pretty fast. I suppose I'll be lucky if I get just one furlough before I go across," Bob wrote to his brother John.

He described a day set aside for psychological evaluation as "eight hours of hell."

"Well, one of my biggest worries is over—or just beginning. I took my mental today and it was truly out of this world. I don't see how anyone could possibly devise anything so complicated. I hope I passed and kinda think I did. We take our psycho-motive Monday. It's the one that tests nerves and coordination. The ARMA and Physical come last. The ARMA is an interview by psychologists and psychiatrists. It's all about our past history. All of the tests combined last four days. Then it's a few days before you know whether you classified or not."

His commanding officer promised the group a beer party if they passed the rigorous test.

"He says he is going to get five barrels of Budweiser and the sky's the limit." The party would be a welcome relief from the rigors of flight training.

"If you know anyone that is planning to join the Air Corps tell them to study Algebra and math," he wrote.

Bob was on his fourteenth combat mission when he died on January 28, 1945, exactly one month after Tom, Vic, Scotty, and Chuck had flown their thirty-fifth and final mission on December 28, 1944. He wrote his last letter to his mother and father on the evening of January 27, the night before he flew his last mission. It was a hopeful and optimistic letter, containing no gloom of war or premonitions of death, but noting wistfully the good fortune of a hometown acquaintance who was getting out of the Army.

"I just got another letter from Bobbie Bridger telling of his discharge from the army—what a lucky guy he is—if he only knew," Bob wrote.

He inquired about his father's farming business that year and whether he would be planting tobacco. And he urged his father to use some of his military pay that he was sending home if his family needed it for farm expenses. He ended on an optimistic and brave note:

"Don't worry about me as I am in the finest of shape. Write soon and take good care of yourself. Love always, Robert."

The previous night, he had written to his much-loved and respected brother-in-law, Livious B. Lennon, who had married Bob's sister Nolie. The two men, both well-read and prone to compose poetry and tease each other with chivalrous banter, always addressed each other as sir, like two medieval knights might have done.

"Sir, Sir, Lady & Loyal Subjects, Here's trusting you are in the cream of health and happiness and dwelling off the fat of the land. Sir Shakespeare could not hold a jerry's chance to you Sir Shakerod, I shake your hand, yea thrice verbally. Your great poetry has brought gladness into this war torn realm of existence, namely England. I could just see myself on that hunt with you—me stumbling along scaring all the game while you and Sir Breedy Stark-Stalker camouflaged a volley of curses under a broad smile and a jolly lie. Great men are all like that, always full of fun as Capt. Dewey used to say. By the way, where is the old boy now?

"Sir, I often have a hankering to strike forth with poetry of the old countries but it doesn't come as freely and lively as it used to be. It shouldn't be too long off before I am on home grounds and I'll be the happiest boy in the world. They're going to have one hell of a time getting me to leave that place called home again."

His observations about the English were more colorful than those Tom sent home, but nonetheless wistful for their rural farming homes, which were similar.

"England's quite a quaint place. Some places may even be considered beautiful. It's very gray over here, houses with thatched roofs, muddy roads with stone fences that wind round and round and finally end up no where. Old men wearing overcoats, flat top caps, and Colin Singletary specialty boots. Little red-cheeked kids running around and invariably have the same line: 'Any gum Chum?' My answer: 'Nope Dope.' In London you find the plutocrats who dress and act as their forefathers did and always will, they live on tradition alone, kinda like Julia Bridger. After all these things, England is the most beautiful island in the world when you are just returning from the east. Just a little hunk of island but right now it's home, a place to eat and a pretty good sack to sleep in. It's a wonderful feeling to set foot on solid mud after a little hop where things are pretty hot. I have thirteen such hops in now.

"Nolie, how have you and the boys been these days? I would give anything to see you. I'll bet that Jerry boy is a big fellow when I get home. He probably won't know me. I wouldn't be surprised if I look a little older than my age, or I did look. It was two years ago the 28th of this month, two years, long ones too, that I've been in this army. Seems like a long time in some ways but a lot of invaluable experience. Almost my bed time so I'll say thanks again for that really swell letter and answer it again, soon. Love to all, Sir Bob."

But Bob had dark premonitions about his fate in combat that he did not share with his parents. The weekend before he was due to ship out for England, he called his sister Louise. He could get a flight to Charlotte, North Carolina, if she would pick him up and drive him home to Bladenboro. Louise, as a USO worker, had access to cars and the scarce, rationed fuel to run them. "USO workers could pull strings and get privileges," she said. (After traveling to Arkansas to see Bob graduate from flight school and receive his commission, she had pretended to be his wife for the return trip because unattached civilians were not supposed to take up a seat on the train.) On his last trip home before leaving for Europe, Louise picked Bob up in Charlotte at 10:00 PM. They drove all night, arriving in Bladenboro on Saturday morning. He wanted to see Wilmington one more time, so he and a friend took Louise's car and drove to the coast. "When he left, he kissed me on the cheek and said 'thanks for the use of your car'," Louise said. "I had assumed I would take him back to catch the train. Late in the afternoon, he said our brother John would take him."

Louise later learned from John that Bob was very emotional on the drive to Charlotte. "I asked John why he didn't want me to take him to the train. He said, 'Bob does not think he's coming back'." Bob gave John names and addresses of people to contact in the event he was killed.

Louise received her last letter from her baby brother a week before he died. He had flown combat missions on Christmas Eve and Christmas Day.

"Life under these conditions make a person's heart turn to stone. Sometimes I feel like all I want to do is kill someone, especially the mess sergeant," he wrote.

After the family learned of Bob's death, Louise began to use her USO connections to try to learn what happened to him. She had the name of Lt. Thomas Hammond, whom Bob had known in the Ninety-fifth Bomb Group. On February 26, Tom wrote to Louise to offer his help in learning how Robert died. He noted that he and Bob had lived in the same barracks, and he gave Louise the name of an officer who was still with the bomb group in England, Lt. Jack Benrube.

On March 8, 1945, Lieutenant Benrube of the Ninety-fifth Bomb Group wrote to Louise, who then lived in Durham, North Carolina, to tell her what he had learned about the circumstances of Bob's death.

"On January 28th the boys went out to their target in the Ruhr Valley about 20 miles north of Cologne. Lt. Mercer was flying No. 2 position or deputy, which is an important position. (Bob was a very good pilot and had been asked numerable times to try for Lead Crew but knowing that his crew would most likely 'break up' he refused.) The target was well protected with anti-aircraft guns. Bob's ship was hit badly; two of his engines were gone with another one threatened. Bob was coaxing the ship toward home when his third engine went out. There was a small fire on one of the wings; the ship was losing altitude quickly now, so the last resort was to bail out over France.

"The only way the men could bail out was for the pilot (Bob) to hold the plane steady. The officers and enlisted men bailed out and landed in Tournai, France. All the men had minor injuries. The co-pilot, Lt. Taylor, did not know that his chute had been hit by a piece of flak. On pulling the ripcord his chute disintegrated in the air. Meantime Bob could not get the plane into complete control to enable him to also 'hit the silk,' so therefore his only alternative was to crash-land it. He crashed in the center of Tournai. Both Bob and Lt. Taylor are buried in France."

Mercer's commander recommended him for the Distinguished Flying Cross, but there is no evidence that it was ever awarded. Benrube noted that Robert's promotion to first lieutenant arrived on January 29, the day after he died.

"Bob was the best-liked man in the barracks. We have 16 officers in our barracks and there was always a great deal of anguish going around. Bob was the peacemaker. In his own quiet way he crept into the hearts of all the men here. We lost the finest and nicest guy I have ever met. He did his duty like a good soldier," Benrube wrote to Louise about her brother.

Later, the seven crew members who survived because of Mercer's heroism recalled how it happened in an exchange of letters. Their accounts, and eyewitness accounts from citizens of Tournai, differ somewhat from Benrube's account. For example, researcher Jacques De Ceuninck believes Taylor's parachute was not damaged, but that he simply waited too late to exit the plane, which was at too low an altitude for him to open his chute.

Approaching their target at Duisburg, near Cologne, Germany, at 27,000 feet, the airplane was struck by as many as four bursts of flak, three of them directly under the cockpit. Bob Mercer ordered Fackrell to unload the bombs, which he did, and the pilot peeled off to the left and descended to 16,000 feet.

"I came out of the ball turret and got on the interphone in the waist. The pilot told us to put on our chutes but said not to worry, that he would get us out. That little bit of conversation gave me confidence. We all calmed down and sat tight," said Jack German, the ball turret gunner.

But the aircraft was struggling and Mercer along with it. Mercer feathered number four engine. Engines number two and three were windmilling. The ship had just one of its four mighty Wright-Cyclone engines still running.

Mercer tried to land at Brussels, the capital of Belgium, but was ordered to continue to the designated emergency landing field at Merville, France. Halfway there, the number two engine began to burn, and the plane began to vibrate terribly. Mercer ordered the crew to bail out to save themselves, while he stayed at the controls to keep the aircraft steady until they escaped.

Donald Hupp, the waist gunner, wrote to his fellow survivors that "all the time every one on board was encouraging each other that we would get out of it all right."

Hupp said fire broke out in the cockpit, where Mercer was wrestling the badly broken plane's controls as the flight engineer tried to extinguish the fire.

The plane was in its death throes. Leonard J. Loucks, the flight engineer, said the number two engine was falling apart and burning; the landing gear on the right wing dropped off, and the top turret was shot away. The cockpit was filling with smoke.

"Then number two engine started to fall apart and smoke a little about five minutes after the engine caught fire. That is when the pilot gave the order to bail out. I was the first to go out the waist door. Then the radio man and tail gunner. The rest of the men were up in the nose fighting the fire up there, then went out the nose door," Hupp said.

"I looked up into the cockpit to see the pilot vainly trying to steady the ship so the crew could safely jump," said Fackrell.

"The navigator (Warren B. Detering) hit me several times on the back to get my attention and then started to jettison the hatch there and motioned for me to bail out. It seemed like a few seconds after my chute opened, and I looked at the plane, that the number two engine vibrated off and went down in flames and the whole left wing was on fire and the ship was losing altitude rapidly and it disappeared in the broken overcast," said Loucks.

"It seemed to me that the pilot did an extraordinary miracle when he held the ship up as long as he did and got us safely in allied territory and held the ship steady for us to all get out of the ship," said Loucks.

Mercer and co-pilot Charles R. Taylor were killed on January 28, 1945, while flying B-17 number 339055. The aircraft came down in Belgium, and was destroyed.[296]

Taylor died when his parachute failed to open. Mercer was trying to coax the dying aircraft to a landing at a French airfield at Merville, designated for emergency landings, and to keep it from striking innocent civilians in the numerous small villages beneath his flight path.

The plane crashed at Kain Village, north of Tournai, Belgium, about ten kilometers from French-Belgian border. Mercer's bravery allowed seven of his crew to escape death, but he went down with his ship.

Scotty Alexander, who lived in the barracks with Bob Mercer, remembered him for the packages he received regularly from home. "We'd go to the mess hall to eat, and on the way out, I'd tell the cooks we needed a pound of butter. Bob Mercer's family would send him five-pound boxes of popcorn, and we'd use the butter to pop the corn on the kerosene stove in our barracks," Scotty said. Bob's family was constantly sending him food. "Dad probably grew that popcorn," said his sister Nolie. Bob acknowledges in his letters from his training bases receiving a cake from Nolie and a package of fresh grapes grown on the family farm.

In November 1945, Walter Taylor of Kalamazoo, Michigan, wrote to Bob's brother John to inquire what the Mercer family had learned about the crash that killed Mercer and Charles Taylor. "We hope these boys have not gone in vain, but sometimes I wonder. Perhaps all we can hope for is that the boys coming back will use these experiences as an influence in shaping this world's future," Walter Taylor wrote about his son Charles and about Bob.

Myrtle Jolly said Callie Mercer, Bob's mother, could not summon a tear when she learned about her youngest child's death. When told, Callie placed her forehead silently on the table. Her hair began to turn white from that day, and her health began to fail. She never again had the vigor she possessed when Bob was alive. "For the rest of his life, our daddy could not talk about Bob without crying," Nolie said.

Livious Lennon, Bob's much-loved brother-in-law, was not a crier, but he missed his fallen kin terribly. On V.E. Day 1945, he composed a poetic tribute to Bob:

To Sir Bob

With heavy heart and tearful eye
I now take up my pen
And write for you a verse or two
A brother and a friend

It was good to have you with us, Sir
Though it seemed so short a while
I'll miss that hearty handshake
Yes, I'll miss that beaming smile

The day we all looked forward to
when you would be coming home
Was just a day much hoped for
Which we know will never come

Now you've gone beyond the Shadows
From a world of Hell and Blood
to take up life unending
In a land both fair and good

The guns have fallen silent now
No more the "flak" will rise
Your victory now is won, Sir
There is freedom in the skies

I'll see you in my dreams, Sir
Otherwise it cannot be,
So Long! I'll not forget you
Blest be your memory

• Sir Buster

The mourning for Bob Mercer's family did not end in 1945. He and his co-pilot were buried in a military cemetery in France. In 1947, Bob's remains were disinterred and returned to his home in Bladen County, North Carolina. His casket arrived aboard the first shipload of soldiers' remains to be returned to the United States from the European war. The ship carrying 6,248 caskets with soldiers' remains arrived in New York City, where Louise was living with her new husband, a paratrooper from New York she had met while working in the USO. Louise attended an elaborate memorial service for the fallen American soldiers and airmen that included her brother. An Army transport, the Joseph V. Connolly, docked at Pier 61, West Twenty-first Street, and a representative coffin was placed on a caisson to be carried to Central Park. Wreaths lined the quay where the ships docked, as soldiers and sailors worked to bring their dead comrades home. West Point and Annapolis cadets followed mounted New York City police escorts, as soldiers of the Eighty-second Airborne Division marched sharply up Fifth Avenue. More than 400,000 people covered the meadow of Central Park and lined city streets, as a distraught mother would periodically cry out the name of her dead son. Eleanor Roosevelt, the wife of President Franklin Roosevelt, attended the ceremony as Army cannon boomed out artillery salutes to the fallen Americans. In the days following the memorial service, the caskets, including Bob's, were put aboard trains for the final legs of trips home to North Carolina and many other states.[297]

The Mercer family held a funeral, with full military honors, two years after they first mourned his death. The cigar box that holds Bob's letters in Nolie Lennon's house also contains fading pictures of the mountain of flowers surrounding the flag-draped casket in the small cemetery beside Big Swamp. Callie Davis Mercer joined her youngest child there in 1962. Charles Oliver Mercer was laid to rest with his wife and son in 1978.

Louise's treasured memorabilia about her brother, including the letter she received from Tom in 1945, are stored in a tin bread box in her attic. Like Nolie's cigar box, and thousands of similar boxes across the nation, they are at last giving up their secret sadness to the history books, as relatives of long-dead Americans seek to refresh the memories of their sacrifices.

"Bob and I corresponded frequently while he was in England. From his letters I could tell life was not a bowl of cherries. In one letter he told me his hair was no longer red—after the missions it turned white.

"It has been sixty years since Bob was killed, but I still have difficulty discussing his death. We have a son named Bob, the only grandchild named after him," Louise Toumbacaris wrote in a letter accompanying copies of her brother's letters.

Figure 15: Tom Hammond, in Detroit, Michigan, after returning home from England and marrying Callie. (Photo from Tom Hammond's collection.)

Chapter 50

▼

Moon Over Miami

Tom continued to try to coax Callie to visit him in Miami. On Monday afternoon, February 26, Tom wrote to Callie:

"I sho was mighty glad to get those two letters today. One was written Friday night and the other Sat. morning. By the way, how did you find the great metropolis of Greer?

"I'm glad you got to see that picture you'd been wanting to see. I'll bet it was pretty good and I'd like to see it. Maybe it will get down this way one of these days. I did see *Stage Door Canteen*.

"I haven't been outside for two days now, I've just been resting up. There was about five days in a row that I was out playing golf and after that I guess two days rest won't do any harm. I'll probably be out again tomorrow if it's pretty.

"I don't know how much longer I'll be down here, honey. I imagine about another month before I leave here for my next base. Think you can make it before that. I sure hope so darling, you don't know how much I want to see you. I assure you we'll have a lot of fun.

"It's just getting dark and I can see a great big round moon coming up over there. It's sure going to be a mighty nice night. I sure hate to see it go to waste. Well, maybe it isn't going to waste either for it makes me think of you all the more. It would be much nicer, though, if you were here darling."

On Tuesday night, February 27, Tom wrote to Callie:

"Here comes that moon again. It seems that every time I write you the moon is just coming up. So what, I like it that way and I'm sure you're watching too.

"I got a very sweet letter from you today and the more I get the better I like them. I've been thinking about you all day and wondering if you were working very hard; I hope you're not doing that. I can't have my gal getting herself worked down when it isn't necessary.

"I'm sorry to hear about Carroll's bad luck, but I guess he was lucky that he was just wounded. So many of the boys are much worse off and won't be getting well at all. There are sure some pitiful cases down here from all the fighting fronts that we have.

"Thanks for sending me Donald's picture. He and I were in the same class at Taylors. It's sure too bad about him; he sure was a smart boy. I always envied him because he always seemed to learn much easier than I did. Maybe it was because he studied a lot and I didn't."

On Wednesday, February 28, Tom wrote to Callie:

"Well, here it is another day gone by and almost another month gone. I guess tomorrow will be officially springtime.

"I sure was glad to get your letter today. That is about the only thing that keeps me going around here. I don't know what I'd do if I didn't have your letter to look forward to. Didn't do very much today, just played a little golf this morning and rested the rest of the day.

"I'll bet you can't guess who dropped in to see us here at the hospital today. Well, it was none other than Sammy Kaye and his orchestra. I really did enjoy it and I sure wish that you could have been here to see him. You'd have enjoyed Billy Williams and Nancy Norman. They were all good and I'd sure like to see them again. I know you would have enjoyed it too.

"I don't know what my chances are of getting home after I get out. If you can talk your folks into letting you come down, darling, please do, for I want to see you so much, and believe me, I'll keep all my fingers crossed.

"They had Sammy and his boys set up down by the pool today where it was cool. It sure was nice, I only wish he'd stayed longer.

"The moon hasn't come up yet but it should most any time now and until then I'll be thinking about you and wishing that we could watch it come up together."

On Thursday, March 1, Tom wrote to Callie:

"I didn't get that looked-for letter today, and I'm kinda blue, but that just makes me look forward to tomorrow all the more. Really, honey I've been thinking about you all day.

"You may think I've been having a swell time down here but I haven't. It's true, I do enjoy going out and playing golf and things like that but even then I keep thinking about you and wishing that you were along with me. Like tonight, the Red Cross put on a movie for us and it was very good too, but I didn't enjoy it near as much as if you had been with me. I know you would have liked this. The name of it was *Sunday Dinner for a Soldier*.

"The doc won't give me any hint as to how much longer I'm going to be kept here but it looks as if it may be some time yet before I'm out. I don't care much; only I get so darn lonesome just hanging around all the time. If I had a job to do maybe it would help a little."

On Friday, March 2, Tom wrote to Callie:

"Heah, I is again and I sho very glad to get that letter from you again today. I was a little disappointed in not getting one yesterday but this one made up for it.

"I just got back from a movie downstairs a few minutes ago. It was very good too. *Tonight and Every Night* was the name of it. I sure enjoyed it a lot. The setting took place in a theatre in London. I've been in the same theatre, that this was supposed to represent, a number of times.

"I've felt better today than I have in a long time. I think it was your letter that did it; in fact I'm sure of it.

"How about you, have you been taking advantage of those rare pretty days that you've been having? It's good for you to get out and get a little fresh air once in a while and I know how you like to. You know what I'd like to do? I'd like to go on a good old fashioned picnic in the mountains. Wouldn't you like that? Somehow I've always liked the mountains more than anything else. Remember the time we went up to River Falls?"

On Saturday, March 3, Tom wrote to Callie:

"It doesn't look as if I will be getting out of here for some time. They just moved me down here to the fourth floor yesterday and it looks like it may be permanent quarters for some time. You'd think they were making money on us to be keeping us here so long. I can hardly realize that I've been in here almost a month. How time flies.

"You know, darling, I've never been in one place so long before without at least going to town every day or so. I just haven't had any desire to go at all. All I want to do is eat, sleep, and look forward to your letters. I haven't even seen any of Miami. It looks as if you're going to have to come down if I'm to get to see any of the sights. Besides, I'm pretty sure I won't be getting any more leaves after the twenty-one days that I've had already. Please do come Darling, if you possibly can. I'd be the happiest guy in the world. The moon comes up later every night, doesn't it? You know what happened last night? I woke up sometime in the night and there was the big old moon staring me right in the eye. It was so pretty that I guess the man in moon woke me up so that I could have a good look. That was strange for I'm not in the habit of waking up at such hours."

Callie worked at Piedmont Shirt Company. She had been working there since she finished high school, and it gave her a glimpse of the world outside the farm, in addition to cash income to share with her farming family.

On March 3, Callie wrote:

"Well, I did work today all except an hour, went up the street late this afternoon. I buttoned up Army shirts, and thought of you, all day. My fingers are sore from buttoning about a dozen buttons per shirt on ten dozen shirts. But it is good old Friday again and my work for the next two days will be a little different. I might even sleep a little late in the morning, imagine that!

"Oh yea! Received a sweet letter from you today and oh boy. I sure was glad to get it. Like you, I like 'em better and look forward to them more every day.

"That old man moon is being mean to me tonight. I can't seem to locate it. You haven't got it hid down there have you? Come on share it with me. For when I'm moon gazing you're always right here with me.

"Darling, I want to see you more and more every day. Keep sweet and I do hope you can come home soon. Night"

On Sunday, March 4, Tom wrote to Callie:

"Did you have a good time today? Hope it was nice out today. It was mighty nice out and I just had to get out and work off some of this pent-up energy playing golf.

"The swimming pool is right under my window and I could hardly keep from going in. The doctor hasn't said that I could go in yet so I didn't.

"I was just thinking how nice it would be if I just had my leave over again and still have as much fun as we had. Darling, I enjoyed being with you more than you know and I wish more than ever that we were together right now.

"Oh yes, remember I told you last night that I woke up where the moon came shining in my window. It happened again last night. I don't mind, though, for I love to lay here looking at the moon and thinking of you."

Tom received orders in March 1945, after he recovered from his nose surgery, to Goodfellow Field, San Angelo, Texas, where he was assigned to become a flight instructor.

On Monday, March 5, Tom wrote to Callie:

"And how did my gal make out today? I was just wondering if this was blue Monday for you. It sure has been for me due most of all to the fact that I haven't had any mail from you for the past two days. You don't realize, Darling, how much your letters cheer me up.

"I went into town for an hour or so this afternoon for the first time since I had my operation. I just went in to take some clothes that needed cleaning so I only stayed a couple of hours. I got back here in time to see the movie for tonight. It was really a good one and I really did enjoy it. The name of it was *'Thunderhead,'* and it was the story of a horse. I sure wish you could have seen it. There was some of the most beautiful scenery of the Rocky Mountains. I do want you to see it if you get a chance.

"As per usual, I played a little golf again this morning."

On Tuesday, March 6, Tom wrote to Callie:

"I played a little golf again this afternoon and then went for a swim in the pool. It was the first time I'd been in but I sure did enjoy it. You don't know what you're missing.

"I guess I'll be getting out of the hospital in two or three days and then I'll probably be sent back over to Miami Beach for about a week or maybe more. Do you think that you will be able to make it down before I leave Darling? It doesn't look as if I will be able to get home and I sure do want you to come if you possibly can.

"Incidentally, this is the third day that I haven't heard from you and I'm just about to go crazy."

On March 7, Tom wrote to Callie:

"You don't know how happy I was to get two letters from you today, especially after three days without a word from you. Darling, I was getting frantic to put it mildly. It did make me realize how much your sweet letters mean to me. I just hope that you won't forget about me.

"I bet you'll soon be getting tired of seeing Army shirts.

"I'm sure glad to hear that it has decided to turn warm at home. Bet you like that a lot. Remember the night we went to that basketball game at Mountain View and most froze to death in the car. Even so, I enjoyed that basketball game more than any I ever went to.

"What do you say darling, suppose we plan a picnic next time I get home and go up to River Falls or some place. How would you like that? The more I think of it the better I like it.

"I should be going back over to the beach about tomorrow. The doc said that I would be all done here tomorrow and I'll be glad, too, for I'm getting tired of just laying around all the time. After they send me back to the Beach I'll have about a week to just lie on the beach and improve my sun tan. Keep your fingers crossed Darling, and let's hope that I won't be sent too far away. I sure get to feeling mighty blue when I think of not being able to see you again for a long time."

Tom had been in the army more than three years. He had too much time on his hands in the Miami hospital. And he was already starting to contemplate life without war, and with Callie. On March 8, Tom wrote to Callie:

"I got a letter from you today that was dated December 31. It went to England and then came back here. That sure seems a long time ago.

"It seems a long time, too, since I saw you last.

"Well, I'm leaving the hospital for sure in the morning and I'm going back over to the beach. I'm kinda glad to get out of here for I'm not used to sitting around all the time. I'm going back to the Beach for about a week, I suppose, then I'll be off for some other place. I sure hope that it won't be too far away.

"The war news looks better in Europe all the time doesn't it? I sure hope that it is soon over there, don't you darling? Maybe we can dare to plan a little toward what we can do after we have peace again. It seems such a long time since I was ever near anything but the Army. It's going to be hard to realize that we are free again when all this is over with."

Finally, Tom was transferred out of the hospital, and back to the beach hotel. On Thursday, March 9, Tom wrote to Callie:

"And how are you tonight? I'll tell you how I am, I'm mighty lonesome, and you know who I'm lonesome for. I'm back at the Beach now, I was discharged from the hospital just this morning. I'm in the same hotel that I was in when I first came here. I haven't done much today except move. I did go out on the beach a while this afternoon and sun a little while.

"The doc didn't see fit to give me a few days leave. He seemed to think that I am disgustingly healthy and I guess he's right. Even so, Darling, I would give my right arm to be with you now."

On Tuesday, March 13, Tom wrote to Callie:

"Say! I really hit the jackpot today. I got a total of six letters from you and was I glad.

"Thanks a million for the pictures darling and I think they're swell. I knew you wouldn't forget. I told you last night that I was having some made here. I had planned to go see the proofs today but I had a couple of Army lectures to listen to and didn't get there after all. I am going tomorrow for sure.

"Darling, as much as I want to see you, I guess it's best that you don't try to come down at this late date. I'd sure hate to see you get down here and then me be gone. The housing problem is pretty bad and it would be hard to find a place to stay, at a moment's notice. When I get to my next station we'll plan on seeing each other then, OK? I'm glad you spoke to Helen about the trip. I wouldn't want you to try it by yourself and I know she would like it very much."

On Wednesday night, March 14, Tom wrote to Callie:

"I'm counting on having you come to see me when I get established at my next base. Sure, things won't be so crowded there as they are down here, now. I sure wish I'd known sooner just how long I was going to be here so that you could be with me now. I'd be the happiest guy in the world if you were here.

"I met two fellows down here that went to primary flight training with me. Both of them are just back from overseas, and one of them I saw once while I was over there. It sure is good to meet someone you know once in a while.

"Since I came back to the beach I have a private room all my own and no one to disturb me. There are two other beds in here, but, as yet, no one occupies them. I hope it stays that way until I vacate."

On Thursday night, March 15, Tom wrote to Callie:

"I spent the afternoon on the beach again. It's getting to be a habit now. I'll sure miss this if they send me way out in the desert.

"I sure am lonesome tonight, darling. This is one of those days where I am especially lonesome and just can't help it. Usually I can find something to do to pass the time but not today. Darling, I sure do miss you a lot and I can hardly wait until I see you again."

On Friday, March 16, Tom wrote to Callie:

"It's another one of those nights that makes my heart sad, when it's going to waste. We'll make up for these when we do get together again. Agree with me? I should be getting my orders any day now and then I'll know what my fate is to be. Just keep your fingers crossed and maybe it won't be too bad. Let's hope for the best anyway.

"You know what darling; I'm in love with you. Hope you don't think I'm crazy for I'm very serious, more so than I've ever been before. I just want you to know how I feel for I didn't get around to telling you before I left. It wasn't until I left that I realized how much you mean to me. I must close darling and I'm looking forward to an answer to this."

On Sunday night, March 18, Tom wrote to Callie with a very special request:

"I'm very unhappy tonight as I think of where I'll be in two or three days. It's happened; they're sending me to Texas. Guess I'll be singing, 'Don't Fence Me In,' in a day or so.

"They weren't satisfied with just Texas, but they're sending me way down in the southwest corner of the state, down near the Mexican border. San Angelo is the name of the town.

"Darling, it breaks my heart to think of being that far away from you. I wouldn't think of having you make that long trip, unless of course, you would consent to come out there for good. That would make me the happiest man in the world. I do love you very much, Darling, and I want you to marry me. I don't suppose this is the usual way for a fellow to ask a girl to marry him, but due to present circumstances, I don't see any other way, and I just have to know darling. I have been thinking of you constantly my dear.

"Did you see the moon tonight? It's still kind of new but it was there just the same and it made me wish all the more that you were going to be on that train with me when it leaves tomorrow night. I saw a very good show last night. *I'll be Seeing You* was the name of it. It was very good but kind of sad. It kind of suited my mood though. Shirley Temple is getting to be quite a grown up young lady isn't she?

"Guess I'll have to get up pretty early in the morning in order to get all packed up and ready to go. My train leaves at eight tomorrow night, and I'll have all day to get ready, but I don't want to rush around too much. I'll have a Pullman all the way or so they tell me, and it shouldn't be such a bad ride. I really have a nice tan now and I shouldn't lose it out in Texas for it's probably warm enough there too. I am going to miss this nice beach. Hope they at least have a swimming pool there. That will help some."

Tom took the train to Texas, and settled into flying training aircraft such as the AT-6 to sharpen his skills following his long furlough and hospital stay.

On March 21, 1945, Callie responded to Tom:

"I sure am a sad little gal tonight, after reading your letter of Sunday night. It really makes my heart sad to even think of you being so far away from me. Will you have to stay out there very long darling? I hope not so long. I don't think I can bear not seeing you much longer. It seems like years since I saw you last.

"I hope you had a nice trip out to the lone star state. Only wish it had been possible for me to have made that trip with you. Guess I'll have to build a big fence around Texas (so they can't steal my baby away).

"You make me happier every day darling. I didn't realize that you feel this way about me, but darling I'm so glad you do. There is no place in the world I'd rather be than with you, always. I love you so much! I'll have to think this all out, about joining you, and let you know later. And I guess you really let yourself in for something by asking me that other question. Darling, meet the future Mrs. Tom Hammond! You know what? I kind of like that name. I just wonder how you're going to take this answer? Really darling, I have never meant anything more in my life."

On April 12, Callie wrote to Tom about her fears for the country after news that President Franklin Roosevelt had died that day:

"Isn't it terrible about the president being dead? I can't seem to realize it. I'm so afraid this will prolong the war, do you think so darling?"

On April 14, Callie noted the pall that had settled over the country with President Roosevelt. She wrote to Tom:

"Everything and everybody are in sort of a sad mood tonight. I guess it's due to the loss of our president. His body came through Greenville (from Warm Springs, Georgia) about seven o'clock this evening, enroute to Washington.

"But darling I'm anything but sad tonight on account of when I got home this afternoon, there were three letters for me from you. Boy, that fifteen days sounds good to me, sure hope you get them soon."

Tom looked for and found a room in a nearby town where they could live, and he took the train back to South Carolina for the wedding. Tom and Callie were married at Mountain View Methodist Church on April 29, 1945. It was the first wedding held in the new church building that literally has a view of the mountains from its front steps.

Tom had bought a road-weary Ford car, purchased a new engine for it from Sears Roebuck Co., and he and his father had installed the engine in the car when Tom was home in January. Tom and Callie drove the car to Texas, where Tom was accused of being absent without leave because he had overstayed his originally authorized furlough. Fortunately, he had telegraphed the base for permission to return late, had received authorization by return telegraph, and he had kept that message. While Tom was away from San Angelo, the rapidly changing circumstances of the war nearing an end caused many servicemen to receive new orders. Tom was no longer needed as an instructor pilot and was given orders to join a utility squadron in Detroit, Michigan. He and Callie drove the old Ford to Detroit, where Tom spent the rest of his active service ferrying aircraft.

Tom made several flights in old bombers, mostly B-24 Liberators, to desert airfields such as Kingman, Arizona, where now-surplus planes were being parked. He also joined a crew flying a new C-54 cargo plane to British India, where American and British forces were still fighting the Japanese. They flew to Brazil, across the shortest expanse of the Atlantic Ocean to Africa, across North Africa to the Arabian Gulf, and on to Karachi.

On October 2, 1945, Tom's active service ended. He and Callie returned home to South Carolina, where they would live the rest of their lives and raise three children: James Thomas, born October 23, 1946; Claude Michael, born February 1, 1949; and Susan Ruth, born January 12, 1957. Tom held a variety of jobs, from working at a farm supply company, to finally owning a picture framing business. Callie worked for many years as a seamstress at a garment manufacturing company. Later, she worked as a secretary at North Greenville College. They retired in the 1980s.

Chapter 51

▼

Seeing Germany on the Ground

In the autumn of 1988, Tom and Callie traveled to Belgium to visit me, my wife, Elizabeth, and our children, Sarah, and Thomas. We tried to show them a bit of life in Europe. I was eager to take them to see Paris. But Tom wanted to see Germany on the ground for the first time. He had not been in Europe in more than forty years, and he had never seen the country on the ground that had been his enemy so long ago.

Strolling through the streets of Koblenz, a medium-sized German city at the confluence of the Rhine and Mosel rivers, Tom, age sixty-six, was silent for a long time. He looked about at the 1960s vintage apartment blocks and the modern office buildings. Like many Americans seeing Europe from the ground level for the first time, he seemed puzzled and a little disappointed that all the buildings did not date from the eighteenth century. Finally, he looked at me and said, "But it all looks so new." There was a real disconnect between what he was seeing and what he had done forty-four years earlier. "Well, Pop, you gotta remember you were part of this urban renewal program," I said to him. In that bleak winter of 1944, the Eighth Air Force destroyed three-fourths of Koblenz. Two of Tom's thirty-five missions, including the final flight on December 28, targeted Koblenz.

Chapter 52

▼

The Last Trip Home

In May 2004, we all knew that Tom, at age eighty-one, was losing strength and becoming increasingly passive. He would sit for hours before the television, oblivious to what was on it and speaking only when spoken to. In retrospect, I think he knew he was dying, but he never spoke of it. Callie told us that doctors had said he had "a touch" of emphysema, but I never took that to mean it was life-threatening until his crisis in the spring. Callie feared he had pneumonia. When he collapsed to his knees on the way to the bathroom, she took him to his pulmonary doctor, who immediately had him admitted to the hospital. My brother Mike called me with the news, and I left Columbia immediately to meet them at the hospital. I arrived in the evening to find him in a temporary room in the trauma center, stripped of his own clothing and clad only in an immodest hospital gown. He recognized me, but already, he seemed disoriented. The bathroom was the next door to the right, and six feet away, but he could not remember where it was, and would wander off to someone else's room when he came out of the room if someone did not intercept him.

About midnight, my brother arrived to relieve me. We had learned from a previous hospitalization that Tom could not be left alone in the hospital at night. He quickly slipped into what I came to describe as a vertical coma. He would not stay in bed, but neither was he conscious of his actions. He lapsed into robot-like movements of his arms, hands, and fingers, seeming to be doing work he had done for years. He appeared to measure and assemble invisible objects, much like the picture frames he had been making for his customers. The second night, my sister Susan stayed with him, and by morning was near despair. His rambling grew worse. Efforts to keep him in the hospital bed only resulted in wrestling matches, with him standing on the bed in unconscious defiance.

By the third day, my mother, brother, sister, and I were ready to break him out of the hospital and return him home where he had previously regained his grip on reality. A well-meaning, but inexperienced young doctor told me with perfect sincerity that my father was going to get well, and then he could go home. Finally, on Saturday, Tom's regular doctor, Angelo Sinopoli, came to see him. I knew of his humanity from my friend Maggie Jones, whose husband Dr. Sinopoli had treated a decade earlier in the terminal stages of lung cancer. Dr. Sinopoli lingered with Tom after examining him, engaging him in conversation, and trying to assess the condition of his lungs. He stood beside the old veteran with his arm over his shoulder, and said, "I just hate to send him home if there is something we can do here to make him better."

I asked him to ask Tom what he wanted to do. When he inquired, Tom suddenly focused, looked squarely at the doctor, and said, "I reckon I'd just as soon be at home."

I motioned for Dr. Sinopoli to speak to me outside the room. "He's not going to get better, is he?" I said to him. He lowered his eyelids in quiet agreement. "Then listen to the patient," I said. He immediately agreed to discharge Tom, and we discussed the options that we faced, including in-home hospice care. He said he would send a hospital social worker to help us find and engage the people with the most experience in end-of-life care. That afternoon, we took Tom home, with a wheelchair, oxygen bottles, and appointments for a hospice nurse to visit and begin helping Callie provide the intensive care he would need for the coming months. We had no idea how many months the disease would take to run its course.

In my fifty-eight years with my father, he had never talked about how his combat experience made him feel. He just talked about the flying, which he loved. But once, during the final days of his life, Tom was sitting at the kitchen table as he often did, his eyes shut, seemingly oblivious to conversation between me and his brother-in-law, Robert Huff. He had married Tom's sister Helen after the war. As Robert and I discussed his service in the Ardennes during the Christmas 1944 Battle of the Bulge, and the killing that took place, Tom suddenly opened his eyes, looked around at us, and said, "I killed a lot of people." He shut his eyes and said no more. It was the only time he ever let on that the human toll of the war still weighed on his mind.

Tom clung to Callie like a life preserver those last weeks of his life. He would not stay in bed. He wanted her close to him all the time. Callie had been his anchor in 1945 and the early years of their marriage, when he would awake, sweating, and screaming about the nightmares caused by Tom's war. Despite the presence of their children and others who were willing to assist with Tom's care, she devoted every minute to making him as comfortable as possible. When she should have been resting, she would lie down with him on their bed. It brought him a little peace, but at terrible cost to her well-being. She got little sleep for several months. We moved a bed into the living room at the other end of the house, so that she would have a separate place to lie down. But she seldom used it, preferring to be close to Tom. She tried to feed him when he ceased to be able to take food. She administered medication to ease his pain and tried to moisten his cracked lips. The night before he died, she seemed near the end of her ability to stay awake all night, as she had done so many nights. I was there, and I insisted she go into the living room and try to sleep, which she did, about midnight. A short time later, Tom sprang from his bed as he did every fifteen to thirty minutes. By the time I got to him, he was in the hall, headed to the living room. I gently put my arm around his shoulders, formerly strong and muscular, but now shrunken and weak, and I asked him where he was going. "I'm going to find my wife," he said. It broke my heart to turn him away from the love of his life, but we had reached a point of choosing between his wishes and Mom's health.

On September 21, 2004, Tom died at his home in rural Greenville County, following a difficult fight with emphysema and heart disease. He was just nine weeks short of his eighty-second birthday. Almost sixty years had passed since he observed his twenty-second birthday the day after he flew his twenty-seventh combat mission. He often spoke proudly of his accomplishments in the United States Army Air Forces, rising from poor farm boy to become an officer and pilot. He lived most of his life after the events he clearly viewed as the high point of his life. He suffered harder than most the disappointments in his work following World War II. It often seemed to his family and friends that he overlooked the very real accomplishments of those years. He fathered three happy and successful children, and was grandfather to three talented grandchildren. He and Callie made a warm, comfortable home and were productive members of Mountain View Methodist Church, where he was admired and loved.

In his workshop at the back of the house, a calendar hung on the back of the door, March 1995 still the page displayed. My sister Susan said it was the month when time stood still for our father, when he began to lose his grasp on time, reality and the ability to control his own life. It began a decade-long descent into dementia that robbed him of his ability to make picture frames, or to cut out wooden ducks on his band saw, or to operate his cherished machines such as the garden tiller or the riding lawnmower.

In his final months of life, he seemed to fight harder than many who see the end of life looming ahead of them. He would not sleep, restlessly prowling the house for hours during the night. Susan said that it almost seemed as if he thought he could outrun death. But it was in his nature to struggle against cruel fate, as he had done sixty years earlier in the cockpit of his B-17 bomber, determined to stay alive in aerial combat that snuffed out the lives of 26,000 fellow airmen.

Chapter 53

▼

Finding Scotty

I felt for much of my life that I knew Scotty Alexander because my father talked about him so much. Actually, the Scotty I knew for so long was forever twenty-three years old, a hard-drinking Yankee from Orange, Massachusetts, who had nerves of steel when under fire by German fighter planes or flak guns. He and my father were friends and crew mates in the fall and winter of 1944 while they checked off the necessary thirty-five combat missions to be able to return to the United States. My father was the crew's co-pilot; Scotty was the navigator. Many of their comrades in arms did not return home.

As a veteran newspaper reporter, I had long felt there was little information, or any person, I could not track down. But I tried for years to find Scotty for my father's sake, and I failed to do so while my father was alive. But my mother's gift of her letters to my father and his letters to her rekindled my desire to find out what had become of Scotty. I went back to step number one—looking for traces at his last known residence in Orange, Massachusetts.

I thought of trying the local government veterans' affairs office, but I could find no telephone number. A veteran's medical clinic in a neighboring county told me to call the county clerk in Orange. When I called that office, the clerk was not there. So on a long shot, I quizzed the woman who answered the telephone about Scotty. At first she said nothing. Then I mentioned the last address I had for Scotty. The woman, Shirley Page, gasped, and said, "That's my house. That's where I live. I bought my house from the Alexanders forty-two years ago."

It is the sort of serendipity success one cannot plan, nor expect. It sometimes comes as a result of dogged re-plowing of old ground until the gold springs from the Earth. Shirley directed me to Janice Lanou, a retired librarian and the wife of the nephew of Scott's post-war bride, Lucille. Janice had never met Scott, but she knew of him, and promised to call me back if she found any contact information. Within an hour she called with his telephone number.

Scotty answered the telephone, and seemed a bit cautious in reaction to the information I was spewing about who I was, about my father's recent death, and about my interest in their wartime experience. But he was cordial, and promised to talk to me further after I sent him some of my research. That afternoon, I carried the document to the UPS Store and instructed them to get it to him by noon the next day at his home on the Chesapeake Bay near Annapolis.

When I called him again three days later, he had received my incomplete story, and had read it. "I believe I can help you straighten out a few things," Scotty said, with decidedly more excitement in his voice than I had detected three days earlier.

"I'll tell you a secret," Scotty said, and explained that he had deliberately kept his wartime experiences in the past, choosing not to contact any of his old combat crew. He had no contact with any of them for sixty years, until I called him on the day before my father's eighty-second birthday. He explained that he thought it was better to go on with life than to dwell on the past.

I arrived at Scotty's home on a rainy December day, a week after I had first talked to him. Judy met me at the door and said she was happy I had come. "I hope you can get him to talk. He never talks about the war." I did not know what to expect, whether he would be suspicious of my motives, whether he would talk openly about his experiences with my father sixty years ago, or whether his memories of those months would be full and sharp. When he entered the room, an eighty-three-year-old man, a bit overweight, with far less hair than in the photos in my father's album, he had a sly grin on his face. "I feel like I've come to meet Elvis," I said, seeking to break the ice. He smiled more broadly, sat down on a kitchen barstool, Judy handed him his morning coffee, and he began to tell long-kept secrets about his war.

"One day, Delcroix needed to take a crap. We found him a bucket to go in. 'What do I do with it now?' he said. I said, 'Dump it out the escape hatch.' He was afraid to open the hatch, so I said, 'Get out of the way, I'll do it.' Well, I had to listen to the ball turret gunner the rest of the mission, because we forgot to tell him to turn his turret around when we dumped the bucket."

Scotty went on like that for almost three hours, until lunchtime came, and he had to take a break. Judy's eyes widened with each new tale. "I've never heard any of that," said Judy, Scotty's companion of twenty-two years.

"I remember the funny things that happened. The bad things I tried to forget, I made an effort to forget them. It took me a long time to get it all out of my system. Stayed drunk the best part of a year. When we got home, I didn't give a rat's ass about anything. Hurray, I'm here, let's go have fun. That's just the way it was," Scotty said.

Judy told me she believed he, like many of his generation, had difficulty coming to terms with the fact he came home while others did not. Scotty, however, would not attribute it to survivor guilt. "It could be that, it could be anything. I don't know."

"My father and Dickie Hickman's father said, those kids haven't told us anything about what they did during the war. We got together with our fathers at my father's house. I brought a bottle. Dickie bought a bottle. Dickie finally took his father home, and I took my father upstairs to bed. We never told them anything about the war, we just got them drunk."

"We had a good group of friends in Massachusetts. My father gave me the use of his car. I remember bringing it home, putting it in the garage and crawling up the back stairs because I couldn't stand to get to my bed. The next morning, I'd jump up and run downstairs to see if I'd put any scratches on it."

"In the morning, we'd go to Jackson's drug store. Mark Jackson would say 'drink this,' give us our morning fix. We'd play golf in the afternoon, then figure out where to go that night."

Life in those months was one long binge of trying to forget the war.

"Once, we crashed the ladies bridge club. Donnie Olsen walked over to one of the women, and asked what she was drinking from her fancy little stem glass. 'Oh no, not the whole thing,' she said. It went downhill from there. We were playing cards with the ladies. I was playing with the wife of the chief of police. Dickie Hickman was playing with a doctor's wife."

Whatever was the social convention, Scotty was drawn to do the opposite thing.

"After I got the idea to pretty much forget the whole thing, I don't think it affected me any. During that time, I just didn't give a damn about anything."

There was recognition for what they had done.

"One night, I walked up to Tommy Dorsey in New York and said 'Play a song for me.' He said, 'Sure, what you been doing, flying in the Eighth Air Force?'" Scotty said.

Tom admired Scotty a lot. In an interview that my son recorded with Tom some years ago, Tom described Scotty this way: "He was our navigator and he was very good. He was one of the coolest guys under fire. It didn't matter to him. He did his job and it didn't seem to affect him."

Scotty admitted the danger affected him: "I was scared, of course. But it was something we had to do. If I wanted to be in it and do it, I couldn't say, don't shoot guns at me, I'm scared. We just did it. When I got through with the whole thing, I was a little different," Scotty said.

And he was reminded of what it was like to be under fire. Scotty worked for the Naval Aviation Logistics Command, and traveled throughout the world setting up bases for Navy and Marine aviation units.

"I went to Vietnam three times working with Marine Air. That's when I knew I was faster than anyone else. The first time the rockets started coming in, I was first in the shelter, underneath a pile of Marines."

Chapter 54

▼

Frank Nutt,
Ball Turret Gunner

After World War II, Frank was an armament instructor at the Air Force Academy in Colorado Springs, Colorado. He won the Commandants Award, given for the highest degree of demonstrated leadership ability while at the Non-Commissioned Officers Academy.

Service was a tradition in Frank's family; he had a sister and three brothers who also served in World War II.[298]

Frank always led with his humor, joking in a March 28, 1993, letter to Tom Hammond that as the crew members passed away, "We'll all meet again someday in the Big One and head for the pub." He never lost his love of flying, telling Tom that even in his seventies, he was looking forward to a ride in a two-seater P-51 fighter plane. He had also recently flown in the Confederate Air Force's restored B-17 Sentimental Journey. He never forgot the exhilaration and terror of their combat missions over Germany. In a December 10, 2000, letter to Tom, Frank recalled their mission against Politz: "Remember the flak was so thick they say you could get out and walk on it! Hell, I tell them all it was so thick, you lowered the gear and we taxied over it. How about that, eh? Ho-Ho-Ho."

When I first contacted Frank's son, Dudley M. Nutt, to learn more about his father's life, he responded as enthusiastically as his father had when I first called him years ago.

"Dad had such memories, and a lot of them were good, humorous, and I know that Dad lived aviation to the fullest.

"Dad had a heart of gold, and spent the last several years taking care of the older generation (eighty-five-plus in years), and made sure that they made all their doctors appointments, and drove them wherever they needed to go.

"Dad died with a smile on his face, and the people who attended to him in Loma Linda Hospital wrote my Mother a great letter expressing their sorrow and especially amazement and appreciation in his good humor."

Dudley's wife, Chloe, was similarly fond of her father-in-law: "Frank was a sweetheart of a man. We miss him greatly. Always smiling, always joking, always a cheerful comment or phrase, even when he was not feeling his best, he made you laugh."

Born August 23, 1922, and raised in Rouses Point, New York, on Lake Champlain, Frank worked in a hardware store. Dudley said his father found a dollar bill on the floor and gave it to the owner, who in turn explained to him that he had put it there to see how honest he was. "I learned a lot about ethics from my dad with that one!" Dudley said.

Frank's interest in technology came at an early age. He worked at the Round House down the street, keeping boilers lit and driving the trains in and out for maintenance. He also understood hard work. He dug graves for the local funeral home.

He was a state champion athlete in gymnastics in high school, and he attended the 1938 New York World's Fair to stage an exhibition with the rings.

Frank and his brothers crossed the Canadian border to join with the Royal Canadian Air Force, but his father, Frank Sr. stopped them, and being an Irish boxer-dairyman-farrier, "I guess you can say that they learned a valuable lesson that day, too," Dudley said.

"Dad was the kid who left the dinner table when he heard a plane overhead (so do I), and sometimes he would run out to the field and take care of a barnstormer's plane and get a ride. He also remembered the Hindenburg over upstate New York, as well as all the great and big airships of the day! How I envy what Dad saw," Dudley said.

After retiring as a chief master sergeant, Frank lived in Apple Valley, California, and worked with the Apple Valley Sheriff's Department Senior Citizens Volunteer Station. He was the national historian for the Pearl Harbor Survivors. He died at age eighty-one at Loma Linda University Hospital on December 10, 2002.

Chapter 55

▼

Sam Clay, Flight Engineer

As the Internet began to offer the possibility of nationwide directory searches in the early 1990s, I began to help Tom explore the possibility of finding some of his former crewmates. He had a general idea where to find some of them, particularly Sam Clay, from whom he had received some news over the years in Christmas cards. I generated a list of all the Sam Clays listed in Alabama, Louisiana, and Mississippi. Tom ran his finger down the list and stopped on one whose residence was Hammond, Louisiana. "I think I'll try this one," he said with a serendipity glint in his eye. A few minutes later, he was talking with his old flight engineer buddy.

After their combat tour, Sam was first reassigned to Gulfport, Mississippi, to prepare to go to the Pacific. But the war ended before he was ready to ship out for the struggle against Japan. After his combat tour, Sam was accepted for training to become a pilot. He went to Clemson University for six months, taking courses for pilot training. He then went to Nashville. But he never made it to flight school because of the war's end.

On April 13, 1994, in a letter to Tom, Sam talked about his life after the war:

"Sorry it's been so long since we have had contact. Martha died on February 3, 1994. I have been trying to get my life adjusted to being without her. After 52-plus years you might imagine what it is like trying to do things without having someone to tell you 'what to do, when to do it, where to do it, how to do it, etc.' I'm confused and besides, when I make a decision and it's wrong, I don't have anyone to blame it on."

I visited Sam twice, in 2003, and again in 2005. A spinal abnormality, undiagnosed in his youth, had taken its toll on his health, leaving him bent and in constant pain. But he refused to allow it to keep him homebound. He did volunteer work regularly and had a circle of friends who would check on him. In 2005, when Hurricane Katrina struck Louisiana, Sam rode it out at his Hammond, Louisiana, home, then endured almost two weeks of late summer heat without electricity.

Chapter 56

▼

Victor Clarence Radke, Chief Pilot

Vic died on October 13, 1996, in Dallas, in the home he and Erna had occupied most of their married lives. His primary hobby was home improvement on the small house they bought on Northwood Road. He added a den onto the dwelling, and later added a wing, doing most of the work himself.

Vic never piloted a plane again after the war. He would sometimes take Erna to an air show so that she could see the antique bombers that groups such as the Confederate Air Force and the Collins Foundation keep flying.

After trying a couple of jobs that he did not like, he settled into sales for PPG. He traveled the length and breadth of Texas, taking orders. His children remember the week-long business trips and his return home for the weekends. Erna raised their three children, Vic Junior, Susan and Tricia, who always hoped to see their father return on Thursday night, because that meant a big meal to welcome him home. Susan recalled her father always dressed impeccably, even though he was going to be spending the day in the car.

Sometimes on weekends, Vic would take his family to Lake Texoma to enjoy their boat together.

Vic and Erna worked hard to keep their family in North Dallas. Vic painted other people's houses to earn extra money. Erna taught piano lessons for sixty years.

Vic shared a passion for gambling with his middle child Susan. Vic, Erna, and Susan would travel to Las Vegas once or twice a year and all three share a room to indulge their joy of gambling. Vic had a poker table in his garage in north Dallas, fully outfitted with poker chips, cards, and everything else needed for the weekly Friday night poker game with his male friends. Vic was a skilled poker player, and Susan often felt he could have made a living gambling if he had chosen that path.

Vic was eighty when he died. He had a son, two daughters, and five grandchildren. He lies at Restland Memorial Park, where he was buried following his memorial service at Preston Hollow Presbyterian Church.

Chapter 57

▼

Edward K. Smith, Gunner

After their combat tour was finished, Ed Smith asked to remain in England so that he could marry Olga, the English woman he had met at a dance at the Ninety-fifth Bomb Group's base at Horham. He transferred to a non-combatant position. When the Ninety-fifth was dissolved at the end of the war in 1945, he transferred to the sister group, the One Hundredth Bomb Group. To marry an English citizen required the permission of the American commanding officer and the base chaplain. Ed was Catholic, and Olga was not, and the chaplain tried to discourage Ed from marrying her. "Why don't you just wait and go home and marry a nice American girl?" the chaplain said. Ed insisted he had found the love of his life, the chaplain relented, and so did the commanding officer. Ed and Olga were married at Felixstowe in the Catholic church on April 11, 1945. During their honeymoon, they heard the news that American President Franklin Roosevelt had died. Ed remained in England until after his daughter Karen was born in 1946.

Ed remained in the Air Force for thirty years, rising to the rank of chief warrant officer.[299] He lived in the Tampa/St. Petersburg area after he was assigned to MacDill Air Force Base in 1965. Following World War II, he had given up flying for a career as a weather forecaster and had assignments in England, Florida, Germany, Louisiana, New Jersey, and at Shemya in the Aleutian Islands.[300]

After he retired in 1972, Ed maintained contact with old comrades as a member of the Ninety-fifth Bomb Group Association. He also was a member of St. Joseph's Catholic Church, Knights of Columbus, and the St. Vincent de Paul Society. In retirement, he volunteered at Immaculate Conception Preschool, American Stage, the Historical Society, and Meals on Wheels.

In a February 11, 1990, letter, Ed wrote about his life to Tom:

"Yes, it's been a long time. Sorry we lost touch. It was a memorable time and I often think of when we were together. Kept in touch with Sam Clay for a number of years but Vic was only one to the present day.

"Anyway a brief history since you and rest of crew returned to the States in January 1945.

"Olga and I became engaged in December 1944 just before we finished our missions. So when you left I went to work in personnel office of Ninety-fifth Bomb Group. No more flying for me.

"We were married in April 1945. When the war ended in Europe and the outfits began to go home, I was able to remain in England by transferring. As a base was closed I transferred to another that was still open. I closed more bases in England than you can imagine.

"Our eldest daughter, Karen was born in Felixstowe, Olga's home, January 1946. I was still stationed in England. Finally had to make a transfer to Bremen, Germany to stay in that part of the world. Olga and Karen flew to States in July 1946 and stayed with my parents in St. Charles until I returned from Bremen the end of August.

"I had 60 days leave coming so when that was up I re-enlisted and stayed with the service for over 30 years retired in 1972 as Chief Warrant Officer.

"Olga died September 1985—certainly miss her. I am thankful for the 40 good years we had. I keep busy and don't sit around mourning—Edward (Ed's grandson) and I have done lots of traveling during his summer holidays from school—Australia, England, France, Germany, and so forth. I try to get to England and Felixstowe every year and visit with Olga's friends."

Ed died Wednesday, July 24, 1996, at his home in St. Petersburg, Florida, where he had lived since his retirement from the Air Force in 1972. He was eighty-one years old at the time of his death.

Chapter 58

▼

Charles M. Delcroix,
Bombardier

After the war, Chuck Delcroix returned to his home in Pittsburgh. In 1948, he graduated from Duquesne University. He became a stockbroker, married Joy, and became a member of Assumption Church in Bellevue. He worked as a stockbroker, and later as an advertising executive for Mail Marketing Services in West Mifflin. Chuck and Joy had three sons and a daughter.

Chuck died on Tuesday, May 12, 1987, at age sixty-three, of cancer. He rests in Allegheny County Memorial Park in McCandless.[301]

Chapter 59

▼

Joseph Hagerty, Radio Operator

Following the war, Joseph A. Hagerty III used his GI Bill benefits to resume his education at the University of Pennsylvania Law School, graduating in 1948. He clerked for Judge Michael J. O'Donnell prior to beginning a law practice that lasted four decades. His friends said he habitually set his fees according to what his client could pay and made a specialty of representing the poor, the troubled, and the downtrodden. Hagerty enjoyed studying the Civil War and World War II, according to a feature obituary in the *Philadelphia Inquirer* by Donna St. George. He loved golf and won the Seniors Golf Championship in 1985 at the Whitemarsh Valley Country Club, where he served on the board of directors. Joe was a member of St. Philip Neri Church; a member of the Law Review at the University of Pennsylvania; and belonged to the Philadelphia and Pennsylvania Bar Associations. He was also secretary treasurer of Provident Building Loan.

After the war, he married his sweetheart, Willella Harvey. They were married for forty-three years, had two daughters, and Willella died in 1988. Joe died March 30, 1989, at age sixty-six. The *Philadelphia Inquirer* described him as "a witty, articulate lawyer who was remembered for combining legal skill and empathy in a one-man Center City practice."[302]

Chapter 60

▼

William C. Galvin, Tail Gunner

Bill Galvin's fellow crew members described him as a loner and learned little about him in the six months they were together. After his discharge from the Army Air Forces, Bill stayed for a time with his brother and sister-in-law. He was a compulsive gambler, showing up at times with pockets laden with cash, then returning days later penniless. In the decades that followed, Bill drifted to the western states, living in the southwest, then in the northwest. His brother and relatives in Pennsylvania lost track of him. Once in the 1970s, Tom and Callie visited Chuck and Joy Delcroix in Pittsburgh, and then tried to find Galvin in nearby Elwood City. They found Bill's brother, who said he did not know where to find his solitary sibling.

His obituary seems to confirm that impression of the man who flew the solitary tail gunner position in skies over Europe. "No service will be held for William C. Galvin, 83, at his request," said the obituary in the *Spokesman-Review* newspaper of Spokane, Washington, on October 23, 1996. He died the previous Sunday, October 20, 1996. Galvin worked in construction and had lived in Spokane for eleven years and formerly lived in Priest Lake and Liberty Lake, Idaho. The obituary listed only nieces as survivors.[303]

Figure 16: (Left to right) Robert Huff; Tom's sister Helen, who married Robert; Tom Hammond; and Callie Barnette, who married Tom. (Photo from 1949 Hammond Family Reunion, by Ed Hodgens.)

Epilogue

▼

The Army Air Forces base at Hawthorne Field near Orangeburg no longer exists. The only evidence remaining is a historical marker at the entrance to Methodist Oaks, a United Methodist Church retirement home, on Highway 21 south of Orangeburg. The railroad track that was once an important landmark for airman cadets is still there. But the landscape is covered by pines, the Orangeburg waste-water treatment plant, and several industrial plants. Columbia Army Air Base trained the famous Doolittle Raiders who were the first American airmen to bomb Tokyo. It is now Columbia Metropolitan Airport. Shaw Field is today Shaw Air Force Base, one of the mightiest fighter bases in America.

The memory of Americans who helped defeat the Nazis remains alive in the hearts and minds of many in Europe. Some remember the Americans from their own childhoods, while others were born many years after the war ended.

The earliest memories of Jacques De Ceuninck, the retired chief inspector of police in Tournai, Belgium, are of German soldiers occupying his country. When he was seven years old, after the Germans had fled to their own country, an American flier parachuted onto Jacques' street in the village of Kain, near Tournai. The flier's plane crashed in the village, killing the pilot and co-pilot. Jacques has made it his avocation to catalogue the local people's memories of that crash. He has questioned many witnesses with the thoroughness of an Agatha Christie detective. He believes the pilot, Lt. Bob Mercer, saved lives and the village church on that day. The witnesses have told of watching as the stricken B-17, with just one engine running and a wing on fire, careened toward a row of houses and the village's tall, gray, stone church. At the last minute, the plane nosed upward, briefly gaining enough altitude to clear the row of houses, and banked slightly to the left to avoid hitting the church spire. Seconds later, it crashed in an open field a few hundred yards beyond the structures. Jacques says the local citizens credit Bob Mercer with a final heroic act that saved their village from fiery destruction.

Jacques is writing a local history that includes accounts of Mercer's crash. He believes it is important to preserve the memory of the brave young men who fought to free Europe.

In a note following my visit to Tournai, Jacques wrote: "(I was) very happy to have met you, the son of one of those numerous American airmen who help us, Belgians, to find again liberty and peace in 1945."

Of the 405,399 Americans who died during World War II, 78,976 were declared missing in action, without clear accounts of their deaths and without recovery of their remains, according to the American Battle Monuments Commission. A large portion of those missing in action were sailors, who sometimes disappeared with their ships by the hundreds at a time. But many others were airmen.

Efforts to recover the remains of missing airmen began even as the war raged. Associated Press reporter Kenneth L. Dixon caught up with one such sleuth in 1944, a former Army major who continued his search for lost airmen in World War I into a similar quest in World War II, a quarter century later. Fred Zinn had been in the fledgling American Army air corps in the first Great War. When the conflict ended in 1919, more than 200 American airmen remained missing. Zinn asked permission to remain in Europe to investigate those MIA airmen. He searched the forests and fields of northern France, Germany, and Belgium, studied records on both sides of the conflict. He ended his quest in July 1919, having accounted for all but six of the missing airmen in World War I. In 1944, at age fifty-two, Zinn was back at his old mission, working alone as a volunteer, to identify lost airmen. His quest took him from North Africa, to Sicily, and Italy. He had no official status, nor any official military transportation. But the increased importance of military aviation and the larger number of men involved meant the numbers of men lost without an accounting was much larger than in the last war. Zinn left his seed business in Michigan to seek out the lost airmen.[304]

Today, Congress commits millions of dollars annually to recovery of missing soldiers, sailors, and airmen. A specialized unit based in Hawaii still travels to remote regions to recover newly discovered remains. Occasionally, changing political regimes open up suspected crash sites for recovery. One such recovery took place in 2002, when the U. S. Army Central Identification Laboratory confirmed the crash site of Lt. Bill Lewis in Germany's Thurlingian Forest. Lewis was flying escort for Eighth Air Force bombers attacking oil refineries at Ruhland on

September 11, 1944, when his P-51 Mustang fighter was shot down. The crash site was marked by a German citizen, but the U. S. Army was unable to confirm Lewis died there for a half-century because the region fell behind the Iron Curtain of East Germany until the reunification of Germany.[305]

In 1951, remains of Lt. Joseph Earle Johnston of Stone Mountain, Georgia, were recovered from the crash site and reburied in the United States. He lies in a common grave with other members of his crew, since individual airmen could not be identified.

After the war, tail gunner Jewel Spruell's family obtained his remains and returned them to the United States for burial.

Except for Spruell, only fragments of remains of the five crewmen trapped in the airplane were recovered. On April 4, 1951, remains recovered from the primary crash site outside Kovarska were buried at Jefferson Barracks, Missouri. Five separate caskets were presented for burial for the sake of the mothers who had come to say a last good-bye to their sons. But the five were memorialized with a single plaque. The mothers sat on a hard bench with bare wooden slats under a cold April sky as the military rites were pronounced for their boys. Mrs. Johnston, the smallest of the sad women, seemed dwarfed by a large overcoat protecting her from the chill. A large, round hat with a fan of artificial flowers covered her head. Several large trees, still bare of leaves, stood sentinel on the windblown hillside over row upon row of plain, white stone grave markers.

A visit in 2005 to the site where Earle died that autumn day in 1944 was no easy task. The German-Czech border crossing at Barenstein is so little used by tourists that Deutchebahn service agents in Dresden had to get out their schedule manuals to see how to direct me there. Even so, they sent me to another town of the same name, costing me two hours and causing me to miss the connection that night. Staying a night in nearby Dresden gave me a glimpse of this phoenix rising from the ashes of World War II and fifty years of Communist stagnation. Just up the street from a group of dilapidated Communist-era buildings was a gleaming new Wal-Mart. The train station was undergoing renovation. A pedestrian shopping mall opposite the train station offered anything retail that is available in the Western world.

I took the morning train to Barenstein and its Czech sister city across the river, Vejprty. The German train climbed effortlessly through the mountains, where small towns and villages dotted the landscape every three to five miles. Each seemed to have a factory building that was closed, falling apart and its windows smashed.

At the Czech frontier, a border guard and a local policeman looked at my passport and waved me on toward the ancient diesel locomotive pulling one little passenger coach. The conductor was not accustomed to dealing with foreign visitors, but despite a complete language impasse, we managed to work out my fare in Euros, the new common currency in the European Union, not yet used by the Czechs.

The train rumbled through the snow-covered evergreen forest shrouding the mountains. I imagined a wounded, terrified American airman descending into the forbidding, Nazi-occupied countryside. Escape for an American airman would have been near impossible here. "When captured by the Luftwaffe, they might have a chance for a good dinner. If captured by the Army, they might have a very good chance to survive. But if captured by civilians, angry civilians, they were only the *terrorflieger*, or terrorist flyers. Many times, the civilians could be very hostile," said Jan Zdiarsky. One P-51 pilot, who made contact with Czech partisans, remained free for eighteen days before being captured by the German army, he said.

Jan's Czech hometown of Kovarska remains testament to the ideals that Tom Hammond, Earle Johnston and Bob Mercer fought for in 1944. It was part of the Sudetenland, a region that before World War II was in the Czech nation, but which was home to many ethnic Germans. Adolf Hitler made it the prize of one of his early land grabs, arguing that the ethnic German population made it a natural part of the German Reich. During the German occupation, ethnic Czech residents were forced out of their homes and towns. After the war began, many took up arms as partisan fighters, and many were killed.

Today Kovarska is a sleepy, economically stagnant mountain town trying to start an Alpine skiing business that will attract affluent western European tourists. Jan Zdiarsky and his friend Petr Frank have attracted small gatherings of German and American veterans who come to see the museum they built about the great air battle that took place above the town on September 11, 1944. Jan and Petr cherish the freedom they enjoy today from the German and then Soviet occupation of their country that lasted a half-century. They can see that hope exists for a new Czech nation, one that will determine its own destiny. But they also know that a terrible price was paid for the freedoms they enjoy.

Jan and Petr volunteer their time to maintain the museum, excavate the crash sites of five B-17s that fell on their village in 1944, and research and write that history. The town government provides the rooms, heating, electricity, and other expenses.

Jan, in 2005, a thirty-three-year-old Czech citizen with a Ph.D. in computer science was bitten by the history bug as a small boy when workmen uncovered flying clothes and identification papers of an American flier inside a wall at his school in Kovarska. The tail section of an American bomber had landed on the school's roof in 1944.

"It is important to keep the memory of the men who fought for our freedom. This is part of the history that was almost forgotten, and we must save it. And we must show to people that any war is a great tragedy for people who do not want the war," said Jan, whose grandfather fought with the Czech partisans against the Nazi army. "I am affected personally by what happened here. For twenty years, we have been working to remember what happened here."

On a warm, late summer day in 2006, Frances and Neil Goddard traveled with Jan along a narrow, winding road into the Czech mountains above Kovarska, to visit the site where Earle Johnston's bomber crashed sixty-two years earlier. High above the village, they parked the car and walked into a grove of trees. They emerged into a grass-covered glade in the forest about one-third the size of a football field, which Jan identified as the place where Earle's bomber crashed to Earth. There was nothing obvious to mark it as the place where five men died in a violent, fiery crash on September 11, 1944. But the debris of war was still there, mingled with the grass. Jan scratched about in the turf and soon came up with several bits of metal, one large and distinct enough to be identified as a link torn from a .50-caliber ammunition belt on a B-17. Neil, a retired Marine, collected the bits of Earle's plane to take home to North Carolina.

The previous day, Neil and Frances had toured Dachau, the monstrous Nazi death camp that had starved, tortured and killed thousands of Hitler's political enemies, clergy, intellectuals and Jews. For the first time in six decades, Frances fully grasped the meaning of her brother's participation in the war and his death in battle against the Nazi regime. She had been only five years old when Earle died. He was listed as missing in action for a long time. As a little girl she clung to the hope she would return to the little farmhouse in Georgia one day and find her beloved brother had come home. Through the decades, Earle's memory faded as she married a career Marine, raised her own family, and then slipped into a comfortable retirement in North Carolina. Then one day in May 2005, she answered a call from me, following my months-long quest to find some of Earle's family. "That's my brother!" she exclaimed when I asked if she was related to Joseph Earle Johnston of Stone Mountain, Georgia. It was the first time anyone had spoken his name to her in years. As we talked by e-mail, telephone and in a personal visit to her home, it was as if Earle had come back to her in very meaningful way.

She dug out photographs of her long-dead brother, all she had been given by her family to preserve of Earle's life and service to his country. As she learned more about his military record, she wrote to the government to obtain his Purple Heart and other service medals. She and Neil agreed they would include a side trip to the Czech Republic on a long-planned vacation to Europe.

On that Czech mountainside, Frances rediscovered the brother she had missed so desperately as a little girl and understood the meaning of his death as never before. "I learned my brother most likely didn't suffer that day. He burned when the plane crashed and didn't lie there injured in this remote spot up on the mountain. I thought about Hitler and what control he exercised over his people, not just Jews, but anyone who did not agree with him, and I understood better why his reign had to end. I am at peace with my brother's death now, and thank God for this experience," Frances said after returning home.

Sources

1. Interviews with Thomas D. Hammond, his letters to Callie Barnette, his Army records, and his pilot's logbook; Scott Alexander, the crew's navigator; Sam Clay, the crew's flight engineer, and Frank Nutt, the armorer and ball turret gunner, and his sons Dudley and Glenn; Callie Barnette Hammond; Herb Hammond, Tom's brother, and Polly Worthy, Tom's sister; Erna Radke, widow of Victor Radke, and their daughter Susan Radke.

2. William D. Strohmeier, who taught flying at Hawthorne Field during World War II, in a telephone interview on September 5, 2004, from his home in Dartmouth, Mass. He also sent me an unpublished essay that he wrote titled "Training in Open Cockpit Biplanes as the Jet Age Dawned."

3. Sarah J. Nachin, daughter of Ed Smith, included her father's memoir in a collection of stories titled *Ordinary Heroes, Anecdotes of Veterans*, (2001, Writers Club Press, Lincoln, Nebraska) about experiences of World War II veterans.

4. *Mighty Eighth War Diary*, by Roger A. Freeman; 1981, Jane's Publishing Inc. New York.

5. *Operational Record of the Ninety-fifth Bomb Group (H)*, by Paul M. Andrews.

6. *The B-17 Flying Fortress Story*, by Roger A. Freeman with David Osborne; 1998, Sterling Publishing Co., New York.

7. *The Lucky Bastard Club*, by Eugene Fletcher; 1992, the University of Washington Press; and e-mail correspondence with Eugene Fletcher 2005-2006.

8. *B-17s Over Berlin*, by Ian Hawkins; 1995, Brassey's of Washington & London.

9. *Contrails*, the Ninety-fifth Bomb Group's book about deployment at Horham, England.

10. *Prop Wash*, the base newspaper of Hawthorne Field, in Orangeburg, South Carolina.

11. Pilot's flight log of Victor Radke, a copy of which Radke gave to Tom Hammond.

12. Casualties were checked against "The Honor List of Dead and Missing," a list published after World War II by the U. S. War Department. Casualties and surviving veterans also where checked against the searchable online database at www.worldwariimemorial.com, which includes the American Battle Monuments Commission burials overseas, the lists of official War Department and Navy Department service rosters held by the National Archives and Records Administration, and those enrolled by the public in the Registry of Remembrances.

13. Newspapers: The *Greenville (South Carolina) News*; *Atlanta Constitution*; the *New York Times*; and *The State* newspaper, Columbia, South Carolina.

14. Mission records (August-December 1944) of the Ninety-fifth Bomb Group (H) of the Eighth Air Force, at the National Archives and Records Administration, College Park, Maryland.

15. World War II Missing Air Crew Reports held by the National Archives and Records Administration, College Park, Maryland.

16. Personal interviews with former Ninety-fifth Bomb Group pilots William C. Bramlett and David M. Taylor; One Hundredth Bomb Group ball turret gunner Nestor "Sully" Celleghin; and B-17 pilot Fred J. Rector of Greer, South Carolina.

17. *Suffolk Airfields in the Second World War*, by Graham Smith, Countryside Books, Newbury, Berkshire, England, 1995.

18. *Norfolk Airfields in the Second World War*, by Graham Smith, Countryside Books, Newbury, Berkshire, England, 1994.

19. Visit to Kovarska, Czech Republic, site of crash that killed Earle Johnston and five more of his crew on September 11, 1944; and interview with Jan

Zdiarsky, director of the Museum of Air Battle Over the Ore Mountains, A. E. Trommer Str. 696, 431 86 Kovarska, Czech Republic. www.museum119.cz.

20. Visit to Tournai, Belgium, site of crash that killed Robert Mercer on January 28, 1945; interview with Jacques De Ceuninck, retired chief inspector of police of Tournai and local historian of the crash.

21. Interview with Robert Galvin, nephew of William C. Galvin.

22. Interviews with family and friends of Joseph Earle Johnston, including his brother, the late Howard Johnston; his sister, Frances Johnston Goddard; his uncle, Vance Percy; and Melba Holcombe Harris, a childhood friend.

23. Accounts of Robert Mercer's last flight, written by crew survivors after the war, copies of which were provided by Lyle Graesser, son of radioman Lyle Graesser.

24. Interviews and visit to Bladenboro, North Carolina, with members of Robert Mercer's large family, including his sisters Nolie Lennon and Louise Toumbacaris, his nieces Myrtle Jolly and Beverly Bryant, and Nolie's son, Joe Lennon.

Notes

1. *The Lucky Bastard Club*, by Eugene Fletcher. University of Washington Press. 1993. Page 428. Also, *Mighty Eighth War Diary*, by Roger A. Freeman. Page 305. Jane's Publishing Inc. New York. 1981.

2. The Honor List of Dead and Missing, a list published in 1945 by the War Department; from the National Archives online collection, www.nara.gov.

3. The *Greenville News*, January 2, 1945, page 3, "11,900,000 in Armed Forces."

4. By the war's end, almost 3,000 American and more than 1,000 French pilots graduated at Hawthorne School of Aeronautics.

5. September 5, 2004 interview with William D. Strohmeier, who at age twenty-five was an instructor pilot at Hawthorne Field.

6. "Training in Open Cockpit Biplanes as the Jet Age Dawned," an unpublished essay by William D. Strohmeier.

7. *Prop Wash*, January 26, 1943 issue. The newspaper of Hawthorne Field, held in collection of South Caroliniana Library.

8. *Prop Wash*, June 30, 1943 issue.

9. *Prop Wash*, September 15, 1943 issue.

10. August 24, 1943 letter written by William D. Strohmeier, the public relations director at Hawthorne School of Aeronautics. The letter is part of the collection of papers of Harold Libby Foster at the South Caroliniana Library at the University of South Carolina.

11. *PropWash*, June 30, 1943 issue.

12. *PropWash*, January 15, 1945 issue.

13. The *Greenville* (S.C.) *News*, December 6, 1944, edition; page 5.

14. The *Greenville* (S.C.) *News*, December 8, 1944, edition.

15. *The State*, January 12, 1944, "U. S. Fighter has Longest Range."

16. *The State*, Page A-1, January 17, 1944.

17. *The State*, Page B-3, February 6, 1944.

18. *The State*, Page A-1, February 29, 1944.

19. The name was later changed to Donaldson Air Force Base.

20. *Ordinary Heroes: Anecdotes of Veterans*, by Sarah Nachin; 2001, Writers Club Press, Lincoln, Nebraska. Also, a letter Ed Smith wrote to Tom Hammond.

21. *Philadelphia Inquirer*, March 31, 1989; Obituary of Joseph A. Hagerty III, by Donna St. George.

22. *Ordinary Heroes*, by Sarah Nachin.

23. Official U. S. Air Force history of the Eighth Air Force, featured on the Eighth Air Force Headquarters Web site.

24. The *Greenville News*, January 26, 1944, United Press report quoting Chairman Charles Wilson of the Aircraft Production Board.

25. The *Greenville News*, March 30, 1944, page 10.

26. *The B-17 Flying Fortress Story*, by Roger A. Freeman with David Osborne, 1998, Sterling Publishing Co., New York. Boeing Co. Web site, http://www.boeing.com/history/boeing/b17.html.

27. Most of the planes that survived combat or accidental destruction were flown back to the United States after the war ended, stored briefly at desert airfields in Arizona and New Mexico, and then scrapped in short order. A

few were operated as target drones for newer aircraft and Boeing's Bomarc missiles.

28. The *Greenville News*, March 30, 1944, page 6.

29. The *Greenville News*. Editions of February 19, February 23, March 9 and March 28.

30. The *Bend* (Oregon) *Bulletin*, Obituary, January 21, 2003. Payne returned home at the end of the war. He married Betty Goughler on July 12, 1945, in Greenville, became a high school coach and teacher, and was athletic director at Bend High School, Bend, Oregon. He was an avid golfer and fisherman. He died January 20, 2003, at age 82, and his memorial was held at the Christian Life Center in Bend.

31. The *Greenville News*, November 5, 2002, obituary. Jameson returned home after the prison camp was liberated by the Russian Army in 1945. He already had graduated from Clemson in 1942, where he played in the 1940 Cotton Bowl. He also had played on the first State Championship football team, was named All State and played on the first Shrine Bowl team. Following the war, Jameson received his Masters Degree from North Carolina State University. He retired as Professor Emeritus in the College of Engineering at Clemson University after teaching 34 years. He never forgot his glory days on the football field. He was inducted into Easley High School Athletic Hall of Fame, and when he died November 4, 2002, asked that memorials be made to the 1940 Cotton Bowl Team Scholarship Fund.

32. Interview with Fred J. Rector. When the war ended, Fred returned to his wife, whom he had married in 1939, and his job with the Post Office in Greer.

33. *Suffolk Airfields in the Second World War*, by Graham Smith, Countryside Books, Newbury, Berkshire, England, 1995. PP. 35-39.

34. Pilot's flight logbook of Lt. Victor Radke, a copy of which Radke gave to Tom Hammond.

35. Missions records of the Ninety-fifth Bomb Group, Thirteenth Combat Wing, Eighth Air Force. August 18, 1944. At the National Archives and Records Administration, College Park, Md.

36. Ninety-fifth Bomb Group records. NARA. August 18, 1944.

37. Interview with Scott Alexander.

38. Ninety-fifth Bomb Group records. NARA. August 18, 1944.

39. Ninety-fifth Bomb Group records. NARA. August 18, 1944.

40. Ninety-fifth Bomb Group records. NARA. August 18, 1944.

41. Ninety-fifth Bomb Group records. NARA. August 18, 1944.

42. Ninety-fifth Bomb Group records. NARA. August 18, 1944.

43. Tom Hammond's combat flight log.

44. Ninety-fifth Bomb Group records. NARA. August 24, 1944.

45. *The Lucky Bastard Club*, by Eugene Fletcher. Page 376.

46. Ninety-fifth Bomb Group records. NARA. August 24, 1944.

47. Ninety-fifth Bomb Group records. NARA. August 24, 1944.

48. *Mighty Eighth War Diary*, by Roger A. Freeman. Page 331.

49. Ninety-fifth Bomb Group records. NARA. August 24, 1944.

50. *The Lucky Bastard Club,* by Eugene Fletcher. Page 376.

51. Flight logs of Tom Hammond and Vic Radke.

52. *Mighty Eighth War Diary*, by Roger A. Freeman. Page 332.

53. Interview with Scott Alexander, December 2004.

54. Interview with David M. Taylor, June 2005.

55. Interview with Sam Clay, May 2005.

56. Ninety-fifth Bomb Group records. NARA. August 25, 1944. Also, Missing Air Crew Reports 8279 and 8280, NARA.

57. Interviews with Tom Hammond, Sam Clay, and Scott Alexander. Also Ninety-fifth Bomb Group records, NARA. August 25, 1944.

58. *The B-17 Flying Fortress Story*, by Roger A. Freeman with David Osborne, Sterling Publishing Co., 1998. New York. Page 162.

59. August 31 letter from Tom Hammond to Callie Barnette.

60. Tom Hammond's flight log.

61. Tom Hammond's flight log.

62. *Mighty Eighth War Diary*, by Roger A. Freeman. Page 336.

63. Ninety-fifth Bomb Group records. NARA. August 30, 1944.

64. Ninety-fifth Bomb Group records. NARA. August 30, 1944. Also, Vic Radke's flight log.

65. *The B-17 Flying Fortress Story*, Page 214.

66. Tom Hammond's flight log.

67. Ninety-fifth Bomb Group records. September 1, 1944.

68. Ninety-fifth Bomb Group records. September 1, 1944.

69. Ninety-fifth Bomb Group records. September 3, 1944.

70. Ninety-fifth Bomb Group records. September 3, 1944.

71. *Mighty Eighth War Diary*, by Roger A. Freeman. Page 338.

72. Ninety-fifth Bomb Group records. September 3, 1944.

73. Interview with Scott Alexander, December 2004.

74. Ninety-fifth Bomb Group records. September 5, 1944.

75. Ninety-fifth Bomb Group records. September 5, 1944.

76. Ninety-fifth Bomb Group records. September 5, 1944.

77. Interviews with Tom Hammond and Scott Alexander.

78. Flight logs of Tom Hammond and Vic Radke.

79. Ninety-fifth Bomb Group records. September 8, 1944.

80. Ninety-fifth Bomb Group records. September 8, 1944. Also, flight log of Vic Radke.

81. *Mighty Eighth War Diary*, by Roger A. Freeman. Page 341.

82. Ninety-fifth Bomb Group records. September 8, 1944. Also, flight log of Vic Radke.

83. Tom Hammond's flight log.

84. *Mighty Eighth War Diary*, by Roger A. Freeman. Page 342.

85. Ninety-fifth Bomb Group records. September 9, 1944. Also, flight log of Vic Radke.

86. Ninety-fifth Bomb Group records. September 9, 1944.

87. *B-17s Over Berlin*, by Ian Hawkins; 1995, Brassey's of Washington & London, Page 232.

88. Ninety-fifth Bomb Group records. September 9, 1944.

89. *The Lucky Bastard Club*, by Eugene Fletcher. Page 386.

90. *Mighty Eighth War Diary*, by Roger A. Freeman. Page 344.

91. Ninety-fifth Bomb Group records. September 11, 1944.

92. Ninety-fifth Bomb Group records. September 11, 1944.

93. September 21, 1944 letter Tom wrote to Callie Barnette.

94. March 25, 1945 letter Tom wrote to Callie Barnette.

95. Interviews with Frances Johnston Goddard, her uncle Vance Percy, and their neighbor Melba Holcombe, 2005.

96. Yearbooks of Georgia Evening College, an earlier name of present-day Georgia State University, at the GSU Library.

97. U. S. Army enlistment records, on the internet site of the NARA.

98. Interview with Frances Johnston Goddard, Earle Johnston's sister.

99. Interview with Nestor Celleghin, June 2005.

100. Army records of Nestor Celleghin.

101. September 21, 1944 letter Tom wrote to Callie Barnette.

102. Interview with Nestor Celleghin, and his Army records.

103. "Lt. J.E. Johnston," published in the DeKalb *New Era* newspaper, Decatur, Georgia, September 7, 1944.

104. Interview with Nestor "Sully" Celleghin, ball turret gunner of Johnston's crew.

105. Letter written October 2, 1944, by George Prater's mother to Jewell Spruell's mother.

106. Ninety-fifth Bomb Group records. September 11, 1944.

107. Interview with Nestor Celleghin; letter written by George Prater after his release from POW camp.

108. *Mighty Eighth War Diary*, by Roger A. Freeman. Page 344.

109. One Hundredth Bomb Group Foundation Web site http://www.100thbg.com/

110. Interview with Nestor Celleghin, June 2005.

111. Interview with Nestor Celleghin, June 2005.

112. Interview with Nestor Celleghin, June 2005.

113. Interview with Nestor Celleghin, June 2005.

114. Interview with Nestor Celleghin, June 2005.

115.Letter by George Prater to Mrs. Jewell Spruell, June 22, 1945, a copy of which was obtained from Nestor Celleghin.

116.*Black Monday over the Ore Mountains*, by Jan Zdiarsky; 2001, Museum of the Air Battle over the Ore Mountains. Also, interview with Jan Zdiarsky, January 2005, during visit to Kovarska, Czech Republic.

117.*Black Monday over the Ore Mountains*, by Jan Zdiarsky.

118.Prater, Dolby, and Celleghin, the only three of the nine crewmates to survive the battle of September 11, 1944, were reunited briefly at an American camp in France after the war.

119.Interview with Nestor Celleghin, June 2005.

120.*The Lucky Bastard Club*, by Eugene Fletcher. Page 388.

121.*Atlanta Constitution*, September 12, 1944, Page 1, Associated Press, "Americans Invade Germany Proper; Last Nazi Line in France Cracks."

122.*Mighty Eighth War Diary*, by Roger A. Freeman. Page 345.

123.Ninety-fifth Bomb Group records, September 12, 1944.

124.Ninety-fifth Bomb Group records, September 12, 1944.

125.Ninety-fifth Bomb Group records, September 12, 1944.

126.Ninety-fifth Bomb Group records, September 12, 1944.

127.Ninety-fifth Bomb Group records, September 12, 1944.

128.Ninety-fifth Bomb Group records, September 13, 1944.

129.Ninety-fifth Bomb Group records, September 13, 1944.

130.Ninety-fifth Bomb Group records, September 13, 1944.

131.Ninety-fifth Bomb Group records, September 13, 1944.

132.Ninety-fifth Bomb Group records, September 13, 1944. Also, Tom Hammond's flight log.

133.*Mighty Eighth War Diary*, by Roger A. Freeman. Page 346.

134.Ninety-fifth Bomb Group records, September 13, 1944.

135.Tom Hammond's flight log.

136.*B-17s Over Berlin*, by Ian Hawkins. Page 233.

137.Interview with Scott Alexander, December 2005.

138.Ninety-fifth Bomb Group records, U. S. Air Force Archives, Maxwell Air Force Base, Montgomery, Al.

139.Ninety-fifth Bomb Group records, U. S. Air Force Archives, Maxwell Air Force Base, Montgomery, Al.

140.Ninety-fifth Bomb Group records, U. S. Air Force Archives, Maxwell Air Force Base, Montgomery, Al.

141.Ninety-fifth Bomb Group records, U. S. Air Force Archives, Maxwell Air Force Base, Montgomery, Al.

142.Interviews with Tom Hammond and Scott Alexander.

143.Interviews with Ed Smith's daughters, Sarah Nachin and Karen Sayko.

144.The *Greenville News*, Associated Press Report from London, January 1, 1945, page 6, "Thousands of British Brides of U. S. Soldiers Coming to U. S. A."

145.Flight logs of Tom Hammond and Vic Radke.

146.Tom Hammond's flight log.

147.*Mighty Eighth War Diary*, by Roger A. Freeman. Page 354.

148.*The Lucky Bastard Club*, by Eugene Fletcher. University of Washington Press. 1988. Page 397.

149.Ninety-fifth Bomb Group records, NARA. September 27, 1944. Also, Interview with Allan Johnson, an English resident of Horham during WW II, regarding the paint on the bombers.

150.Tom Hammond's flight log.

151.*Mighty Eighth War Diary*, by Roger A. Freeman. Page 357.

152.Ninety-fifth Bomb Group records, NARA. October 2, 1944.

153.Ninety-fifth Bomb Group records, NARA. October 2, 1944.

154.Interview with Tom Hammond. Also, Ninety-fifth Bomb Group records, NARA. October 5, 1944.

155.Ninety-fifth Bomb Group records, NARA. Also, interview with Tom Hammond.

156.Interview with Scott Alexander, December 2005.

157.*Mighty Eighth War Diary*, by Roger A. Freeman. Page 360.

158.Ninety-fifth Bomb Group records, NARA. October 6, 1944.

159.Ninety-fifth Bomb Group records, NARA. October 6, 1944.

160.War diary of Staff Sargeant Gerald Hoefert.

161.Ninety-fifth Bomb Group records, NARA. October 19, 1944.

162.Ninety-fifth Bomb Group records, NARA. October 19, 1944.

163.*Mighty Eighth War Diary*, by Roger A. Freeman. Page 368.

164.Ninety-fifth Bomb Group records, NARA. October 19, 1944.

165.Ninety-fifth Bomb Group records, NARA. October 19, 1944.

166.Ninety-fifth Bomb Group records, NARA. October 19, 1944.

167.*Mighty Eighth War Diary*, by Roger A. Freeman. Page 370.

168.Ninety-fifth Bomb Group records, NARA. October 25, 1944. Also, Vic Radke's flight log.

169.Ninety-fifth Bomb Group records, NARA. October 25, 1944.

170. *Mighty Eighth War Diary*, by Roger A. Freeman. Page 371.

171. *The Lucky Bastard Club*, by Eugene Fletcher. Page 428.

172. Ninety-fifth Bomb Group records, NARA. October 25, 1944.

173. *Mighty Eighth War Diary*, by Roger A. Freeman. Page 371.

174. Ninety-fifth Bomb Group records, NARA. October 26, 1944.

175. Ninety-fifth Bomb Group records, NARA. October 26, 1944.

176. *Mighty Eighth War Diary*, by Roger A. Freeman. Page 372.

177. Ninety-fifth Bomb Group records, NARA. October 28, 1944. Also, Vic Radke's flight log.

178. Ninety-fifth Bomb Group records, NARA. October 28, 1944.

179. *Mighty Eighth War Diary*, by Roger A. Freeman. Page 375. Also, United States Strategic Bombing Survey (European War), September 30, 1945.

180. Interview with Scott Alexander, December 2004.

181. Vic Radke's flight log. Also, Ninety-fifth Bomb Group records, NARA, November 2, 1944.

182. Ninety-fifth Bomb Group records, NARA, November 2, 1944.

183. *Mighty Eighth War Diary*, by Roger A. Freeman. Page 376.

184. Ninety-fifth Bomb Group records, NARA. November 4, 1944.

185. Ninety-fifth Bomb Group records, NARA. November 5, 1944.

186. *Mighty Eighth War Diary*, by Roger A. Freeman. Page 377.

187. Ninety-fifth Bomb G records, NARA. November 5, 1944.

188. Ninety-fifth Bomb Group records, NARA. November 5, 1944.

189.Ninety-fifth Bomb Group records, NARA. November 5, 1944. Also, Vic Radke's flight log. Also, *The B-17 Flying Fortress Story*, by Roger A. Freeman with David Osborne. Page 214.

190.Ninety-fifth Bomb Group records, NARA. November 5, 1944.

191.Ninety-fifth Bomb Group records, NARA. November 5, 1944.

192."2,500 Bombers Pound 5 Cities in West Reich," by the Associated Press, published in the *Atlanta Constitution*, November 6, 1944.

193.The *Atlanta Constitution*, November 8, 1944, Page 1, Associated Press, "Nazis Fight To Bar Road to Cologne."

194.The *Atlanta Constitution*, Page 4, November 6, 1944, United Press, "80 Per Cent of Cologne Erased, Says German."

195.Ninety-fifth Bomb Group records, NARA. November 9, 1944.

196.Ninety-fifth Bomb Group records, NARA. November 9, 1944.

197.*Mighty Eighth War Diary*, by Roger A. Freeman. Page 379.

198.Ninety-fifth Bomb Group records, NARA. November 9, 1944.

199.Ninety-fifth Bomb Group records, NARA. November 9, 1944.

200.U. S. Eighth Air Force Headquarters, tactical mission report, November 9, 1944, field order number 1,299, operation number 707, documents at the National Archives and Records Administration, College Park, Md.

201.Ninety-fifth Bomb Group records, NARA. November 9, 1944.

202.Ninety-fifth Bomb Group records, NARA. November 9, 1944.

203.Interview with Scott Alexander, December 2004.

204.Interview with Tom Hammond.

205.The *Atlanta Constitution*, November 13, 1944, United Press report, "Two Spaatz Air Arms Claim 15,210 Planes."

206.*Mighty Eighth War Diary*, by Roger A. Freeman. Page 384.

207.*Operational Record of the Ninety-fifth Bomb Group (H)*, by Paul M. Andrews.

208.Ninety-fifth Bomb Group records, NARA. November 21, 1944.

209.Vic Radke's flight log. Also, Ninety-fifth Bomb Group records, NARA. November 21, 1944.

210.The *Greenville News*, Page 2, November 24, 1944.

211.Missing Air Crew Report 11199, NARA.

212.Alumni records, The Citadel. Also, *The Bulldog*, Citadel yearbook, 1940. Also, *The Nautilus*, yearbook of Greenville High School, 1935 & 1936. Also, interview with Horace Crouch, August 2005.

213.Alumni records, The Citadel.

214.MACR 11199.

215.U. S. Army Air Forces Missing Air Crew Report, number 11199, on microfiche at The Mighty Eighth Air Force Museum, Pooler, Ga.

216.MACR 11199.

217.Interview with Paul Nally.

218.The *Greenville News*, November 26, 1944, edition, Page One.

219.The *Atlanta Constitution*, Tuesday, November 28, 1944. Associated Press from London, "239 Germans Downed by 8th U. S. Air Force."

220.Tactical report, headquarters, Thirteenth Combat Bomb Wing, Mission to Hamm marshaling yards, November 29, 1944. Records of Ninety-fifth Bomb Group at the National Archives and Records Administration, College Park, Md.

221.Interview with Tom Hammond. Vic Radke's flight log.

222.*Mighty Eighth War Diary*, by Roger A. Freeman. Page 387-388.

223. Ninety-fifth Bomb Group records, NARA. November 29, 1944.

224. Ninety-fifth Bomb Group records, NARA. November 29, 1944.

225. Ninety-fifth Bomb Group records, NARA. November 29, 1944.

226. Ninety-fifth Bomb Group records, NARA. November 29, 1944.

227. *Mighty Eighth War Diary*, by Roger A. Freeman. Page 388.

228. Ninety-fifth Bomb Group records, NARA. November 30, 1944.

229. Ninety-fifth Bomb Group records, NARA. November 30, 1944.

230. Tactical report, Thirteenth Combat Wing, November 30, 1944, mission reports of the Ninety-fifth Bomb Group, NARA, College Park, Md.

231. Ninety-fifth Bomb Group records, NARA. November 30, 1944.

232. Ninety-fifth Bomb Group records, NARA. November 30, 1944.

233. Payne survived the war in a German POW camp, and died February 12, 2000, at the age of 83. He became a retail salesman after the war, and was a member of the Ninety-fifth Bomb Group (H) Association.

234. Ninety-fifth Bomb Group incident records, published in *Operational Record of the Ninety-fifth Bomb Group (H)*, by Paul M. Andrews.

235. Truesdell was a thirty-six-year-old West Point graduate, the son of Army Maj. Gen. Karl Truesdell. He remained in the Air Force and became a major general himself in 1954.

236. Interview with Scott Alexander, December 2004.

237. Ninety-fifth Bomb Group records, NARA. December 2, 1944.

238. Ninety-fifth Bomb Group records, NARA. December 2, 1944.

239. Ninety-fifth Bomb Group records, NARA. December 2, 1944.

240. Callie had bought a pair of warm leather gloves, carefully packaged them for the overseas mail, and sent them to Tom for a Christmas gift. When Tom

received the package, it had been opened, and there was nothing in the box. Someone in the chain of military post offices was wearing his gloves, most likely. But he did not tell Callie that he did not receive the gift until after they were married.

241.Ninety-fifth Bomb Group records, NARA. December 4, 1944.

242.Ninety-fifth Bomb Group records, NARA. December 5, 1944.

243.Ninety-fifth Bomb Group records, NARA. December 5, 1944.

244.Interview with Bill Bramlett. May 2005.

245.Interview with Bill Bramlett. May 2005.

246.Interview with David Taylor. June 2005.

247.Tactical bombing report for December 5, 1944, Ninety-fifth Bomb Group records, National Archives and Records Administration, College Park, Md.

248.Tactical bombing report for December 5, 1944, Ninety-fifth Bomb Group records.

249.*Mighty Eighth War Diary*, by Roger A. Freeman. Page 391.

250.Ninety-fifth Bomb Group records, NARA. December 5, 1944.

251.The *Greenville News*, December 7, 1944, edition.

252.The *Greenville News*, December 1, 1944, edition. Page 15.

253.The *Greenville News*, December 18, 1944, edition.

254.Ninety-fifth Bomb Group records, NARA. December 12, 1944.

255.Ninety-fifth Bomb Group records, NARA. December 16, 1944.

256.Ninety-fifth Bomb Group records, NARA. December 16, 1944.

257.Ninety-fifth Bomb Group records, NARA. December 16, 1944.

258. Crew interrogation report for Lt. Victor Radke's crew, mission of December 16, 1944, in Ninety-fifth Bomb Group mission records, National Archives and Records Administration, College Park, Md.

259. Interview with Col. David M. Taylor, U. S. Air Force (retired), at his home in Charlottesville, VA, on June 6, 2005.

260. Ninety-fifth Bomb Group records, NARA. December 12, 1944.

261. U. S. Army Air Forces Missing Air Crew Report.

262. Recollections of Eugene Fletcher, shared with the author in correspondence.

263. Recollections of Eugene Fletcher.

264. Missing Air Crew Report 10418. NARA.

265. Missing Air Crew Report 10418. NARA.

266. Interview with Robert Huff. September 2004.

267. Following the war, Robert Huff married Tom Hammond's sister Helen.

268. *The Lucky Bastard Club*, by Eugene Fletcher. Page 472-473.

269. *Mighty Eighth War Diary*, by Roger A. Freeman. Page 399-400.

270. Ninety-fifth Bomb Group records, NARA. December 24, 1944.

271. *The Mighty Eighth*, by Roger A. Freeman, Cassell & Co., London, 2000; Third Air Division Intelligence Report, National Archives, College Park, Md.

272. Ninety-fifth Bomb Group records, NARA. December 24, 1944.

273. Ninety-fifth Bomb Group records, NARA. December 24, 1944.

274. Ninety-fifth Bomb Group records, NARA. December 24, 1944.

275. Ninety-fifth Bomb Group records, NARA. December 24, 1944.

276. Ninety-fifth Bomb Group records, NARA. December 24, 1944.

277. Ninety-fifth Bomb Group records, NARA. December 25, 1944.

278. Ninety-fifth Bomb Group records, NARA. December 24, 1944. Also, Interview with Scott Alexander, December 2004.

279. Tom Hammond's flight log. Also, *The B-17 Flying Fortress Story*, By Roger A. Freeman with David Osborne. Page 214.

280. Ninety-fifth Bomb Group records, NARA. December 27, 1944.

281. Ninety-fifth Bomb Group records, NARA. December 27, 1944.

282. Ninety-fifth Bomb Group records, NARA. December 27, 1944.

283. Ninety-fifth Bomb Group records, NARA. December 27, 1944.

284. Ninety-fifth Bomb Group records, NARA. December 27, 1944.

285. Ninety-fifth Bomb Group records, NARA. December 27, 1944.

286. Ninety-fifth Bomb Group records, NARA. December 28, 1944.

287. *Mighty Eighth War Diary*, by Roger A. Freeman. Page 407.

288. *The B-17 Flying Fortress Story*, By Roger A. Freeman with David Osborne. Page 248.

289. *The Lucky Bastard Club*, by Eugene Fletcher. Page 285.

290. Tom Hammond's Army records.

291. The *Greenville News*, United Press Report, January 1, 1945, page 2, "29,000 Airmen of Eighth Lost in '44."

292. Interviews with Tom Hammond, Scott Alexander and Sam Clay.

293. Interview with Scott Alexander, December 2004.

294. http://www.historical-museum.org/collect/world_war/ww2-2.htm.   From Update, v. 8, number 4 (November 1981). © Historical Association of Southern Florida, 1981. Article titled "Miami 1941-1945: From VIP Suites to GI Barracks," by Daniel Markus.

295. "Taylors Sergeant Sacrifices Life for Remainder of Crew," The *Greenville News*, February 16, 1945.

296. *Operational Record of the Ninety-fifth Bomb Group (H)*, by Paul M. Andrews.

297. The *New York Times*, October 27, 1947, "Transport Docks with 6,248 coffins." Also, "400,000 in Silent Tribute As War Dead Come Home," by Meyer Berger, Page 1.

298. Obituary, published December 24, 2002, in the *PressRepublican.com*, Apple Valley, Ca.

299. Obituary, *St. Petersburg Times*, Florida. August 7, 1996. Edward K. Smith. Page 5, 7B.

300. Interviews with Ed Smith's daughters, Sarah Nachin and Karen Sayko.

301. *Pittsburgh Press*, May 14, 1987, Obituary, Charles M. Delcroix.

302. *Philadelphia Inquirer*, March 31, 1989; Obituary of Joseph A. Hagerty III, by Donna St. George.

303. *Spokesman-Review*, Spokane, Washington, Obituary, William Galvin, October 23, 1996; Idaho edition.

304. *Greenville News*, March 5, 1944, "Zinn Hunts Missing Fliers In This War As In Last," by Kenneth L. Dixon, the Associated Press.

305. *Los Angeles Times*, November 2, 2002, "The Final Mission Is Completed."

Index

978-0-595-41539-7
0-595-41539-3

Printed in the United States
79233LV00007B/106-108